The Quest for Shakespeare's Globe

The Quest for Shakespeare's Globe

JOHN ORRELL

Professor of English, University of Alberta

Cambridge University Press

CAMBRIDGE

LONDON   NEW YORK   NEW ROCHELLE

MELBOURNE   SYDNEY

Published by the Press Syndicate of the University of Cambridge
The Pitt Building, Trumpington Street, Cambridge CB2 1RP
32 East 57th Street, New York, NY 10022, USA
296 Beaconsfield Parade, Middle Park, Melbourne 3206, Australia

First published 1983

Printed in Great Britain at the University Press, Cambridge

Library of Congress catalogue card number: 82–9445

British Library Cataloguing in publication data
Orrell, John
The quest for Shakespeare's Globe.
1. Globe Theatre—History
I. Title
792'.09421'64   PN2596.L7G/
ISBN 0 521 24751 9

For Wendy, Kate and David

Contents

	List of Plates	*page*	viii
	Preface		xi
1	The topographical glass		1
2	The printed panoramas		32
3	Looking at the Globe		70
4	Measuring the Globe		84
5	The plans of the Fortune and the Globe		108
6	Seating and capacity		127
7	The Globe and the sun		139
	Appendix A: Speculations		158
	Appendix B: The theatre at Christ Church		168
	Notes		172
	Index		185

Plates

1   The Globe (left) and the Hope, from Wenceslaus Hollar's
    Long View of London, 1647. Guildhall Library   *page* 1

2   Wenceslaus Hollar, 'West part o[f] Southwarke toward
    Westminster.' Yale Center for British Art, Paul Mellon
    Collection   2

3   Wenceslaus Hollar, 'East part of Southwarke, towards
    Grenwich.' Reduced. Yale Center for British Art, Paul Mellon
    Collection   5

4   Wenceslaus Hollar, view of west London. John Rylands
    Library, Manchester   6

5   Wenceslaus Hollar, 'London.' Master and Fellows, Magdalene
    College, Cambridge   7

6 ⎫   8

7 ⎬   9

8 ⎪   10

9 ⎪ Wenceslaus Hollar, *Long View of London*. Guildhall Library   11

10 ⎬   12

11 ⎪   13

12 ⎭   14

13 Wenceslaus Hollar, 'London and Old St Paul's from the
    Thames.' British Museum   16

14 Wenceslaus Hollar, 'London and Old St Paul's' plotted on
    sightlines drawn to positions traced from a modern map   17

15 Detail traced from Hollar's 'London and Old St Paul's' showing
    the cathedral and, circled below it, the Upper Frater at
    Blackfriars   19

16 A drawing frame, from John Bate, *The Mysteryes of Nature, and
    Art*, 1634. British Museum   24

17 A topographical glass in use, from [Jean Dubreuil,] *Perspective
    Practical*, 1672. Victoria and Albert Museum   27

18 Wenceslaus Hollar, 'London by Milford Staires.' Master and
Fellows, Magdalene College, Cambridge 29

19 Wenceslaus Hollar, 'London by Milford Staires' plotted on
sightlines drawn to positions traced from a modern map 30

20   32

21   33

22 } Claes Jan Visscher, *London*. Guildhall Library 34

23   35

24 } John Norden, *Civitas Londini*. Royal Library, Stockholm 38

25   39

26 Detail of Norden's *Civitas Londini*, showing the top of St
Saviour's Tower 57

27 Wenceslaus Hollar, diagram of Thames Street. *The Connoisseur* 72

28 Wenceslaus Hollar, 'West part o[f] Southwarke' plotted on
sightlines drawn to positions marked on an Ordnance Survey
map. Crown copyright reserved 82

29 Same as Plate 28, but here the bearings of the Globe, the Hope
and the eastern gable of Winchester House have been deduced
from the drawing 98

30 An enlargement of the Bankside section of Plate 29, showing
the bearings of the theatres and the gable of Winchester House.
Drawn on a sixty-inch Ordnance Survey map 102

31 I   An *ad quadratum* construction from Sebastiano Serlio, *Il
primo libro dell'architettura*, Venice, 1560. University of
Alberta Library

II   John Thorpe, plan for a house on a round terrace. *Country
Life* 118

III   John Webb, the Cockpit-in-Court at Whitehall. Provost
and Fellows of Worcester College, Oxford

32 C. Walter Hodges, 'Diagrammatic projection from the
drawing': the plan of the Globe deduced from Hollar's sketch.
Oxford University Press 123

33 The theatre in the hall at Christ Church, Oxford, in August
1605. British Library 130

34 The hall at Christ Church, 1605. Diagram showing the
rearrangements made in the auditorium after Suffolk's
intervention, with descriptive comments by Stringer and Wake 133

35   Andrea Palladio, drawing of a Roman theatre made to illustrate
     an edition of Vitruvius. R.I.B.A. Drawings Library   141

36   I John Webb, the Cockpit-in-Court at Whitehall. Stage area.
        Provost and Fellows of Worcester College, Oxford   144
     II John Webb, the Cockpit-in-Court at Whitehall. Survey plan.
        Provost and Fellows of Worcester College, Oxford   145

37   The *homo ad quadratum* in Vincenzo Scamozzi, *L'idea
     dell'architettura universale*, Venice, 1615, p. 40   148

38   John Webb, 'The designe of ye Chirurgions Theater 1636.'
     Provost and Fellows of Worcester College, Oxford   150

39   Detail of Plate 38, showing the anatomy table   151

40   The orientation of the Globe's façade deduced from Hollar's
     'West part o[f] Southwarke'. Yale Center for British Art, Paul
     Mellon Collection   153

41   The Globe with twenty-four sides. Diagram based on Hollar's
     'West part o[f] Southwarke'. Yale Center for British Art, Paul
     Mellon Collection   165

Preface

Although the title of this book refers to Shakespeare's Globe as if there had been only one such building, there were in fact two. The first was made from the timbers of London's earliest permanent playhouse, the Theater, when it was dismantled in 1598–9 and carried across the Thames from its original site in Shoreditch to a new one in Bankside. This notable relocation took place at that time in Shakespeare's life when he was about to embark on the great tragedies that begin with *Hamlet* and are foreshadowed in parts of *Julius Caesar* and *Henry V*. The second Globe, which was promptly constructed to replace the first after it had been destroyed by fire during a performance of *Henry VIII* in 1613, marked no new outburst of creativity in the playwright, but surely reflected in the details of its design many of the practical lessons of stagecraft that he and his fellow actors had learned in the intervening years. That Shakespeare himself developed so variously over those years is a persuasive reminder that the design of playhouses can hardly have failed to change too, at least to some extent. Recent scholarship has convincingly shown that there was no such thing as a 'typical' Elizabethan playhouse, and it is at least likely that the second Globe differed markedly from the first.

Yet I have retained the singular 'Globe' in my title because much of the evidence adduced here shows that there appears to have been a standard plan for the large wooden frames of most of the public theatres of Shakespeare's time. Such frames, which housed the galleries and access passages of the auditorium and formed the setting in which the jewel-like tiring house, stage and 'heavens' were mounted, were complex structures and hardly likely to have been planned in an *ad hoc* way every time a new one was needed. They left plenty of scope for the evolution of new ideas about the stage and its adjuncts, but very little for radical reworkings of the auditorium proper. I shall contend, therefore, that the second Globe, for all its undoubted theatrical evolution, substantially resembled its predecessor, and that this was in turn similar – so far as its main structural frame went – to the Theater of 1576.

The argument in the first half of the book is based on a drawing of the second Globe made by Wenceslaus Hollar in about 1640, and is concerned with the size and proportions of the theatre. Since this building which Hollar saw and so meticulously described with his quick pen had been built on the foundations of the first Globe it follows that the drawing has something to tell us about the size of the earlier theatre too. But the argument craves confirmation from an independent source, and in chapter 5 this is found in the allusions to the first Globe in the well-known Fortune theatre contract of 1600.

The book therefore is about what the two Globe theatres had in common rather than their differences. I do not for a moment deny the great importance of these last, which would be all the more wonderful to discover because they must surely have been prescribed by Shakespeare himself, but I have no new evidence about them and could only rehearse once more what is already widely known. It would in any case be a rash man who tried to improve upon the fascinating, rich eclecticism of J. Cranford Adams's *The Globe Playhouse* or the careful, brilliant charm of C. Walter Hodges' *The Globe Restored*, both works of compendious scope.

I have sought rather to offer only new evidence or new ways of looking at the old, and my conclusions are severely limited to what can be justified by the fresh information. They have to do mostly with the size, shape and orientation of the main frame of the second Globe; but there are strong implications for the first Globe too. These are matters of prime importance to anyone who wishes to reconstruct either theatre today – and there are well-advanced projects to do so at Southwark and at Detroit – but not without significance also for the reader of the Elizabethan and Jacobean drama. For the theatre which emerges in the following pages is a larger, less intimate house than was once thought likely, truly capable of holding the three thousand spectators of contemporary report, and requiring a wide range of abilities from its actors, who had both to fill it with rage and to quell its yard and galleries to an expectant stillness. In developing the arguments of this book I drew strength from the knowledge that Richard Hosley, surely the most meticulous scholar to address himself to this problem, had already concluded that the second Globe was about 100 ft across, a figure with which I entirely agreed, but which challenged earlier thought on the matter. Richard Southern had proposed something altogether smaller and more like the 80 ft wide Fortune playhouse, while C. Walter Hodges in *Shakespeare's Second Globe* described the later theatre as about 92 ft across. Both Hosley and Hodges based their arguments, as I do in the earlier part of the present book, on the evidence of Hollar, whose reliability as a topographical reporter is so astutely assessed in the opening pages of Mr Hodges' book.

My particular approach to Hollar was suggested by an unpublished seminar paper given at the Shakespeare Association conference in Toronto in 1978 by Sidney Fisher, though both my evidence and my conclusions are different from his. I have had the invaluable assistance of Richard and David Orrell in mathematical matters, and of Douglas

Hube in astronomical. Parts of chapters 1 and 4 have been summarized in *The Third Globe: Symposium for the Reconstruction of the Globe Playhouse*, edited by C. Walter Hodges and others (Detroit, 1981), and chapter 5 has appeared in a slightly modified form in *Shakespeare Survey 33*. Some of the material in chapter 1 has appeared in *The Burlington Magazine*.

One of the great pleasures of working towards an understanding of Shakespeare's theatre, I have discovered, is the good company of others who are interested in it. To both Richard Hosley and Walter Hodges, who have given me every encouragement and much good advice, I owe debts of friendship which I must not compound with whatever errors this book contains: they are all mine, but the principal goodwill is theirs.

1 The topographical glass

And I haue seene the Globe burnt, and quickly made a Phoenix.
Henry Farley, *The Complaint of Paules*, 1616

At the opening of Henry Farley's little book there is a blank space, evidently intended for a woodcut of St Paul's that did not arrive at the press in time to be included in the printer's forme. The loss of the illustration is doubly regrettable, for while other printed words crowd alongside the gap left for the cathedral's central tower, the line about the Globe runs across the bottom of the space, suggesting that the new theatre itself was to have been pictured at the foot of the composition. Here, after all, was a notable and galling contrast: in the background the huge pile of Paul's, running sadly to decay, the object of the long-standing neglect that Farley's pamphlet campaigns against; and

1. The Globe (left) and the Hope, from Wenceslaus Hollar's *Long View of London*, 1647. Working on the etching in Antwerp, Hollar mistakenly transposed the names of the two playhouses.

1

in the foreground the newly built second Globe, promptly and enthusiastically erected by the players on the foundations of its predecessor, victim of the notorious fire of 1613. According to John Taylor, the water-poet, this new playhouse was 'a stately theator';[1] the tatler John Chamberlain heard that it was 'the fairest that ever was in England.'[2] The rebuilding took less than a year, the expense – about £1400 – was almost scandalously high, and already the profits were flowing in. Meanwhile the stones fell from St Paul's and men were in risk of their lives when they pissed against its walls. It was to be many years before Farley's agitation met with success. In 1620 Inigo Jones began the task of surveying and designing, but not until the next decade did he recase the cathedral in Portland stone. In the year of

2.   Wenceslaus Hollar, 'West part o[f] Southwarke toward Westminster.' Approximately original size.

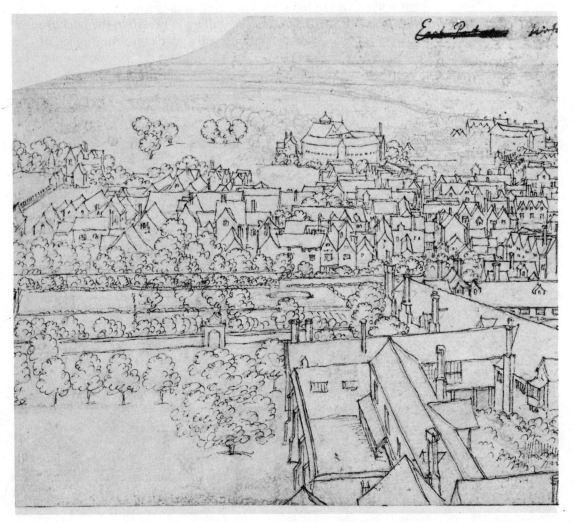

Shakespeare's death the deplorable contrast between gorgeous theatre
and depressed cathedral was obvious for all to see.

Farley's book is written in the voice, and from the point of view, of
St Paul's herself. We have no picture of the Globe theatre as seen from
her heady viewpoint, but it happens that we do have no fewer than
three as seen from the area of St Saviour's in Southwark, now
Southwark cathedral. All three are by the noted topographer Wenceslaus Hollar; two are drawings and one is the famous depiction of the
theatre in the *Long View of London*, etched in Antwerp in 1647 [Plate
1]. Here, ignominiously mis-labelled 'Beere bayting h,' the theatre is
shown as a great round frame, its central courtyard half open to the
sky, half covered by a twin-gabled structure crowned by an ogee-
capped timber lantern. The roof is of tile, where the first Globe had its
dangerous and fatal thatch, the gables of the superstructure have a hint

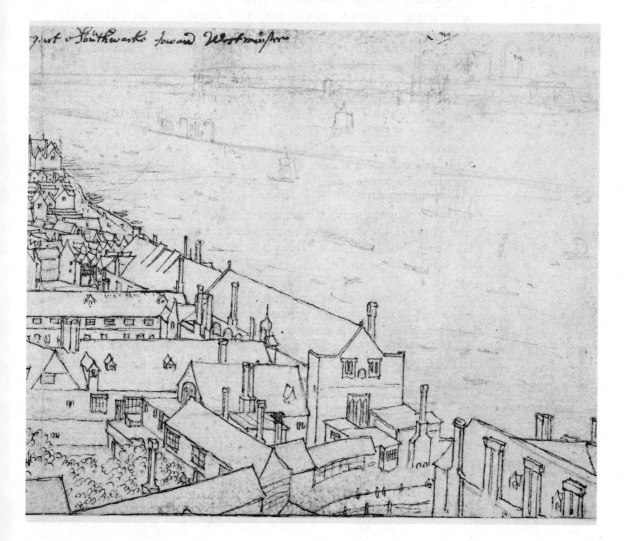

of half-timbering indicated in the etched lines of Hollar's shading, and the curved outer wall appears to be rendered in plaster, there being no sign of the timber frame itself. Here is Taylor's 'stately theator' in all its splendour: a theatre designed by the men who acted Shakespeare's plays while the author himself looked on, or trod the boards with them in person.

It is a tantalizing image, this finely etched depiction, so precise in its treatment that it offers a line of a dozen small windows visible to the left of an attached staircase turret; we conclude that they mark the level of one of the galleries within. Two windows lower down, just above the bushes that fringe the theatre's base, perhaps indicate the level of the lowest gallery. The roofline of the superstructure can be followed down almost – but not quite – to the point where it presumably meets the eave of the frame on its inner, or courtyard side. Three faces of the polygonally planned lantern are visible, two of them showing the upper parts of lights: we conclude that it was indeed a lantern meant to illuminate some area beneath, and that its plan was an octagon. A second stair turret is shown just beyond the curve of the wall of the frame: it seems to be a quarter-circle further round from the first, apparently symmetrical with it about an axis which runs through the central gulley between the superstructure's twin ridges. A roof of a house intervenes to prevent us from seeing whether there were doors at the foot of each of the staircase turrets. In short, although we can quiz this splendid little picture for hours, and with great profit, almost every piece of information it provides leads persuasively to another question. How big was the stage, not visible here? Was the heavy superstructure supported by posts, or could it span the whole width of the yard without intermediate support? What treatment of the interior caused the talk about town that made Chamberlain report that the Globe was 'the fairest that ever was in England'? And, above all, how big was its frame and in what tradition of architectural design was it rooted?

The interpretation of the etching cannot lead to answers to these questions by itself – some of them, indeed, cannot yet be answered at all – but we are helped in our quest by two other images of the Globe made by Hollar. These are both drawings; the one rather loose and lackadaisical, the other deliberate and precise. This latter, careful, drawing is well known [Plate 2]. It first turned up at an auction at Sotheby's in 1931; there it was bought by Iolo Williams, who published a photograph of it in *The Connoisseur* of 1933.[3] It went unnoticed by theatre historians until I. A. Shapiro called attention to it in the *Shakespeare Survey* of 1949.[4] It has now passed into the collection of Mr and Mrs Paul Mellon, and is kept at the Yale Center for the Study of British Art.[5] The sheet is 128 mm by 308 mm (about 5 in. by 12⅛ in.) along its right and bottom edges, and just a little wider (309 mm) overall. The medium is pen and ink over pencil, with some chalk. The top left corner is cut away, but the view is splendidly clear for the most part: the river Thames sweeps diagonally down across the sheet from left to right, and most of the buildings on its nearer side, the south bank, are meticulously inked in over the foundation of a pencil sketch. Among them the Globe and its neighbour the Hope form a centre of visual interest in the middle ground; close-to the courts of Winchester House dominate the view.

The image of the Globe in this drawing differs just a little from that in the etching. The superstructure looks smaller, and extends less far into the yard. Its lantern seems relatively larger in diameter, and stands a little further forward. The staircase turrets, though still symmetrical about a central axis, are more widely spaced, and while only one level of windows can be seen in the frame it extends to both sides of the closest staircase. One or two marks may indicate small windows in the gables of the superstructure, which are decorated with pointed finials. A horizontal band or beam stretches across the gables at the same height as the ridge of the evidently circular frame. The further staircase turret is curiously drawn as if in X-ray or else simply out of perspective, and it is topped by an object that may be a drooping flag or else a chimney.

The buildings on the far bank in this drawing are represented by only the faintest of lead marks: there is a suggestion of the shoreline, with St Paul's to the right of the view and other structures shown here and there along the north bank, but none is inked in. A similar emphasis is found in a companion piece, also at the Yale Center.[6] This is a view of the east part of Southwark, looking towards Greenwich [Plate 3]. It is much the same size as the Globe drawing: 140 mm by 311 mm (about $5\frac{1}{2}$ in. by $12\frac{1}{2}$ in.) including an additional strip at the

3.   Wenceslaus Hollar, 'East part of Southwarke, towards Grenwich.' Reduced.

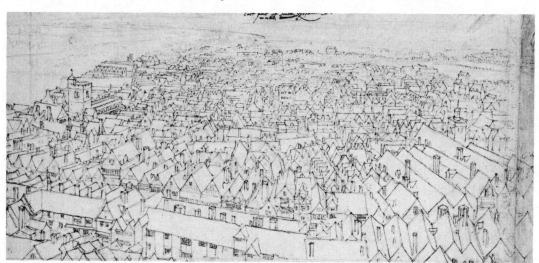

right added by the artist. The medium is pen and brown and black ink over black chalk and lead. Here the river cuts across the top left corner of the view, while in the foreground the roofs of Southwark appear in a jostling mass, all carefully inked in. St Olave's church is prominent amongst them, and on the far side of the river a few chalk lines show the position of the Tower of London. Clearly this drawing and its companion are studies made in preparation for the *Long View*, and it seems likely that the facts they report about the scene in Southwark are more reliable than those contained in the etching, which was composed miles away in Antwerp. Anyone who sets out to discover all that can be known about the Globe theatre must try to learn just how to read these drawings, for clearly they are eyewitness reports of the scene, including a small but deliberate rendering of the Globe itself. Because the two sketches so obviously belong together any techniques we find used in one may very well help us to understand the other, and for that reason we must keep both well in mind as we attempt to plumb the mysteries of Hollar's fascinating art. For, as we shall see in the following pages, these little sketches contain truths as yet unguessed-at by the historians of Shakespeare's theatre.

Another sketch of the Globe by Hollar was published recently in *Shakespeare Survey* by Graham Parry [Plate 4].[7] In size and technique it is quite different from the Yale studies, though it covers an area somewhat similar to that presented in the west Southwark view. It is contained in a book of Hollar drawings which once belonged to the diarist John Evelyn, and indeed appears to have been assembled by him; the volume is now in the John Rylands Library at Manchester.[8] At 85 mm by 193 mm the sheet is smaller than the Yale views, and in

4.   Wenceslaus Hollar, view of west London.

general the handling of the drafting – in pen and brown ink – is much looser. The drawing is undated, but it clearly forms one half of a panorama of London the companion of which we discover among the papers of another diarist of the seventeenth century, in the Pepysian Library at Cambridge.[9] This sheet [Plate 5] is roughly the same size as the Rylands Library one (80 mm by 180 mm) and the medium is again pen and brown ink. A careful comparison of the two drawings shows that they are exactly contiguous. The Pepysian view extends from the Tower to the right as far as St Lawrence Jewry to the left. In the foreground it shows many of the rooftops surrounding St Saviour's, and judging these against the similar ones shown in the *Long View* we are able to locate the westward limit of the drawing. Reading leftwards from the church tower we see $2\frac{1}{2}$ neatly drawn gable-fronts in an alley by the river, then $4\frac{1}{2}$ roof ridges before the edge of the sheet. The Evelyn sketch, again judging from the foreground as it appears in the *Long View*, takes up at the right just where the Pepys one left off. In the *Long View* we see the flank of a building with four tall chimneys, while in the sketch the flank is to be seen, though without the chimneys. On the far side of the river at the very edge of the sheet stands the tower of Bow Church. Thus the two views are contiguous and together form a Hollar panorama of London, here identified for the first time since it was split up between two famous collectors in the seventeenth century.

The Pepysian drawing is dated 1638, so the Evelyn one must have been made in that year too. The image of the Globe presented by this newly reunited panorama is regrettably loose: we see the double gable, but not the lantern; the row of windows, but not the staircases;

5.   Wenceslaus Hollar, 'London.'

the neighbouring Hope has a flag, but the Globe does not. We shall not discover much about the theatre from this hasty depiction of it; the interest of the new panorama lies rather in its status as a preparation for the *Long View*. The two Yale studies, with their similar sizes and media, represent one kind of preliminary drawing, in part very

Plates 6–12.
Wenceslaus Hollar,
Long View of London.

detailed, in part the merest note of an outline. The Evelyn/Pepys panorama is altogether looser in technique but more evenly stated: the north bank receives as much attention as the south, and because the two parts are contiguous – unlike the Yale studies – they comprise a

7. full sweep of the view from Whitehall to the Tower. Their purpose

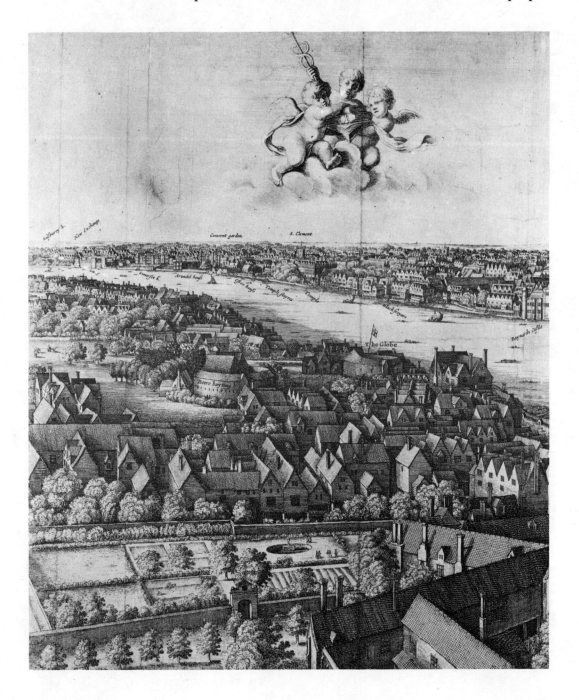

seems not to have to do with the details of buildings so much as their placement in the panoramic range. They are, that is to say, a compositional study.

For *pace* the *Long View*'s apparent realism it is as much a composed work of art as a Kokoschka. One need do no more than glance at

8.

Hollar's representations of west Southwark in quick succession to see that he has played with the relative position of the major elements of the view in order to change the character of his picture. Consider the roofline of Winchester Hall, the large gabled building flanking the Thames in the foreground. In the *Long View* [Plate 8] its ridge slopes

9.

only gradually up towards the horizon, so that we seem to see the building almost sideways-on. The compositional sketch collected by Evelyn [Plate 4] exaggerates this effect, while the Yale study [Plate 2] does the reverse: it angles the ridge more sharply upwards, giving the impression that the Hall recedes more abruptly away from the viewer.

10.

A similar effect is seen perhaps more clearly in the courtyard ranges extending southward from the Hall: in the Yale study their ridges are almost horizontal, while in the *Long View* they slope upwards to the right, and in the Evelyn sketch they do so quite sharply. We may note, too, the varying alignments of the Hall gable with the crossing of St

11.

Paul's on the far side of the river: in the *Long View* the crossing is almost directly above the peak of the gable; in the Evelyn sketch it is well to the left, while in the Yale study it is equally well to the right. In each case it seems that the *Long View* is a kind of *via media* between the extremes of the Evelyn sketch on the one hand and the Yale study on the other.

12.

Another way of describing these variations on the Winchester House theme would be to say that in each picture the point of view differs, were that not to prejudge a matter to which we shall now have to give some rather close attention. As a sort of shorthand it will do to say that the point of view in the Evelyn sketch is much further to the left than that in the Yale study, while the *Long View* represents as usual a compromise between the two extremes. A glance at the map suggests that the etching intends to convey the idea that it represents the panorama of London as seen from the top of St Saviour's tower: one looks down into the courts of Winchester House to the left and onto the roof of St Olave's to the right, so it is evident that one's perch is high up. Of St Saviour's itself there is no sign, but the proximity of the river and Long Southwark (Borough High Street) shows that the reason we cannot see it is that it is so close; it lies beneath our feet.

The Evelyn/Pepys panorama, with its different alignments and apparent point of view, actually shows the head of St Saviour's tower in the foreground. It seems, then, that this view is an imaginative composition, for Hollar could not have made it from an actual eyrie looking down upon St Saviour's, which was by far the tallest building in the neighbourhood in his time. The imaginary viewpoint seems to be about 50 yards south of St Saviour's tower, and the surprising thing is that Hollar has shown the various landmarks in the view in their correct alignments as they would be seen from such a point in reality. A moment with a straightedge and a map is enough to show that he was correct to put St Olave's to the left of the Tower of London, the tall spire of St Dunstan's-in-the-East in line with the near side of the Bridge, the tall square-headed tower of St Michael's in Cornhill straight over the centre of St Saviour's tower, with the spire of St Lawrence Poultney appearing to its left. None of these alignments is correct for lines of sight taken from the tower itself; each accurately compensates for an imagined shift of the observer's position some way further south. From this same southerly point of view the Guildhall would appear, as Hollar shows it, in line with Coldharbour on the north shore of the river; the east end of St Paul's would appear where he puts it, above the gable of Winchester Hall; while the west end of the cathedral would line up, as here, toward the west end of the Hall. This new panorama shows both Hollar's readiness to adapt his eyewitness information for the purposes of composition, and his extraordinary ability to recast the whole townscape consistent with an imaginary point of view. It is something of a technical *tour de force*.

The penmanship of the panorama is free and relaxed; that of the Yale studies is much more disciplined, even constrained. If the panorama shows, for all its ease of handling, such deliberate attention to the topographical facts, what sort of truths will these more tightly controlled studies have to offer? Like the *Long View* itself, they clearly

imply a point of view atop St Saviour's tower, and another moment
with straightedge and map shows that their alignments correctly
convey the literal truth about the sightlines from that spot. We shall
return to this matter later on, in rather more detail; for the moment we
may observe merely that the two studies appear to offer actual
eyewitness reports of the skyline of Southwark as seen from the top of
the church. St Olave's is to the right of the Tower of London and St
Paul's is to the right of Winchester House: both alignments are
consistent with lines of sight traced from the tower of St Saviour's. St
Paul's is seen, as it should be, directly in line with St Saviour's dock
(now St Mary's dock), visible at the foot of the sheet, its footpath
trodden by the only human figures visible in these otherwise
unpeopled, technical studies.

But if these drawings are eyewitness reports and not imaginative
reconstructions made in the studio, how were they made and what
further kinds of literal truth do they contain? These questions are
worth asking for their own sake, perhaps, but if we are to discover the
truth about Shakespeare's Globe theatre it is imperative that we
answer them. Hollar's drawings are the very best evidence we have,
and it appears that they may contain remarkably precise information
whose value has not hitherto been recognized. One of his sketches of
London now in the Print Room at the British Museum is a case in
point [Plate 13];[10] even though it does not show the Globe itself it
offers a decisive clue to our understanding of the accuracy which the
artist was able to achieve by the careful use of a simple drawing aid. It
is catalogued under the title 'London and Old St Paul's from the
Thames,' though to be more precise it shows the view eastward from
a spot we can identify as Durham House. There was no foreshore at
Durham House, which extended all the way to the water's edge. A
close look at the left margin of the drawing shows that it was made
from a point elevated above the river, for we look down onto the
waterline as it runs up to the masonry wall of the Savoy. It may be that

13.   Wenceslaus Hollar. 'London and Old St Paul's from the Thames.'

John Aubrey, in his sketch of Sir Walter Raleigh's life, has described the very room from which Hollar made the drawing:

Durham House was a noble palace; after [Raleigh] came to his greatness he lived there or in some apartment of it. I well remember his study, which was a little turret that looked into and over the Thames, and had the prospect which is pleasant perhaps as any in the World, and which not only refreshes the eie-sight but cheeres the spirit, and (to speake my mind) I beleeve enlarges an ingeniose man's thoughts.[11]

The medium of Hollar's drawing is pen and brown ink; the size 90 mm by 298 mm. Its composition is curiously uninspired for so refreshing a view: the buildings of pre-Fire London line themselves up along the north bank of the river like so many soldiers on parade, and the shoreline itself makes a shallow regular curve on its way eastward from the Savoy at the left to the Tower at the right. The very deliberation with which each church tower or spire is placed in this rather stolid array suggests that Hollar's composition here is not free, but tied to the facts of the landscape before him. In order to test this in a rudimentary way we can draw on a map the lines of sight from the artist's estimated point of view in Durham House, connecting them to

14. Wenceslaus Hollar, 'London and Old St Paul's' plotted on sightlines drawn to positions traced from a modern map. The landmarks located are:

TH	Temple Hall	P	St Paul's crossing
BR	St Bride's	B	St Mary-le-Bow
SEP	St Sepulchre	LP	St Lawrence Poultney
ML	St Martin's, Ludgate	T	White Tower
WT	Bulmer's water-tower		

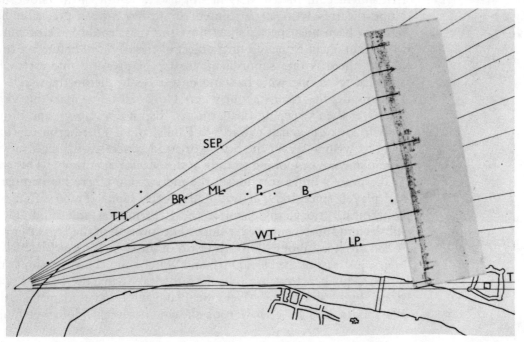

the series of landmarks which figure most prominently in the view:
St Sepulchre's to the left, followed in order by Middle Temple Hall, St
Bride's, St Martin's, Ludgate, the crossing of St Paul's, Bow Church,
Bevis Bulmer's water-tower at Broken Wharf, St Lawrence Poultney
and the north and south faces of the White Tower. The lines of sight to
the Tower cut across the south bank in the area of Paris Garden, so that
a cluster of buildings there obscures the view of the Bridge further on.
To check Hollar's drawing against the map we have merely to mark
off the intervals between the appropriate buildings on a strip of paper
and then lay this across the radiating sightlines we have drawn. There
are other, more sophisticated, tests that might be appropriate if this one
fails: perhaps Hollar plotted his townscape with a surveying instrument of some sort and reproduced the findings on paper through some
intermediate process. But the simplest, most direct question we can
ask of him is whether he has set down the view exactly as it presented
itself to him as he worked in the prospect room at Durham House. So
we proceed with our innocent game, juggling the scaled strip of paper
across the map of sightlines until, to our delight, it settles neatly into
place. When the line of intervals is arranged on a bearing of about 167°
from true north it fits all the sightlines – all ten of them – which we
have ruled connecting the viewpoint to the landmarks ranging from St
Sepulchre to the Tower [Plate 14].

Here is a discovery which may well have implications for our
interpretation of the all-important Yale studies of Southwark. If
Hollar made a habit of such accuracy as is evidently contained in this
British Museum sketch, may he not also have drawn the Globe and
Hope theatres with an agreement to reality whose precision has
hitherto been unsuspected? Just how the artist could have obtained
such accuracy must be our next object of enquiry, but before we turn
to that there is one subordinate matter of pressing interest to be
attended to. If one were to stand nowadays to the northern side of
Embankment Gardens, about where Hollar stood to make his view
(the river then sweeping further north than it does now), and if one
were to look eastwards towards St Paul's, and if – furthermore – one
were to wish away all the brickwork and concrete of the centuries,
would one not be looking straight at the Blackfriars theatre? This was
Shakespeare's other playhouse, the indoor one where his company
had played since 1609. It was built in the Upper Frater of an old
Dominican priory, dissolved at the Reformation and subdivided,
sub-let and sub-tenanted ever since. The location of the Upper Frater
is known: it lay about 100 yards north of the river bank at Blackfriars
Stairs, just east of the Fleet Ditch and Water Lane. The land slopes up
quite steeply here towards St Paul's cathedral, so that the Upper Frater
stood high above the river. Scholars who have identified the
Blackfriars as a long, low roof shown in several Hollar etchings

running northwards from the river hereabouts[12] have failed to notice this point; the theatre was located close to what the modern maps give as the 10 m contour. The long roof down below by the Fleet is that of the Long Gallery at Bridewell.

In the British Museum view a clutter of rooftops appears in line with St Paul's, crowding the hillside below the church [Plate 15]. At the bottom, by the river, we can see the long roof of Bridewell (it appears also, seen from the other side, in the Evelyn sketch, just above the right side of the Hope). And there, above Bridewell, between it and St Paul's, stands the Upper Frater and Blackfriars theatre, now correctly identified for the first time.

We return to the main argument. How could Hollar achieve the particular sort of accuracy we have found in this sketch of London? For we must notice that there are limits to its accuracy. For one thing, the skyline seems too neatly arranged as a set of towers and spires, many of which appear to out-scale their surroundings. For another, the lantern on Middle Temple Hall seems over-large, leaving doubts about other details of the view. What the artist has got abundantly right are the intervals between the major landmarks: these are presented with all the accuracy of a topographical survey, while the details of the view are subject to the artist's interpretive vision.

15.   Detail traced from Hollar's 'London and Old St Paul's' showing the cathedral and, circled below it, the Upper Frater at Blackfriars.

In 1611 there appeared in London a surveyors' handbook called *Speculum Topographicum: or the Topographicall Glasse*. Its author, Arthur Hopton, was a mathematician, an astrologer, a friend of Selden and the compiler of methodical prognostications for the years 1607–14. He addressed his book to professional surveyors, that rapidly growing class of proficient technicians whose task was to prepare the accurate estate surveys which the landowners of the sixteenth and seventeenth centuries found increasingly necessary for their affairs. For the most part the book follows the usual pattern of such manuals, which were quite common in the period, showing how to calculate the areas of various regular and irregular figures, how to use the surveyor's instruments – the circumferentor, plane table, chain, etc. – and how to set up the estate book for clarity and elegance. Such a book will require, every now and then, a graceful illustration of the main buildings, done in perspective if it is to look up-to-date. So Hopton is led into a consideration of the problems of perspective, though he has no intention of swelling his book with all the complicated rules a regular manual on the subject would require. Even so, his background as a man of science will not let him rest with a cursory account of foreshortening: he must offer a reliable, theoretically sound method of making perspective drawings without the great burden of perspective theory. In his 97th chapter, therefore, he offers 'A briefe discourse how to draw the platforme of any kind of building, or any other thing seene, though you cannot approach vnto the same, and that according to true proportion, according as it appeares or offers it selfe to the sight.' What follows is a description of a device that was well known to Italian artists and perspective theorists of the Renaissance, but had not, so far as I know, been introduced to English readers before:

If you desire to proiect the due forme of any obiect vpon a plaine superficies according as it shal offer itselfe to ye eye at any appointed place & distance, as to describe any town, or citty, any house, any floure, or any other body whatsoeuer, you must do thus.

Take a faire piece of smooth glasse, and fixe the same vpon a perpendicular at the end of a ruler, the which ruler let be diuided into a number of equall parts, next vpon this ruler must be another short perpendicular agreeing to the height of the midst of the Glasse, and in the vpper part of this shorte perpendicular must be a small and round sight hole, which done let ye perpendicular be made to moue equally fromwards or towards the Glasse, or to stand fixed at any diuision vpon the ruler as occasion shall be offered: this so ordered, when you desire the plat of any obiect as house or such like, plant the glasse opposite to the proportion required, the ruler lying paralel, then moue the shorter perpendicular neere to or far from the Glasse, euen as you desire the proiectment to be great or lesse: this done place your eye in the final sight hole noting well through the same how euery particular obiect doth appeare vpon the Glasse, your eye so resting, with your pencel or dyamond,

draw vpon ye said Glasse whatsoeuer you shall apprehend (or at the least whatsoeuer shall be required in your proiectment, and the worke is finished
. . . .

And you must note in all proiectments prospectiuely that you can lay no more downe but what you see, as in a 4 square house, you cannot possibly set downe more then any of the two sides and so much of the roofe as you see and so of cities &c. and therefore you may lay downe so much of any citty as your eye can apprehend, from any place where you plant your Glasse.

(pp. 179–80)

This device enables the artist to secure the two fixed elements required for any regular perspective composition: the so-called 'plane of intersection,' here established by the flat sheet of glass; and the unvarying point of view, here located exactly by the rigidly held eyepiece. In the closing pages of his *Underweyssung der Messung* (Nuremberg, 1525) Albrecht Dürer had included a woodcut showing a glass in use by a portraitist who views his model through an eyepiece set so that he can easily reach the glass itself, on which he works with what appears to be a quill. The glass is securely framed, and held erect at the edge of its table-stand by heavy brass supports. The eyepiece is provided with screw-adjusters which enable it to be moved towards and away from the glass, as well as up and down and from side to side.

Dürer's illustration of so substantial a device, appearing as it did in a treatise on measurement, had far-reaching consequences, especially in topographical art. But the theory of the instrument – though in a somewhat less developed form – had been described by Alberti in his discussion of drawing outlines, which he called 'circumscriptioni':

So attention should be devoted to circumscription; and to do this well, I believe nothing more convenient can be found than the veil, which among my friends I call the intersection, and whose usage I was the first to discover. It is like this: a veil loosely woven of fine thread, dyed whatever colour you please, divided up by thicker threads into as many parallel square sections as you like, and stretched on a frame. I set this up between the eye and the object to be represented, so that the visual pyramid passes through the loose weave of the veil. This intersection of the veil has many advantages, first of all because it always presents the same surfaces unchanged, for once you have fixed the position of the outlines, you can immediately find the apex of the pyramid you started with, which is extremely difficult to do without the intersection. You know how impossible it is to paint something which does not continually present the same aspect. This is why people can copy paintings more easily than sculptures, as they always look the same. You also know that, if the distance and the position of the centric ray are changed, the thing seen appears to be altered. So the veil will give you the not inconsiderable advantage I have indicated, namely that the object seen will always keep the same appearance. A further advantage is that the position of the outlines and the boundaries of the surfaces can easily be established accurately on the painting panel; for just as you see the forehead in one parallel, the nose in the next, the cheeks in another, the chin in one below, and everything else in its particular place, so you can situate precisely all the features on the panel or wall which you have similarly divided into appropriate parallels. Lastly, this veil affords the greatest assistance in executing your picture, since you can see any object that is round and in relief, represented on the flat surface of the veil. From all of which we may appreciate by reflection and experience how useful the veil is for painting easily and correctly.[13]

In the form of a drawing frame Alberti's *velo* was often used by sixteenth-century painters. Dürer, in the *Underweyssung*, shows a man squinting across an eyepiece at a nude, his view interrupted by a network of strings held in a wooden frame. At his hand he has a squared-up paper onto which he is transferring the image he sees through the reticulation of the frame. Although Alberti claimed to have invented the *velo* it was described by Leonardo in a passage on portrait painting; in the same paragraph is an allusion to the perspective glass as a device especially useful for drawing topo-graphical subjects: 'Del Modo del Ritrarre uno Sito Coretto,' runs the heading.[14] Some of the early Florentine city views, made under Alberti's influence, appear to have been composed on the basis of surveys made with a *velo* or glass, reflecting accurately the ratios between major landmarks as seen from a particular viewpoint in the hills around the city.[15] The principle of the drawing frame is described by Vignola in *Le due regole della Prospettiva Pratica*[16] and a reticulated frame, complete with eyepiece and a sheet of squared-up paper, is illustrated by Robert Fludd in his *Utriusque Cosmi Historia* (Oppenheim, 1619).

By the seventeenth century, indeed, the use of the frame, whether filled with strings or glass, was widespread. In a recent thesis A.K. Wheelock remarks of Dutch artists of the period:

They probably utilized artistic aids to a much greater degree than previously realized. The most prevalent aid to perspective was certainly the glass frame. Ever since its appearance in Dürer's *Underweyssung* . . . , the glass frame had been popularized by perspective theorists. It played a prominent role in Marolois' treatise, and when Hendrick Hondius described its use, he wrote that it 'est practiqué par les plus excellens Maistres ordinairement.'[17]

Amongst English authors also the two notions – of the drawing frame and the perspective glass – became commonplace in the seventeenth century. John Bate's *Mysteryes of Nature, and Art* (1634) illustrates a graticulated frame as suitable for making city views [Plate 16]: 'A verie easie way,' he calls it, 'to describe a Towne, or Castle: being within the full sight thereof':

For the effecting of this, you must have a frame made, and crossed into equall squares with Lute strings, and figured at the end of each string: this frame must have a foot, wherein it must be made to be lifted higher or lower as occasion serveth; also you must divide your paper that you are to draw upon into so many equal squares as your frame containeth: having the like figures at the ends of each line that there is on the frame; before this frame must be placed a style or bodkin having a little glasse on the top of it for to direct the sight. Note now that the nearer any thing commeth unto the Center, the lesser it appeareth: hence it is that a Towne of a mile, or more long, or a huge great Castle, at a distance may be comprehended, and that easily within the limits of so small a frame; By the stile direct your sight from one part to another, beginning at one square, and proceeding through the rest in order as they lie ....[18]

While Bate suggests a drawing frame for making townscapes most authors agree with Arthur Hopton that the glass is best for this purpose. Indeed the 'perspective glass' was so well known that other technical writers made casual allusions to it. William Folkingham, whose *Art of Survey* (1610) is an exercise in jargon so pretentious that even Osric could hardly cope with it, begins his feeble section on perspective thus:

For Delineating of Adiuncts, as Edifices and other erections, the Prospectiue glasse is facil & compendious, but for want thereof take this generall Rule.
(p. 55)

And he continues with a wondrously opaque account of foreshortening. Contemporary poetic uses of the phrase 'perspective glass,' such as those in William Browne's *Britannia's Pastorals* (1616), are more likely to refer to a primitive form of telescope, called by that name in Leonard Digges's *Pantometria* of 1571 (sig. Gij[a]). John Norden, the 'performer' of one of the major London panoramas of the early seventeenth century, was first of all a professional surveyor, though he was a poet too, who in his long moral poem *Vicissitudo Rerum* (1600) claimed that Geometry was the mother of all the arts:

> *Geometrie* the mother of all Arts
> Was not at first found by a former Art:
> *Nature* did first deliniate those parts,
> That *Wits* and *Willes* might come vnto her mart,
>   And buy by practise (to adorne the heart)
>   The Principles of Art, as *Archimedes* did,
>   *Archytas* too, and other, to some hid.   (Stanza 144)

Like so many others of his kind Norden certainly knew the sort of instrument described by Hopton, for in his *Surueiors Dialogue* (1610) he makes a passing and casual allusion to it:

A Painter can by his art delineate the proportion of any creature, without vsing perspectiue glasse, or a compasse euen by the eye and serious obseruation: so may a' man, hauing the true vse of any topographicall instrument by rules geometricall describe a Mannor in a kind of forme, without line or chaine, or other measure. But if he will say he doth ..., I will then say he is a rare bird ....
(p. 117)

16. A drawing frame, from John Bate, *The Mysteryes of Nature, and Art*, 1634.

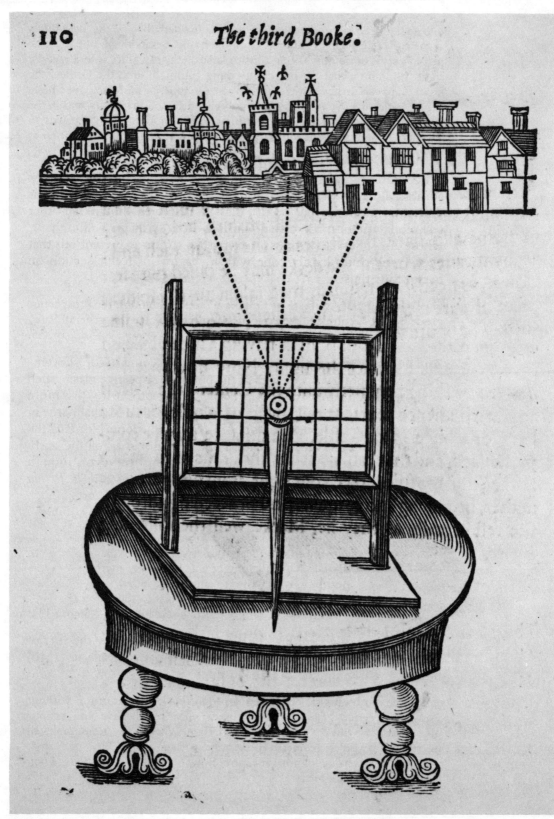

A painter *may* be able to achieve a good perspective by the rules 'without vsing perspectiue glasse,' but if he does he is like a surveyor making thought and calculation stand duty for the hard slog of actual measurement on the ground, to which he ought to be committed. The force of Norden's comparison is perhaps a little obscure, but it is clear that the perspective glass and the compasses will bring exactness to a painter's work just as the actual deployment of a line will make a survey true. Indeed Hopton appears to claim that the perspective glass might be used as a kind of topographical instrument to enable the surveyor to judge, as Norden puts it 'by rules geometricall,' the scale of landmarks in the view before him:

Now if you desire to make a scale for this proiectment, note the equall parts betwixt both the perpendiculars, which call your first number, then let the distance from your eie to the obiect bee your second number, lastly draw a perpendicular vpon the Glasse from the summity of the obiect to the center of the Glasse, or rather to that part of the Glasse that is of the same height from your ruler as the sight hole is where you place your eye, and this shall be your third number, which number is found by applying the length of that line to the equall parts vpon your ruler, these 3 numbers had, multiply the second and third and diuide by the first, so is the quotient the number of feete or inches, that the said perpendicular containes according as the distance of the obiect was expressed in feete or inches, of which make a scale and measure all the rest. (*Speculum Topographicum*, pp. 179–80)

Hopton is perhaps not quite explicit enough for comfort here, but the principle he is applying to the geometry of the glass is that of the proportionality of similar triangles, and his fundamental claim is that a perspective view registered in the way he describes is sufficiently true to make scaling-up from it worthwhile. As a practical consideration this last point is doubtless of little value because one cannot imagine why it should be necessary, except perhaps in wartime, to estimate the heights of buildings in such a roundabout way if access to them is easy, and presumably access is necessary if their distance from the observer is to be measured. But Hopton's claim is merely characteristic of contemporary books of geometry, which seldom failed to illustrate the Euclidian demonstration of the proportionality of similar triangles by showing a man calculating the height of a tower whose top he has lined up with a wand planted in the ground at a known distance and elevation from his eye. Nevertheless it is true that a perspective taken according to the method described by Hopton will in fact contain the sort of precision that he claims for it, and for the reasons that he indicates in his paragraph on scaling. Such a view will be exactly what theorists of perspective mean when they allude to the 'picture plane' or 'plane of intersection,' and the proportions registered on it will indeed bear a relation to the reality depicted which may be analyzed in

Euclidian terms. If the particular claim about scaling is of little real value, the more fundamental claim to accuracy cannot be denied.

No description of the topographical glass from the earlier part of the seventeenth century gives any very helpful account of how the outlines marked on the glass are to be transferred to paper. With a graticulated drawing frame there is no difficulty: the composition is made directly onto the squared-up sheet at the artist's hand. The well-known French manual of mid-century, the so called 'Jesuit Perspective,' has chapters on all kinds of drawing frame and glass, and does go into some detail on this awkward technical point. The English translation did not appear until 1672, when it was illustrated by the earliest picture I have found in an English text of a perspective glass (as distinct from a drawing frame) [Plate 17]. In the accompanying text the author, Jean Dubreuil, describes how to convey the image of a landscape from glass to paper:

... one may mark upon the Glass with the Pen and Ink, and after that all is done, to moisten a little the other side of the Glass for to refresh the Ink and to set on the side, which we shall have traced, a Paper somewhat moist, and then to pass the hand upon it; and the Paper will take, all that which was marked upon the Glass.[19]

Of course this image will be reversed, and it seems unlikely that the print-off method was much used for topographical subjects. In a private letter Mr C. Walter Hodges has shown me how the thing must have been done by practical artists working on the ground. The portable glass is clamped in place before the fixed eyepiece, and the artist traces the outline of the scene upon it with a fine brush or a pen. When he has finished he takes the glass from its brass clamp or frame, clips a sheet of paper to it on the marked side and, holding the resulting sandwich up to the light, retraces the view onto the paper, doubtless using chalk or lead because it would be necessary to hold the work high up and ink could not be expected to flow. Just such a tracing method was advocated by Dürer in the *Underweyssung der Messung*.

Here, then, is an instrument whose use would account for the particular kind of accuracy we have found in Hollar's drawing of the city of London as seen eastwards from Durham House. On the plane of glass, clamped perpendicularly in front of a fixed eyepiece, Hollar might have marked the exact positions of all the major landmarks in their true proportions as they registered at the mechanical equivalent of the picture plane. Only by positing the use of such a device can we account for the extraordinary accuracy with which these intervals are rendered on the paper. Even the very width of the White Tower is exactly stated in relation to the much larger intervals between, say, the Tower and St Paul's, or between St Sepulchre and Bow Church. All

are given precisely where they should occur along a straight intersection of Hollar's lines of sight, and it seems unlikely – to say the least – that such exactness could be achieved freehand, especially since it is a kind of exactness that does not come readily to the unguided eye. Left to its own devices, the eye would rather record the intervals along such an arc of vision as directly proportional to the angles they subtend at the point of view. Hollar's intersection is straight; that of the roving eye is segmental.

We have no very thorough account of the artist's working methods left by his friends and contemporaries. From Francis Place in the eighteenth century comes a report that he held a hand over one eye when he worked,[20] and to this we may add John Aubrey's observation:

He was very short-sighted, and did worke so curiously that the curiosity of his Worke is not to be judged without a magnifying-glasse. When he tooke his Landskapes, he, then, had a glasse to helpe his Sight.[21]

By these words Aubrey evidently means that Hollar used some sort of telescope to survey the scene, but that surely is an unlikely thing for him to have done, except perhaps to check on local details. The alternative meaning, that Hollar used a magnifying glass to see his close-work with the pen, seems to run counter to Aubrey's allusion to his shortsightedness. Possibly the antiquarian's memory is inaccurate or his phrasing not quite exact: for 'taking' a landscape the most useful sort of glass would be the topographical instrument we have described here.

A topographical glass could be set up so that the centre line of the projected drawing was directly opposite the eyepiece, and doubtless that was the normal procedure. It is the one illustrated in all the prints of drawing frames and glasses that have so far come to light, but it is by no means the only possible configuration. If the eyepiece were moved to the left or right the proportions of the view then registered on the glass would alter, and it seems likely that Hollar made use of this characteristic of the device as an aid to his composition, especially in views where one side of the scene had more intrinsic interest that the other. To move the eyepiece leftwards in relation to the glass would be to compress the left side of the resultant view and to expand the right. If the British Museum drawing under discussion represents the whole span of an original pencil study made from the glass – it may, of course, have been cropped to either side – it indicates that the eyepiece was set up somewhat to the right of centre. The view thus compresses the Tower and St Lawrence Poultney, and by comparison stretches the intervals between the Temple and Bow Church, probably because the artist wanted to offer more detail in this passage.

A greater and reverse emphasis is shown in the drawing at the Pepysian Library of London as seen from Milford Stairs [Plate 18]. We can locate the point of view readily enough from the evidence of the riverside buildings shown in the foreground to the left. These appear also in Hollar's *Bird's Eye View of West London*,[22] so that we can fix Hollar's position on a modern map as about the middle of Temple Place at the foot of Arundel Street. Several landmarks are obvious and readily identified: St Paul's central crossing appears above the nearby buildings one-third of the way across the picture from the left; Bevis Bulmer's water-tower rears its conical head just to the left of the tall spire of St Lawrence Poultney; the Tower of London is distinctly visible to the left of the Bridge; and at the right margin of the sheet we can just see the tower of St Saviour's in Southwark. Many other landmarks are visible, but their identification is not as easy as these. When we draw a map of sightlines radiating from the point of view in Temple Place we find that a strip of paper marked with Hollar's intervals fits across them quite perfectly [Plate 19]. Once again the width of the White Tower is exactly correct, as are the larger intervals between St Saviour's and St Paul's and the small one between the water-tower and St Lawrence. But this time Hollar's eyepiece is deflected well to the left in relation to the picture plane, in relation, that is, to the topographical glass. As a result the large buildings in the foreground to the left are compressed in relation to the broad expanse of the river to the right. In the etching which he based on this drawing, Hollar retained the exact proportions of the intervals between the landmarks as established by the glass, trimmed off a great part of the

18.   Wenceslaus Hollar, 'London by Milford Staires.'

left of the view, and extended it marginally to the right so as to include the whole of St Saviour's. Thus he carried further the emphasis he had already established by the particular configuration of his topographical glass and its eyepiece.

And here for the first time we have made the significant transition from preparatory drawing to finished etching. To be sure, this is a minor case: the etching of the view from Milford Stairs is only 168 mm wide. Nevertheless it carries within it the exact surveyed proportions we have found in the sketch. Now we must ask whether the great printed panoramas of the earlier seventeenth century show evidence of a similar accuracy. Above all, is Hollar's own *Long View*,

19.   Wenceslaus Hollar, 'London by Milford Staires' plotted on sightlines drawn to positions traced from a modern map. The landmarks located are:
      P   St Paul's crossing   LP   St Lawrence Poultney
      WT   Bulmer's water-tower   T   White Tower
      S   St Saviour's, Southwark

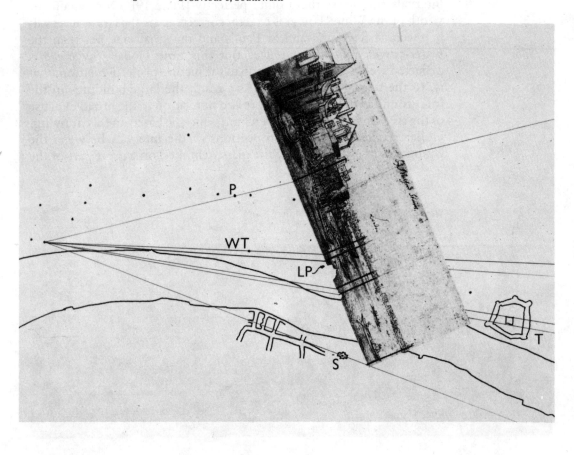

with its tantalizing picture of the Globe and the Hope, the result of surveys made at the topographical glass?

2 *The printed panoramas*

Our object is to find out as much as we can about Shakespeare's Globe theatre, so precisely depicted in Hollar's various views of Bankside. It appears also in Norden and in Visscher, but with rather less visual conviction there, looking altogether too sketchy in the one and too schematic in the other. Possessing some of Hollar's drawings as well as his finished etching, we are unusually well equipped to enquire into the methods by which he worked, and in particular the degree and kind of accuracy he was capable of achieving. The sketches, especially the Yale studies, are our best evidence for the Globe, but in

Plates 20–23. Claes Jan Visscher, *London*.

order to read them correctly we must investigate their relation to the finished state of the print. Hollar, working in Antwerp, did not copy his etching directly from them; rather he adapted and moulded the work as it proceeded, giving artistic authority to material that was hardly more than an accurate topographical survey. Yet his great etching, and the panoramas of Norden and Visscher, incorporated a surprising amount of literal, surveyor's truth, more of it indeed than any of the conventional maps of the period, and if we are to understand their representations of the Globe, and those of the studies on which they are based, we must first discover how they were surveyed.

Although it may now be regarded as certain that Hollar used the topographical glass in some of his preparatory drawings, it would nevertheless be a quite revolutionary step to claim that such precise surveys formed a measured, structural basis of any of the panoramas. Yet that is what I hope, with all the diffidence that the case requires, to

21.

prove in this chapter. Hitherto the consensus has been all the other way: that however good a general idea of the city given by John Norden or Visscher or Hollar, and however accurate some particular details may be, the views are works of art and subject to the constraints of emphasis, balance and contrast usually to be found in artistic compositions. This is no doubt true, but we must remember that a topographical craftsman working in the tradition of Leonardo or Alberti would include measured accuracy as one of the aspects of his art; far from seeing the precision of a survey as opposed to the claims of expressive pictorialism, a man like John Norden would see both as facets of the one precious stone, for he believed that Geometry was the mother of the arts, not their antagonist. It is not so much that he would aim at a surface verisimilitude, like that achieved by a photographer, but rather that his mental equipment both as artist and as surveyor would predispose him to make a pictorial composition which included the geometry of a survey as a necessary part of its own special

22.

sort of visual form. I shall not therefore claim that the great London views of the seventeenth century give an accurate account of everything that lay spread out before the observer's eyes as he stood behind the parapet at the top of St Saviour's tower in Southwark, gazing across the boat-filled river at this little house or that particular church or market. The merest glance at Visscher's panorama [Plates 20–23] is enough to show that its aims are celebratory and memorial, not literal. Great spires soar above lofty towers, St Paul's rises like a backdrop above the tiny footrows of the houses below it, buildings of note like Coldharbour puff themselves out to fill an altogether disproportionate space, and the river straightens to make a convenient stage for all this civic drama. Yet for all their show, the most important of the buildings are set exactly in their right places: the surveyor in Visscher has seen to that.

Visscher's fine panorama of London is only one of a great number of such views. The list of them compiled by Irene Scouloudi in 1953

23.

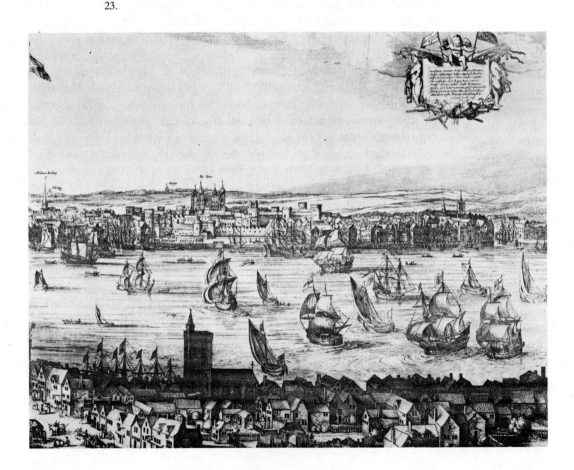

contains 110 different entries, covering the years 1600 to 1666 and including a few later adaptations.[1] They range from Harrison's rather compressed and schematized representation at the head of an arch of triumph (1604)[2] to Hollar's 'Trve and Exact Prospect' of 1666,[3] which records the devastation caused by the great Fire. Of course some of the views are of slight topographical interest, and many are in any case merely redactions from others, so that Miss Scouloudi was able to reduce the 110 items to twelve groups, of which only three are of immediate interest to us here as possibly deriving from original surveys. These are the *Civitas Londini*, 'performed' in 1600 by John Norden but apparently engraved and printed somewhat later, about 1615; Claes Jan Visscher's view published in Amsterdam in 1616; and Hollar's *Long View* of 1647, together with their redactions. Another Visscher panorama first published in the middle of the seventeenth century, the so-called 'Visscher excudit' view, and certain of Hollar's later pieces, while not directly derivative from their authors' earlier work are nevertheless so indebted to it that they hardly constitute independent classes. The views of Harrison, Hondius, Holland and Merian,[4] while not clearly derivative from any single particular source, are evidently too imprecise to command our attention here, and we may properly restrict ourselves to the great seminal works of Norden, Visscher and Hollar.

John Norden's view of London [Plates 24–25] is extant only in the four sheets held in the Royal Library at Stockholm (in the de la Gardie collection, no. 89). The British Museum has the two central sheets,[5] but these are from a late pull, possibly as late as the middle of the seventeenth century, for the plates have been worked over. Assembled together, as they are in Stockholm, the sheets make a view 35.7 cm by 125.3 cm. It is characterized by a very curious method of composition, for London appears as if mounted on the top of a globe, with the central part highest up and the extremities east and west falling away precipitously to either side. Yet one notices that although the ground seems to slope downwards from the centre with increasing steepness toward the edges, Norden generally maintains the verticality of his upright lines, with the result that buildings in Whitehall to one extreme and beyond the Tower to the other are represented as if in some fancied approximation to an isometric projection. The result is very odd and quirky to look at, as if Norden had been puzzled by the problem which every maker of panoramas has to face sooner or later: how to reduce a very wide angle of view to the discipline of a two-dimensional picture plane.

Visscher appears to solve that problem in a direct, even a cavalier, way [Plates 20–23]. He composed his view as if it were seen along a river whose banks were straight and parallel. The near, southern, shore is an even band along the bottom of his composition; the far, northern, shore is equally straight, though its horizon is somewhat relieved by the undulations of the hills of Middlesex. The northward turn of the river beyond Wapping is not included, and the southward turn toward Whitehall is indicated by the merest dip of the shoreline to the left of the panorama. The character of the engraving is therefore quite different from Norden's. Where the *Civitas Londini* is a tumbling world of great pregnant curves, Visscher's *London* is all horizontals and verticals, an even town whose energy goes into spires and towers. Visscher's sheets are therefore wider than Norden's: again there are four of them, but joined together they make a rectangle 42.3 cm by 215.9 cm.

Both Norden and Visscher include a view of the south bank, and both show the tower of St Saviour's church, now Southwark Cathedral. It is of some significance that they should do so, for the third of our subjects, Hollar's *Long View* [Plates 6–12], makes it quite clear that the point of view from which the panorama was made was the top of St Saviour's tower. In a later but related work, the 'Trve and Exact Prospect' of 1666, Hollar makes the explicit statement that the survey is taken from 'St. Marie-Overs [i.e. St Saviour's] Steeple in Southwarke.'[6] The proportions of the *Long View* are much the same as Visscher's: Hollar has seven sheets, though the first and last are only half-plates. Each full sheet is 47.6 cm by 39.4 cm, and the view takes up about 45.7 cm by 38.8 cm so that the entire panorama is 45.7 cm by 232.8 cm. The composition, however, is very different from Visscher's. As in Norden, the river swells as it approaches the point of view and diminishes as it recedes away from the observer to west and east. Its meanders on the way to Greenwich are shown, and although the curve southward past Whitehall seems oddly flattened it is nevertheless clearly indicated. Of the three views this most readily suggests that the reality of the town has met a satisfactory convention for its depiction; the horizontality is less rigid than Visscher's, yet more convincing than Norden's great hummock, the sweep of the river looks much as it might do were it registered on the screen of a *camera obscura*, and above all the emphasis on major buildings, though obviously not forgotten, does not seem to lead to their physical overstatement. Compared with the others, Hollar's *Long View* simply looks businesslike and accurate.

Hollar's is the only one to bring the foreground into an apparently satisfactory relation to the view of the far bank, and indeed it has long been established that Visscher's account of the south bank is merely a rendering in perspective of the information – much of it false – given in the so-called 'Agas' map of London. As with so much having to do with these maps and views, the precise debt is difficult to ascertain, for the extant copies of the 'Agas' map were not published until 1633, well after Visscher's view had appeared.[7] Yet it shows London for the most part as it would have looked very much earlier, probably about 1560, and indeed in recent years two copper plates[8] have come to light bearing parts of what is almost certainly the source of the 1633 map, itself a crude woodcut. No plate has yet been discovered showing the south side of the river, but while we live in hope we may assume that it would bear the same close relation to the 'Agas' map as the two extant plates do, and we may therefore further assume that Visscher had this source before him as he worked on his panorama. If it was indeed like the 'Agas' map it would have shown the ponds of the King's Pike Gardens reduced from their many and irregular shapes to a few schematic rectangles. The 'Agas' map shows Maid Lane as a dead end, and marks two animal-baiting arenas. All this Visscher closely reproduces, merely replacing the arenas with polygonal theatres, one of them the Globe, and supplying a third theatre – the Swan – in a vacant space by the river, although in fact it is known that the Swan was some 400 ft from the bank.[9] Whatever may be true of his picture of the city itself, then, Visscher's Southwark is something of a shambles, and certainly not based on an independent and accurate survey. Of course this is not to say that it contains no useful information: the Bridge Gate is generally correct, St Saviour's is clearly an attempt to render the special character of that building, and St Olave's tower is shown correctly bearing a turret in its northwest corner.

Plates 24–25. John Norden, *Civitas Londini*.

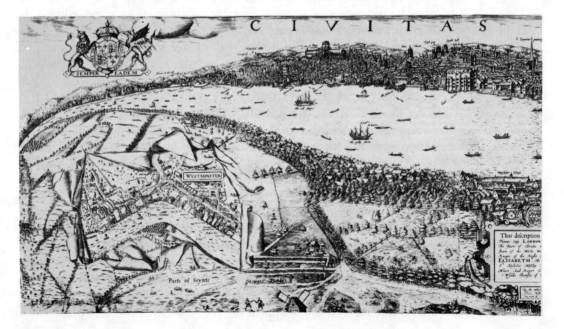

John Norden's south bank offers difficulties of another kind, for inset into the *Civitas Londini* is a map of London quite certainly by Norden himself (it is an updated version of one he had published in 1593[10]) and so far as the south bank is concerned the depictions in the map and the panorama fail to agree. The map locates St Saviour's correctly, while the panorama puts it too far west. In the map Winchester House has no lantern on the great hall; in the panorama it does. Indeed the panorama's depiction of the streets of Southwark is generally incorrect, as is its view of St Saviour's, while the map in these respects is good. Such contradictions as these have suggested to some commentators that the panorama is merely an updated revision of an earlier, lost, original made perhaps to commemorate the mayoralty of Sir Nicholas Moseley, whose name and arms are given prominence on the plates.[11] But in any case Norden was not an engraver, and can only have supplied the cartographic information from which the plates were made. He – or the engraver – is careful to show a human figure at the top of St Saviour's wielding a pair of compasses under the tag 'Statio prospectiua.' If this phrase means anything, it must indicate that the views of the north and south banks are taken from quite separate points, for St Saviour's is certainly not the place from which the southern part of the panorama is seen. Our dissatisfaction with the inaccuracies in the Southwark part of the

25.

engraving must not be visited automatically on the view to the north of the river, for as in Visscher the two parts are probably of separate provenance.

Neither artist presents the Bankside theatres with the unambiguous assurance the patient enquirer seeks. Visscher's narrow octagons representing the Bear Gardens and the Globe are so obviously located in positions dictated by the older map that one would be rash indeed to afford them any credence in matters of structural detail. Norden's panorama sets the buildings more correctly on their proper sites, but shows them in what we may call for convenience sake a cartographer's polygon: the Swan and the Bear Gardens present three faces each, apparently one-half of a hexagon, while the Rose and Globe, seen from above, are given hexagonal roofs. In the plan which forms part of the *Civitas Londini* all the theatres are shown as circular, as they are also in Norden's earlier map of 1593. Later views of the playhouses do little to clear up the muddle: some show the Globe as round, others as octagonal, some show it too close to the river, or confused with the Rose, or too inexactly to make much sense. Until Hollar all seem to be derivative, from either Visscher or Norden, and none gives an independent, unambiguous report of the structure of the play-houses.[12] A quite different view, that discovered in the library of the University of Utrecht and published by Leslie Hotson,[13] shows London as seen from the north and includes at its left edge one of the Shoreditch theatres, rendered as a polygon, probably an octagon, with two very large attached staircases. The main polygon is shown much taller than it is wide. Since windows mark that it had three storeys we may estimate the height to the top of the walls as 33 ft, and if we take the engraving's depiction of it as reliable in such matters we must conclude that the main part of the house was about 24 ft across – this to contain stage, yard, galleries and all. Such a structure would be absurd, and clearly the view is another cartographer's polygon, much like those in Norden's *Civitas Londini*, with whose pictorial style the anonymous North View has other suggestive affinities.

Thus far this review of some of the faults of the panoramas of Norden, Visscher and Hollar would hardly suggest that they have much to offer in the way of topographical exactness. Yet if we shift our attention from the south bank to the north we find something altogether more satisfactory. Here in each case is a simple panorama, a range of rooftops and spires beyond the river line interspersed with the distinctive shapes of a series of familiar and recognizable buildings: the Temple church, St Bride's, St Paul's, the crown on Bow Church, the spire of St Lawrence Poultney, the tall spire of St Dunstan's-in-the-East, the lower one of Allhallows, Barking, and the battlements and turrets of the Tower. For the most part these buildings lie somewhat to the north of the river, so that buildings like Baynard's

Castle or Coldharbour or Fishermen's Hall, which front the river itself, may be aligned with the towers and spires beyond them. Here we notice that as a general rule – there are exceptions to which we shall come later on – these alignments are consistent in all three views with lines of sight taken from the tower of St Saviour's.

This is a simple matter to test, and for this part of our enquiry all we need are a good Ordnance Survey map and a straightedge. If we rule a line between the tower of St Saviour's and a landmark north of the river bank we can plot the point on the bank that would appear immediately below it in a panoramic view, that is to say in line with it. Thus the west side of St Paul's (Old St Paul's, locatable by reference to the standard history of the cathedral)[14] lines up a little to the east of the eastern edge of the mouth of the harbour at Queenhythe, and St Dunstan's-in-the-East is on the same bearing as Lion Quay beside Billingsgate. When we turn to Visscher's view we find that these alignments are exactly reproduced. St Bride's appears, as it should, directly above Paul's Stairs, and the crossing of St Paul's lines up with the Three Cranes at Vintry, at the end of the modern Vinter's Lane. Bow Church is seen slightly to the left of the crane at the Steelyard, a little to the west of what is now Allhallows Lane. Guildhall appears as it should in line with Coldharbour, and St Lawrence Poultney's spire rises just to the west of the Swan, about where Swan Lane now runs. The ornamented tower of the Exchange can be seen to the west of Fishermen's Hall and St Michael's in Cornhill just to the east. Beyond the Bridge St Dunstan's-in-the-East is correctly aligned with Lion Quay, while Allhallows, Barking is just to the right of the South Gate of the Bridge. Thus along the whole range of the panorama from Bride's to Barking at least nine major landmarks are seen in their correct relations to the river bank if viewed from the tower of St Saviour's. At the western extreme of the engraving this trueness no longer holds good: the Temple and St Dunstan's-in-the-West are too far to the left in relation to the buildings on the bank, as if Visscher had compressed the foreshore to give more room for the great houses of the Strand, but left the more northerly buildings in a consistent relation to the rest of the view. St Clement's, for example, appears correctly in line with the western end of Middle Temple Hall.

The alignments we have noted in Visscher are correct when judged against reality, but they are quite at variance with the 'Agas' map and presumably with its source, on which Visscher almost certainly drew for his image of the south bank. Here for example Bow Church aligns with Dowgate at the north bank, well to the left of its position judged on a modern map. Allhallows, Barking is also well to the left of the South Gate of the Bridge in 'Agas,' and while some of the other alignments are closer than these to the modern survey none so precisely coincides with it as the whole array found in Visscher from

St Bride's all the way to Barking. Whatever the shortcomings of his depiction of Southwark, Visscher's north bank gives clear evidence of having been based on a precise eyewitness view taken from the top of St Saviour's, without the intervention of any available map.

But what kind of a view can this have been? The panorama is not a meticulous piece of verisimilitude: Middle Temple Hall is shown with five bays instead of seven, the picture of the Steelyard fails to agree with an extant Elizabethan plan of it in the Public Record Office,[15] the choir of St Paul's has too few bays, the ogee caps on the Tower are grossly exaggerated. The list of particular inaccuracies is endless. Yet because the major alignments of the view are correct we must conclude that it is based on some kind of skeleton survey taken from St Saviour's, and we must now try to discover what kind of a survey that was. It might, of course, simply have been rule of thumb. The alignments we have checked were patently visible from the surveyor's point of view, but he might merely have estimated the actual intervals between the landmarks. If so we should not expect the proportions of the panorama to fit a modern map, the more so since in matters of verticality Visscher seems quite happy to depart from the literal truth to achieve the kind of emphasis he wants.

Yet it can be proved that the skeleton survey on which Visscher's picture of the north bank is based was in fact a careful, precise record of what was actually there in front of the observer, as recorded on a topographical glass or drawing frame. But before we can proceed to the demonstration, or even to the consideration of rival possibilities, it will be necessary to establish the true positions on the ground of the more outstanding buildings shown in the panorama, and in particular their bearings from the point of view at the top of St Saviour's church. Hitherto in our study this question has not been troublesome, but now we must note that the range of landmarks from the Savoy to the Tower is not left to us today as it presented itself to the view in the early seventeenth century. One can take a number twenty-three bus past most of their sites and from its upper deck see a city quite different from Norden's or Hollar's. But as we ride along we shall see that there are parts here and there that have not been lost: the chapel of the Savoy remains, for instance, to remind us of the position of that great cruciform hospital; beneath the handsome building of St Bride's are medieval and earlier crypts; and of course the Tower itself still resolutely stands.

It happens that there is, in the British Library among the Harleian MSS,[16] an odd little description of London which gives a street-by-street account of part of our route as it was seen by an observer long before the days of London Transport. It begins with Whitehall, then moves in the manner of a street directory to Charing Cross and so to the Strand. Here it enumerates taverns, inns and houses including 'yorke howse over against the howse you maie stand and see repairing.' This may indicate that our directory, otherwise undated, was made about 1624, when 2000 tons of Portland stone were given to the Duke of Buckingham by the King for the embellishment of York House, the Duke's London residence.[17] As our bus picks up speed past the Civil Service Stores and the Vaudeville Theatre it is perhaps hard to imagine that once the right side of the street was fronted only by a thin line of taverns and gatehouses, beyond which the courts and gardens of great palaces swept down to the river. To the left the buildings clustered more thickly, and where the Strand widened there was an island of them at the centre. The directory splits all these up into columns:

right hand	left hand
Cranbourne howse ioyning to	Exeter howse ore against the Sauoy
Salsbury near after this	and at the opening of the brod stran
worster howse	White hart In. tav.
iij tunnes tav.	Sayle and child In.
iij cranes tav. ioyning	Helmet In.
to the Sauoy hospitall	Swan In.

and so on, until the centre column fills in: 'Hear in the midst of the street a plumpe [*sic*], a maypole; a Dial Pillar about which are fishmongers shoppes. . . .'

There, then, lay the Savoy to our right; all we can see of it now is the nameplate of Savoy Street, but if we were on foot we could seek out the elegant little Savoy chapel, the last remaining part of this once-great hospital. A plan of the building, erected by Henry VIII and still standing for Norden, Visscher and Hollar to see or know about, was published by George Vertue.[18] From it, and from the position of the extant chapel, we can plot the layout of the whole place, and especially its long river front, which extended all the way from a point east of the present Savoy Hill across Lancaster Place and just into what is now the western part of Somerset House. The western edge of the river front thus lay on a bearing of 281.7° from St Saviour's. (I give the bearings in decimals of degrees, rather than minutes and seconds, because later on we shall be punching them up on a pocket calculator, which deals nicely with the one and hardly at all with the other.)

Today this part of the Strand is pierced by the approaches to Waterloo Bridge, but the old directory has some pretty entries: to the right 'The Queenes backyard,' next door to 'King Henry head tav.' and then 'Denmark howse of old Som. [i.e. Somerset House]' before the 'Mitar tav.,' 'Stran bridge' and 'Talbot In wher the stran beginnes to narroe.' And here too at the centre lay 'the Bar of howses wherein S. Clements church and churchyard standeth . . .,' one of our landmarks. The right side of the way continued with 'Arundell howse,' 'milford lane,' 'Essex howse,' these last two bracketed to the note: 'ore against S. Clements church.' Somerset House did not extend so far west as it does now, and a plan among Sir William Chambers's papers showing the outline of the old building with the present one superimposed[19] gives the position of its western flank at a point whose bearings from St Saviour's is 285°. Arundel House, familiar from Hollar's detailed etchings and his bird's-eye view of this area,[20] consisted of a great court to the northwest, with a small court south of it and a range of buildings stretching westwards to a point where they met the long gallery running up from the river. We take this westward end of the main block as our measuring point, and find from Ogilby and Morgan's map of 1676 that it was located a little south of the present Howard Street, between Norfolk and Surrey Streets. Its bearing from St Saviour's is 288.5°.

Further east the tower of St Clement's still shows signs, in its western windows, of its Gothic origins. Wren rebuilt this church in 1680–2, but used the fifteenth-century fabric of the west tower, acknowledging the debt by either inserting or preserving the pseudo-gothic tracery one notices as the bus sweeps past along the Strand. The tower we see today is therefore the same one that Hollar saw, but reclad. Its bearing from St Saviour's is 294.7°.

On the left the old directory includes, amongst numerous taverns and lanes, 'Cliffordes In of chancery behind S. Dunstans churche' and then 'the Golden Bull a sixpenny ordinarye' before 'fetter-lane.' Further along, in Fleet Street, stood 'Sarisbury [i.e. Salisbury] court where is Dorset howse,' 'Graihound tav. at the east end of broad fleet street wher a narro entry to S. Brides church.' Today as we enter Fleet Street we notice that St Dunstan's-in-the-West is a nineteenth-century church, not at all the building of the Harleian directory. In fact its predecessor, as we can see from Ogilby and Morgan's map, lay some 30 ft south of the present church, and had a west tower whose bearing from St Saviour's can be estimated at 301.6°. The Temple church still stands, on the right, its round tower at 298.5° from St Saviour's. St Bride's, glimpsed only momentarily if at all from the bus, was destroyed in the Fire and rebuilt by Wren, who used the old foundations as much as he could. The old St Bride's had a west tower, built in the early fifteenth century; its bearing from St Saviour's was 306.8°.

Now the bus slows as we grind up Ludgate Hill towards St Paul's, passing St Martin's on the left. After the Fire the street here was widened from 17 ft across at its narrowest to 45 ft, and it has subsequently been widened still further. The old church of St Martin's extended further south than the present one, across what is now part of the surface of the road, and its tower rose hard by the gate itself. The Harleian directory says that on the left side 'The first thing within Ludgate and next to it [is] S. Martines churche,' while to the right 'The first thing within Ludgate and ioyning to it is Ludgate prison.' In most of the London views Ludgate is represented by a cluster of towers, one of which is meant for the west tower of the church, and the rest – sometimes one, sometimes two – for the gate and prison. Like Newgate to the north this was a large structure, substantially rebuilt in 1586 and decorated with statues of Queen Elizabeth and King Lud and his sons. A ballad among the British Library manuscripts describes the experiences of a country newcomer to London:

> when I came first to London Towne
> I was a Novice as most men are
> Methought ye king dwelt at ye sign of ye crown
> & the way to heauen was through ye Starr.

Ludgate had a similar effect on him, as he passed through it on his way from St Paul's:

> To Ludgate then I ran my race:
> when I was past I did backward looke
> ther I spyed Queen Elizabeths grace
> Her picture guylt, for all gould I tooke.[21]

The gate was damaged in the Fire and rebuilt, to be pulled down and sold for its materials in 1760.[22] In his vestry the vicar of St Martin's keeps a silver effigy of Ludgate for use in processions: it shows a three-storey square-headed building. In taking the bearing of Ludgate from St Saviour's we have a little difficulty deciding which part of it to choose as the landmark. I have taken the west tower of the church (a little to the south and west of the present church, at 315.1° from St Saviour's) and have interpreted the more easterly of the cluster of towers shown in Norden, Visscher and Hollar as that of the church as distinct from the gate, to which was attached the substantial prison described by Stow.[23]

Today we have to crane our necks to see much of St Paul's, but the old cathedral was even bigger than Wren's building – it was 585 ft long, even without its porch[24] – though it occupied the same site. It was also more correctly oriented. Most of the extra length lay westward in comparison with the present building: its east end almost exactly coincided with the limits of Wren's choir. High above the complexities of porches and buttresses the gable tips of its west and east ends lay on bearings from St Saviour's of 320° and 328.2° respectively.

A curious building which figures largely in all the panoramas and sketches lay to the south of our bus route, at Broken Wharf. There Bevis Bulmer built his water-tower in 1594: it is the tall, tapering structure shown in the views just west of Queenhythe, in the purlieus of Bygot House. 'Within the gate of this house,' wrote Stow, (now belonging to the citie of London) is lately, to wit, in the yeare, 1594 and 1595 builded one large house of great height, called an engine, made by *Beuis Bulmar* Gentleman, for the conueying and forcing of Thames water to serue in the middle and West parts of the Citie.[25]

It burned in the Fire of 1666, but soon after was rebuilt, as a petition to the Fire Court dated 1671 makes clear. The petition concerned '... all that Cisterne or Cisterne place of stone or receipt for Water at or near unto the place called Broken wharfe thertofore erected by Bevis Bulmore Esq[re]' and it records 'That the said Waterworkes and Engine in the time of the late dreadfull ffire in London were burnt downe, [and] That the Peticon[rs] at their great Charge haue rebuilt the said Waterhouse And have as yett made no profitt thereof...'[26] It was the object of litigation in 1692–3,[27] but by the time of Strype's revision of Stow's *Survey* in 1720 its fortunes had improved:

Broken Wharf. By this is a Water House to convey the *Thames* Water in Pipes. Which of late Years hath been much improved, as to the Revenue....[28]

All these allusions show that the water-tower was rebuilt after the Fire, and strongly imply that the later structure was on the same site as the earlier one. Its position can be found quite accurately in the post-Fire map of Ogilby and Morgan, where it is marked by a heavily hatched square giving it a bearing of 315.9° from St Saviour's.

Past St Paul's our route lies down Cannon Street; to the north, in Cheapside, St Mary-le-Bow punctuates what has become a rather featureless modern thoroughfare. Beneath the church lies an eleventh-century crypt, at the west end of whose southern aisle, now closed off, stand the foundations of the tower shown in the seventeenth-century views, always easily distinguished because of its princely crown spire. The present tower is further north than the original one, whose bearing from St Saviour's was 341.2°. From the bus we shall certainly not see St Lawrence Poultney, which burned in the Fire and was not replaced, but its site between Cannon Street and Thames Street still remains as a little park, though the west tower of the church evidently stood on ground that is now incorporated into a pleasant widening of St Lawrence Poultney Hill at the point where it runs upward to Cannon Street. In Hollar's time the church boasted a magnificent steeple which had been rehung with five new bells in 1631–2. Strype in his revision of Stow gives the site of the church exactly:

... the Place where the Church stood goes by the Name of St. *Laurence Poultney Hill.* Which is an open Place, and leadeth North-westwards into *Green Lettice Lane* [i.e. back up to Cannon Street]; and Southward falleth into *Thamesstreet.*[29]

The bearing from St Saviour's was 5.7° east of true north.

Away to the north of our bus route are St Michael's and St Peter's, both in Cornhill. Both are now rebuilt, but the tower of the former survived the Fire and the present pseudo-gothic of Hawksmoor retains some of the fabric as well as the character of the fifteenth-century original. Its bearing is 19.7°, and that of St Peter 23.2°. The bus does take us close to St Dunstan's-in-the-East and Allhallows, Barking. St Dunstan's had a notable spire, tall enough to be envied by St Paul's in Henry Farley's poem:

> My head should weare the *Crowne* full well I know,
> But that must stand upon the toppe of *Bowe*:
> Or else the shaft or spire that should bee best,
> But that's vpon S. *Dunstanes* in the *East*.[30]

The church was partly destroyed by the Fire and was repaired by Wren early in the next decade. Its tower was rebuilt on the old foundations in 1698,[31] so that its present bearing of 51.0° from St Saviour's remains the same as that observed by the seventeenth-century topographers, despite the fact that the rest of the church was again rebuilt in 1817–18. Allhallows, in Great Tower Street, had the misfortune to be blown up soon after Hollar depicted it in the *Long View*. It had indeed been extensively restored as recently as 1634, but on 4 January 1649/50 a fire in a nearby ship-chandler's house set off his store of gunpowder with the result that a total of forty-one neighbouring houses were either destroyed or rendered uninhabitable, the windows of the church were 'wholly all broken and blowne out,' and the tower itself dangerously shaken.[32] The parishioners subscribed £110 for the 'reparation of the Church much defaced by the blowe of Gunpowder' but the serious-ness of the damage to the tower was not discovered until 1658, and in the next year it was rebuilt. It seems likely that in setting the new tower at the west end of the nave the parishioners were shifting it entirely, for most of the early pictures of the church show its tower and steeple to have been at the west end of the south aisle, some 23 ft south of the present structure. Unfortunately we cannot be quite sure of this, because although twentieth-century digging at the base of the present tower has revealed no sign of an earlier foundation one important print does show the original tower to have been in the present position at the west end of the nave.[33] I have, however, taken the majority verdict and located the steeple of Allhallows some 23 ft south of the present tower at 63.2° from St Saviour's.

The great Fire of 1666 stopped short of Allhallows, whose solid new tower offered a fine vantage point to the observer who preferred to stay upwind of the smoke and the danger. Pepys went 'up to the top of Barkeing steeple' to look westwards across the route we have just travelled, and to see it all in flames and dirt.[34] Behind his back rose the Boughton-stone walls of the Tower of London, untouched by the Fire and even now still squarely placed where they were when Norden and Hollar drew them in their studies of the London scene. One cannot, I think, be very satisfied with any of the panoramas' depictions of the Tower. Hollar's is the best, but although he gets the general proportions right some of his details are amiss, as for example his failure adequately to represent the Traitor's Gate. Of course in interpreting the mass of battlements and bastions shown in the etching we must remember that they are seen from the tower of St Saviour's and not, as in Visscher, from some point across the river to the south near Horsleydown. In the White Tower the second turret from the left is accordingly shown rounded in the *Long View* because it represents the northeast corner of the building, whose turret is indeed rounded in plan.[35] We may use Hollar's etching [Plate 11] as a guide to our interpretation of the view as seen from St Saviour's. The foreground from this angle presents a battlemented high wall with a group of bastion towers to the left, a round tower at the centre and a group of round towers to the right. These last align themselves a little to the left of the closest corner of the White Tower. They are, then, the Bell Tower of the inner curtain with the Byward Tower of the outer curtain in front of it. Further to the left, between the observer and these towers, lies another round structure – the Middle Tower of the main entrance. The battlemented wall is the inner curtain, with the Beauchamp Tower at the centre and the Devereux Tower to the left. Beyond this last, appearing just a little to our right, runs the line of towers on the north side of the Ward: Flint, Bowyer, Brick. The alignment of the Bell Tower just left of the nearest corner of the White Tower correctly represents the view from St Saviour's. To the right the battlemented walls reach past the Wakefield Tower; then the line of the inner curtain cuts inland away from the river and we see the darker, square-headed Salt Tower above the Lanthorn Tower. Lower down, by the wharf, the Well and Develin Towers and the Iron Gate end the composition as seen by Hollar. Of all these points four may usefully be plotted from St Saviour's: namely the left and right extremities of the main Tower group, which can be identified on the map as the Devereux and Salt Towers, and the left and right corners of the White Tower between them. The bearings of these four points from St Saviour's are, reading from left to right (i.e. from northwest to southeast), 71.5°, 75.8°, 78.6° and 82.4° east of true north.

Here we must leave our bus and catch another returning westward; we alight near Cheapside and call in at the maproom of the Guildhall Library to follow up the next stage in this quest for Shakespeare's Globe. Our object is to discover whether any of the seventeenth-century panoramic views of London can be said to have been shaped by the disciplines of the surveyor. Eventually we shall ask this question of Hollar's sketches of Southwark, in which the Globe is represented, but for the moment the enquiry concerns the prints, and is restricted to their depictions of the north bank alone. We begin by spreading Visscher's handsome sheets across the table, using the fine reproductions published by the London Topographical Society [see our Plates 20–23]. It is the work of a moment to establish that the intervals Visscher represents between the landmarks do not correspond to the distances on the ground in any direct fashion. It is about 1100 ft from the Temple church to St Bride's, a distance represented on the panorama by an interval of 158.0 mm, or about 6.96 ft to 1.0 mm. From St Bride's to the east end of Paul's is – or rather was, for we speak of Old St Paul's – about 1935 ft, given in Visscher by the interval of 265 mm, or 7.30 ft to 1 mm, substantially different from the more westerly interval. But that between Bow Church and St Michael's, Cornhill is some 1870 ft, represented by 274.5 mm in Visscher, or 6.81 ft to 1 mm, a scale rather like that between the Temple and St Bride's. Further east the distance from St Michael's to Allhallows, Barking is 1970 ft, for an interval of 377.5 mm in Visscher, or 5.22 ft to 1 mm, much less consistent.

Visscher has evidently not composed his view by translating ground measurements directly to his picture surface, in any case – let us now confess – a most unlikely procedure. He might more plausibly have aimed to represent the intervals between landmarks proportionately according to the angles they subtended at the eye of an observer at St Saviour's. This too would be an unusual procedure – indeed I believe a unique one in 1616 – but it might have been a possibility. The result would have been a view projected onto a segmental surface which, on being flattened out, would have possessed something of the dado-border quality of Visscher's composition. But we need speculate no further, for the scaled-angle theory is as readily tested as the scaled-distance one. The angle subtended at St Saviour's by St Bride's to the left and the east gable of St Paul's to the right is 21.4°, represented by 265 mm on the engraving. Between Bow Church and St Lawrence Poultney the angle is 24.5°, but this greater angle is marked by a smaller spread of the panorama: 187 mm. The 158 mm covering the distance between the Temple church and St Bride's represent an angle of only 8.3° subtended at the point of view. These figures are at variance with one another, and it is plain that whatever regularity the engraving may contain it does not offer equal measures for equal angles subtended at St Saviour's. Something very close to such a view is given in the photographic panorama taken from St Saviour's and published by the Royal Commission on Historical Monuments:[36] its character is altogether different from Visscher.

A third alternative is the one for which I have already cited some theoretical precedent: the method of the topographical glass. It hardly matters whether we think of the surveyor tracing the outlines of the forms he sees directly onto the pane of glass through which he sees them, or whether he transfers the proportions he notes from a graticulated frame to his paper by means of a pair of compasses, the result will be the same. What he sees will be reduced and foreshortened to a two-dimensional form in such a fashion that we who come later can, with a little trouble, reconstruct the essentials of the method he used. Our procedure is simple enough. On a good modern map – I have used the 1:10000 Ordnance Survey sheet TQ 38 SW, though for copyright reasons all the diagrams are reduced from the earlier six-inch survey – we plot lines of sight from St Saviour's tower to the various landmarks of the north bank, ranging all the way from Whitehall to Wapping, making such allowances as we have found necessary for the reconstruction and repositioning of some of them since Hollar's time. At once we see that a single 'take' through a glass could not possibly cover the whole of the range, for the angle of view subtended at St Saviour's is somewhat over 180°, and to represent that on one flat picture plane is not possible. Straight away the solution to the problem of how to reduce so wide a view to two dimensions leaps to the mind: a surveyor will have to set up his glass to make two, three or more separate pictures, just like Hollar's sketches of Southwark, facing in different directions, and then he will join them together to make the whole panorama. In such a view the alignments will all be correct, for everything will have been established by lines of sight from the single point of view, and the proportions of the intervals between the landmarks, while not uniformly consistent throughout, will nevertheless correspond to the real world, though mediated through the methods the artist has used. It is now our task to see if we can trace those methods in the evidence of Visscher's panorama.

We may begin in the simplest way, by toying about with bits of paper. We take a short strip and mark off the relative positions of the major landmarks of the view. Because it is obvious that Visscher or his source must have made any survey in several 'takes' we may restrict this first essay to one part of the whole, say the section from Bow Church to St Dunstan's-in-the-East. On the panorama itself the intervals between the major landmarks of this section are as follows, measured between the centres of the church towers:

Landmark	Interval in mm
Bow	0
St Lawrence Poultney	187.0
St Peter's, Cornhill	113.5
St Dunstan's-in-the-East	214.0

We must reduce these measurements to make them manageable on the map we have chosen to use, and I have made my own measure at

¼ scale. Now we take this strip of paper on which the proportions between the landmarks are recorded in the same proportions as in Visscher, and we attempt to fit it to the radii we have drawn on the map in such a way that the positions of the landmarks and the lines of sight coincide. Of course any set of three points can be made to fit any set of three radii – within certain very broad limits – and were the evidence restricted to so few pieces of information it would tell us nothing. But if we have four or more points coinciding with their correct radii we have sufficient proof that this section of the view was indeed proportioned on a glass or frame and also a clear indication of the angle at which the glass was set up. The line established by our strip of paper as it intersects the lines of sight is parallel to the picture plane of this section of the view (always assuming, of course, that the section we have chosen is indeed the result of a single take, a matter we can only establish by trial and error).

In the event it turns out that the scaled strip fits the bearings not only of the section from Bow to St Dunstan's but also eastwards to Allhallows, Barking, when it is placed across these radii on a bearing of about 106° from true north. This is an experiment that anyone can easily repeat, but it may help to have a diagram of it.

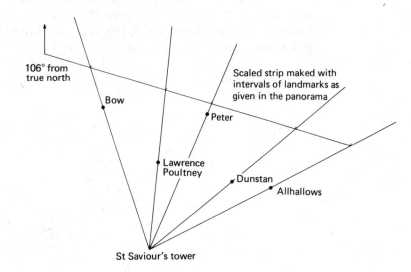

The section west of Bow Church includes St Paul's but seems to extend no further than the cathedral's west gable. Here the picture-plane indicated by a scaled strip laid across the lines of sight is about 96°, but because there are only three checkable points of intersection this finding cannot be adequately confirmed.

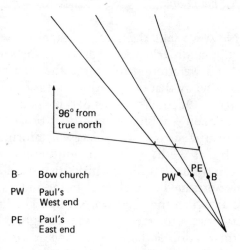

B — Bow church

PW — Paul's West end

PE — Paul's East end

Because this picture plane angle is so close to the previous one it deserves a sceptical reception: the intervals between its three points are hardly more than a slightly inaccurate westward extension of the take from Bow to Barking, and may well have no independent surveyed authority. Doubts about this section are strengthened when we turn to the next one, from St Bride's to the southwest corner of Arundel House. Here the scaled strip indicating the positions of the landmarks in Visscher settles neatly across the sightlines on a bearing about 11° or so from true north. I have used the lines to St Bride's (BR), St Dunstan's-in-the-West (DW), the Temple Church (T), St Clement's (CL) and Arundel House (ARU).

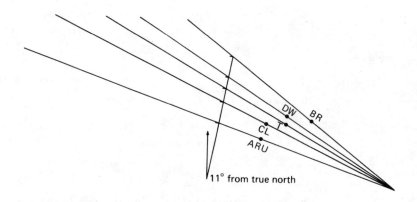

This take is evidently accurate within its own span, but does not extend eastwards to meet the west end of St Paul's, where the previous one left off; nor does it extend westwards to cover the area towards Whitehall. The hiatus between St Bride's and St Paul's represents the place where two takes are joined in the panorama, and seems to have been filled in without reference to a survey. Beyond Arundel House to the west and Allhallows to the east the proportions of the panorama do not fit the radii of the lines of sight marked on a modern map. It would seem that Visscher improvised these passages, and I have already noted that even in the section below the Temple he appears to have crammed the river-bank buildings eastward to make room for the palaces of the Strand. His picture of Whitehall is greatly foreshortened and confused, and while the rendering of the Tower at the other end of the view is sound enough it appears not as seen from St Saviour's, but as from a point opposite it on the south bank, perhaps from Vine Lane. But our findings for the central and major part of the panorama are both secure and of great importance for the present study: Visscher's panorama is, for most of the range between Arundel House and Allhallows, Barking, indeed a true and exact survey.

The nature of its truth is, I hope, now established. The view shows the correct positions, alignments and intervals of the landmarks of the north bank as seen from St Saviour's in two or three separate takes through a drawing frame or more probably a topographical glass. But our methods of demonstration, using fiddly bits of paper and rule of thumb, are not sufficient to prove the exactness of the view. It is possible to confirm our findings, and somewhat to refine them, with the help of trigonometry. For each take we may calculate the bearing of the picture plane by taking any two contingent intervals and the angles they subtend at the point of view, as in the following diagram:

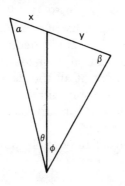

Here x and y are the intervals between landmarks as measured on the engraving, and θ and ϕ are the angles subtended at St Saviour's. Our problem is to discover the angle α, for this will make possible the calculation of the bearing of the picture plane, represented by the line $x + y$. α may be discovered thus:

$$\alpha = \sin^{-1} \left| \frac{\sin(\phi + \theta)}{\sqrt{\left[\dfrac{x \sin \phi}{y \sin \theta} - \cos(\phi + \theta)\right]^2 + \sin^2(\phi + \theta)}} \right|$$

This formula may be applied to calculate the picture plane implied by each of the possible sets of data for each take, and if the results tally closely we shall have confirmation of the accuracy of the survey. Even small inaccuracies in the relative intervals given by the engraving (x and y) will show up in widely divergent values for $\bar{\alpha}$.

Let us take the angles subtended at St Saviour's (S) by Bow Church (B), St Lawrence Poultney (LP) and St Peter's, Cornhill (P):

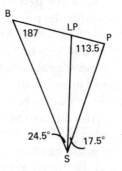

In this figure 187 is the distance in millimetres from Bow Church to St Lawrence on the panorama, and 113.5 is the like distance from St Lawrence to St Peter. The angle subtended at St Saviour's by Bow and St Lawrence is 24.5°, measured on the modern map, and the like angle subtended by St Lawrence and St Peter's is 17.5°. Our problem is to calculate the angle at which the picture plane B–LP–P crosses the lines of sight S–B, S–LP and S–P. If we can discover this angle we shall then be able to compare it with the like angle deduced from the data concerning Allhallows and St Dunstan's-in-the-East, and we may then be able to judge the accuracy of all the data according to the closeness with which our various results agree. In practice it will be convenient to calculate the angle at B for various sets of lines of sight and intervals on the panorama.

To the triangle P–B–S above we may apply our formula thus:

$$\hat{B} = \sin^{-1} \left| \frac{\sin 42}{\sqrt{\left[\dfrac{187 \sin 17.5}{113.5 \sin 24.5} - \cos 42\right]^2 + \sin^2 42}} \right|$$

Thanks to the pocket calculator one may quickly find that the result for $\hat{B}$ is 55.99°. Since the bearing of Bow Church from St Saviour's is 18.8° west of true north the picture plane consistent with the data from Visscher is here 105.21°. A similar calculation may be carried out for the sequence Bow – St Peter – St Dunstan, where Bow – Peter is 300.5 mm and 42°, and Peter – Dunstan is 214 mm and 27.8°. Here the result is an angle at Bow of 55.98°, yielding a picture plane of 105.22°, so very nearly identical with the previous result that Visscher's exactness in this respect is fully confirmed. The angle of the picture plane may be calculated from each of the possible groups of three from the whole series Bow (B), St Lawrence Poultney (LP), St Peter's (P), St Dunstan's-in-the-East (DE) and Allhallows, Barking (AHB). The results tabulated below are derived from the following data:

Landmark	Angle subtended at St Saviour's tower	Interval measured on Visscher's engraving in mm
B	0°	0
LP	24.5°	187.0
P	17.5°	113.5
DE	27.8°	214.0
AHB	12.2°	137.5

Group	Bearing of picture plane calculated in degrees east of true north	
B – LP – P	105.21°	
B – LP – DE	105.22°	
B – LP – AHB	105.63°	
B – P – DE	105.22°	Average 105.61°
B – P – AHB	105.76°	
B – DE – AHB	106.59°	

These calculations are very sensitive, and the smallest change in either the bearings or the measurements of the intervals is enough to change the angle of the presumed picture plane considerably. The results lie within a range of 1.38°, a remarkable testimony to the precision of Visscher's survey. Nothing like such good results could be gained from any extant map of the early decades of the seventeenth century. Evidently the topographical-glass or drawing-frame technique was at this stage capable of giving more accurate results than the cumbersome business, not yet fully perfected, of surveying with chain, circumferentor and plane table.

The westerly extension of the take covers the section from Bow Church to St Paul's, and because only three points may be checked there is only one calculation to make:

Landmark	Angle subtended at St Saviour's tower	Interval measured on Visscher's engraving in mm
B	0°	0
PE	13.0°	143.0
PW	8.2°	119.0

Group	Bearing of picture plane calculated in degrees east of true north
B – PE – PW	96.43°

Both the angle of the picture plane and the scale of the intervals on it are so close to those of the previous take that it seems likely that this section was originally continuous with the other, but has been modified by Visscher in the course of composition.

Further west the take from St Bride's to Arundel House includes St Dunstan's-in-the-West, the Temple church and St Clements. Assessed manually on the map of sightlines the angle of the picture plane is some 11° or so east of true north, but the fit, though fairly close, transverses some very narrow sectors, whose angles are small enough to throw the sensitive trigonometrical calculations into some confusion:

Landmark	Angle subtended at St Saviour's tower	Interval measured on Visscher's engraving in mm
BR	0°	0
DW	5.2°	99.0[37]
T	3.1°	59.0
CL	3.8°	64.0
ARU	6.2°	104.0

Group	Bearing of picture plane calculated in degrees east of true north	
BR – DW – T	32.17°*	
BR – DW – CL	13.77°	
BR – DW – ARU	12.58°	Average, excluding ill-conditioned problems, 11.07°
BR – T – CL	0.21°*	
BR – T – ARU	6.72°	
BR – CL – ARU	11.21°	

The two answers marked with an asterisk are the result of ill-conditioned problems and must be discounted. It will be seen that the calculations can be thrown off very easily if they concern very small angles: it is rather like the difficulty faced by a marksman who wants to calculate the range of a rifle. If he fires it upwards clear of the ground at an angle of, say, 45°, he can confidently predict the nature of the arc that a bullet will trace. But if he lies on his stomach and fires horizontally the range is virtually incalculable, so small is the clearance from the ground even at the beginning. In practice I have found that in

26.   Detail of Norden's *Civitas Londini*, showing the top of St Saviour's Tower.

the sort of calculations we are making here any result derived from an angle subtended at St Saviour's of less than 4.0° is likely to be aberrant. Such is the case with the ill-conditioned problems above, both of which concern angles of less than 4.0° and both of which yield results at odds with the more reliable remainder. All subsequent ill-conditioned problems (i.e. those involving angles of less than 4.0°) will be marked with an asterisk and omitted from the calculation of averages. In the present take, therefore, the results not springing from ill-conditioned data tend to confirm the manual finding, and the presence of five checkable and clearly defined landmarks in the take makes the calculation confirmable and certain. Visscher could not have spaced his composition so accurately without basing it on a precise survey taken at a topographical glass or frame.

This discovery has many implications for the study, not only of London topography, but – what is of greater consequence – of the development of surveying techniques in the seventeenth century. At least one of the London views is not just a pretty picture but a considered exploration and record of certain literal truths about the city. It is not, let me repeat, a matter of surface verisimilitude. We know that in that respect Visscher has many faults. But a view such as his is made of many elements, each the result of a separate study. Individual sketches of particular buildings and parts of the landscape doubtless contributed to a mosaic of information built up in the studios in Amsterdam before the whole work was composed. We have Hollar's numerous pen and ink sketches to show how the thing was done in his case, and there is even a sketch of a part of Westminster reputed to have been made by Visscher[38] as a preparation for the panorama (though whether Visscher ever actually visited London remains in doubt). All this information had to be combined in a single composition, and for that it is clear that the engraver had recourse to various solutions. He based his view of Southwark on the maps he had to hand, adopting an imaginary point of view south of St Saviour's; his picture of the Tower he inserted in roughly the right place but seen from an angle doubtless given him by his preliminary study, quite inconsistent with the rest of the panorama. For the main part of the view he relied on a very precise survey made through a topographical glass or drawing frame in two or three takes from the top of St Saviour's tower. Probably this survey was a mere diagram, a skeleton view showing only the locations, not the detailed appearance, of the main landmarks. In between them Visscher filled as best he could, introducing some quite fanciful buildings and others altogether imaginary, such as the 'St. Hellen' shown to the east of the Bridge.

Visscher is not alone in basing his panorama on an accurate survey, though I believe his is the most precise in this respect of all the early city views. Merian's view of 1627, though based on Visscher, does not

absorb his precision of location and fails to correspond to the actual
proportions of the scene. Other views, such as those by Harrison,
Jacobus Hondius and Holland, are too compressed or merely conventional to attempt the discipline of a survey; but when we turn to John
Norden's *Civitas Londini* [Plates 24–25] we find at least the initial
encouragement of the little figure drawn at the top of St Saviour's
tower holding aloft a pair of compasses beneath the tag, 'Statio
prospectiua.' We have seen that the view of Southwark cannot have
been made from this point and must, like Visscher's, have been
supplied separately. But the alignments of northerly landmarks with
buildings on the north bank are, as in Visscher, substantially
consistent with the point of view of St Saviour's, and the intervals
between major buildings in the city again demonstrate that Norden,
who was by profession a surveyor, based his view on an exact survey
taken through a topographical glass or its equivalent.

Once again we turn to the London Topographical Society facsimile
of the engraving to measure the intervals between the major
landmarks it shows. Following just the same procedure as before we
find, by manipulating a strip of paper marked with these intervals,
that Norden's view is consistent in the range from Bow Church to St
Dunstan's-in-the-East with a picture plane of about 106° from true
north.

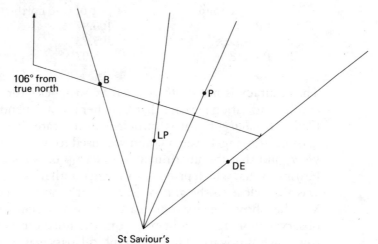

At once we notice something quite remarkable: the picture plane
adopted by Norden is – so far as we can tell from the manual way of
judging it – just the same as that adopted by Visscher for this section of
the panorama. Could it be that Visscher has used Norden for his
survey? On the face of it such a thing seems very likely, for Visscher
certainly made use of Norden for his picture of the north bank, even
misreading Norden's thickened 'e' in one label and reproducing it as
'St. Dunston in the cast.' His rendering of 'The Eell Schipes' and 'The

Gally fuste' in the river closely follows Norden, as I. A. Shapiro pointed out.[39] But we notice that while Visscher's take includes the whole range from Bow to Barking, Norden's stops short at St Dunstan's-in-the-East. His Allhallows, Barking is too far west to fit the scheme. Since in this respect Visscher is accurate and Norden is not, Visscher can hardly have relied exclusively on the *Civitas Londini* print. Could it be that they both had recourse to a skeleton survey, perhaps one made by Norden but from which he departed in the easterly part of his engraving? Such speculations about the interdependence of these views are, however, well beyond the purposes of our present study. What matters for the moment is that Norden, like Visscher, offers a kind of precision in his view of London that has not been recognized hitherto. Again we may check it by trigonometry:

Landmark	Angle subtended at St Saviour's tower	Interval measured on Norden's engraving in mm
B	0°	0
LP	24.5°	144.8
P	17.5°	85.7
DE	27.8	164.75

Group	Bearing of picture plane calculated in degrees east of true north	
B – LP – P	106.97°	
B – LP – DE	105.73°	Average 105.92°
B – P – DE	105.07°	

The accuracy is not quite as good as Visscher's for this same take – another indication perhaps that Visscher is not dependent solely on the *Civitas Londini* – but it is sufficient to indicate that the perspective-glass or drawing-frame method was used to survey this section of the view, and that the instrument was set up on substantially the same bearing as that which provided Visscher with his survey. That bearing was very close to the axis of St Saviour's, so that both Norden and Visscher show the city to the east of Bow Church as it appeared to an observer looking straight out from the northern face of the church tower in Southwark. The topographical glass was set up parallel to the parapet through whose crenellations the surveyors looked to take their views of the north bank.

To the west of Bow Norden made at least two more separate takes, one extending as far as St Bride's and the second to Arundel House. The first of these is not quite satisfactory in the engraving, as we find when we plot the intervals between the major landmarks on the map: Bow Church (B), St Paul's east (PE) and west (PW) gables, the water-tower at Broken Wharf (WT), and St Bride's (BR). All of these points fit a picture plane on a bearing about 47° east of true north, with the exception of the west end of Paul's, which is shown too far east by as much as 4.0 mm. Perhaps Norden located the cathedral on his survey only by reference to its east end, which is correctly placed in relation to the other landmarks. Whatever the cause of this aberration, it will be necessary to leave PW out of our more detailed calculations:

Landmark	Angle subtended at St Saviour's tower	Interval measured on Norden's engraving in mm
B	0°	0
PE	13.0°	81.0
WT	12.3°	69.0
BR	9.1°	53.0

Group	Bearing of picture plane calculated in degrees east of true north	
B – PE – WT	45.29°	
B – PE – BR	47.18°	Average 47.40°
B – WT – BR	49.72°	

The central portion of the *Civitas Londini* is contained in sheets 2 and 3, and in these the north bank of the river is represented as fairly straight and level, though it does tilt rather to the right. But further east and west, on sheets 4 and 1, Norden's acute sweep downwards to either side distorts the landscape and makes measuring awkward. Nevertheless it is quite possible to measure the horizontal intervals between the landmarks, and this I have done, assuming that such would be the intervals suggested to Norden by a graticulated drawing frame or by any use of squared-up paper in transferring the image from a topographical glass. The western take covers the span from St Bride's to the southwest corner of the main block of Arundel House. Clearly identifiable points include the Temple church, St Dunstan's-in-the-West and St Clement's. Further west the downward sweep of the foreshortening is very steep indeed, and we find, when the intervals are plotted on a map, that the Savoy and the Great Hall at Whitehall lie outside the scope of this take, which is made with a picture plane bearing about 20° west of true north. This figure may be confirmed by trigonometric means:

Landmark	Angle subtended at St Saviour's tower	Interval measured on Norden's engraving in mm
BR	0°	0
DW	5.2°	44.5
T	3.1°	24.0
CL	3.8°	22.0
ARU	6.2°	33.0

Group	Bearing of picture plane calculated in degrees west of true north	
BR – DW – T	2.19°*	*Ill-conditioned
BR – DW – CL	18.66°	(includes angles
BR – DW – ARU	18.84°	between DW and T,
BR – T – CL	28.30°*	and T and CL, less
BR – T – ARU	23.42°	than 4.0°)
BR – CL – ARU	19.09°	
		Average 20.0°

Norden's two western takes are on bearings quite different from those set up by Visscher, whose array of landmarks from Bow to Bride's is rather uncertain, but whose range from St Bride's to Arundel House is consistent with a picture plane set at 11.07° *east* of true north (Norden's is 20° *west*). It follows, then, that the Dutchman could not have derived his spatial information about the western part of the view from the same survey as the Londoner, whatever may be true of the broader take from Bow to St Dunstan's-in-the-East. We may conjecture that they used independent surveys, and that the close coincidence of the easterly picture planes at about 106° results from the surveyors' setting up their frames or glasses roughly parallel to the axis of St Saviour's.

If both Norden and Visscher show that they have used quite deliberate surveys to proportion their panoramas of the north bank, we approach Wenceslaus Hollar's great *Long View* of 1647 with renewed interest. Perhaps it too contains the sort of accuracy we have discovered in its predecessors. But at first glance the evidence is disappointing. The foreground makes it plain that the point of view is again the top of St Saviour's tower, but buildings on the south bank do not align truly with those to the north. The site of St Olave's church tower should be seen a little to the right of the White Tower over the river, but Hollar shows the one immediately in line with the other [Plate 11]. Again, his placing of the eastern gable of Winchester House is much too far east in relation to St Paul's beyond it [Plate 8]. Although some variation of these alignments would occur according to the position Hollar actually took up on St Saviour's tower, the relative positions he shows are not consistent with a point of view in the tower at all. Despite the apparent authenticity of his view of Southwark it is clear that he shares with his predecessors the compositional habit of thinking of the two sides of the river separately enough to be able to alter their proportions for aesthetic rather than topographical reasons. St Olave's tower, with its central – and as we shall see in a moment incorrect – cupola, neatly punctuates the right-hand side of the composition at the same point as the Tower of London, and to the left the interest created by the unusual forms of the 'Beere bayting h' and 'The Globe' [Plate 7] terminates an alternating rhythm set up between the Bridge and St Paul's. It is no surprise, then, to discover that the Globe itself (here mis-labelled the 'Beere bayting h') is incorrectly placed in relation to the north-bank buildings visible beyond it. The site of the Globe, long ago securely established within quite narrow limits by W. W. Braines[40] and confirmed more recently by the discovery at the London Guildhall of a local map marking it,[41] lay to the south side of Maid Lane (the modern Park Street) just about at the east side of the area where it crosses under Southwark Bridge Road. A line drawn from St Saviour's tower through the most northerly part of this site (that is, skimming the south side of Park Street) and projected westward until it strikes the far bank of the river does so somewhat to the right of Waterloo Bridge. Of course in Hollar's day the river did not boast a Victoria Embankment, and the shoreline lay much further back than it does now. In fact the northern part of the Globe site, seen from the tower of St Saviour's, was just in line with the river front of the Savoy, whose site straddled the modern Lancaster Place. But in Hollar's magnificent etching the 'Beere bayting h' (i.e. the Globe) is shown far to the right of the Savoy.

Evidently Hollar is no more to be trusted than Norden or Visscher in this matter of the relation of south-bank landmarks to northerly ones. When we turn to his alignments of buildings on the north side itself the evidence is at first equally disappointing. The Temple church [Plate 7] is shown too far west of Blackfriars Dock as seen from St Saviour's; the west end of Paul's [Plate 8] should appear just to the east of the mouth of Queenhythe, but is actually shown in line with its eastern edge; the east end of Paul's is incorrectly aligned with Three Cranes, when it should appear further east; Bow Church [Plate 9] is too far west of the Steelyard; and Guildhall is too far west of Coldharbour. In this whole section of the panorama, then, from the Temple to Guildhall, the northerly landmarks appear too far west of the corresponding points along the river bank. It may be that the buildings further off are shown too far to the west, or that those along the bank are shown too far to the east, or some combination of these two, or even that what we have here is sheer muddle. For the moment we must suspend judgment. Further to the east things look appropriately brighter. St Lawrence Poultney [Plate 9] is a little to the left of the Swan, as it should be; the Exchange appears correctly to the left of Fishermen's Hall, and St Michael's, Cornhill a little to the right; St Peter's, Cornhill is in its true place to the left of the far end of the Bridge; St Dunstan's-in-the-East [Plate 10] correctly appears over Lion Quay and Allhallows, Barking lines up with the right side of the South Gate at the near end of the Bridge. There are no buildings between the Tower [Plate 11] and the river to make a similar judgment possible in its case, but as we saw earlier in the present chapter its turrets appear correctly as they would from St Saviour's, and in this Hollar is clearly superior to Visscher.

The alignments of Hollar's north bank are good from St Lawrence Poultney eastwards; west of that point they are incorrect. We may now test his etching to see whether they depart – as the compositional distortions of the view of Southwark suggest they do – from the disciplines of the survey in order to satisfy aesthetic aims. As before, we may prepare scaled strips of paper marking the intervals between the landmarks and deploy these on an Ordnance Survey map on which the lines of sight from St Saviour's have been plotted. Perhaps it would be as well to tackle the eastern part of the view first, since there at least the alignments have been found to be true. We soon discover that the series from St Dunstan's-in-the-East (DE) to Allhallows, Barking (AHB) and the Tower fits the lines of sight very well. We can make four separate readings for the Tower by taking the bastion at the northwest corner of its inner curtain wall as one point (TL – it is the bastion to be seen to the left in the etching); the northwest turret of the White Tower (TL₁); and southeast corner turret of the White Tower (TR₁); and the southeastern bastion of the inner curtain, seen to the right in Hollar (TR).

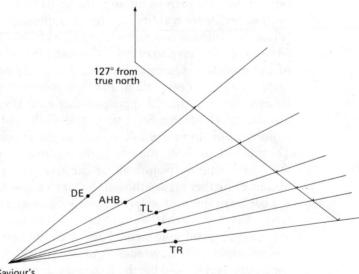

Here is a take which appeared in neither Norden nor Visscher. If indeed it is true – and we shall see in a moment how very precise it is – it indicates that Hollar was either using a survey independent of theirs or else was in this sector following a common survey with much greater fidelity than his predecessors. The former seems more likely, particularly since in Visscher's panorama the segment from St Dunstan's-in-the-East to Allhallows, Barking belongs in a take which extended as far westward as Bow Church and terminated in the east at Allhallows, while in Hollar this same segment appears in a separate take. It happens also that this part of Hollar's etching is particularly precise in its relative placing of the landmarks, as the following calculations will show (I have omitted the readings for the White Tower because the angle they subtend at St Saviour's is too small for sufficiently accurate measurement and offers ill-conditioned data):

Landmark	Angle subtended at St Saviour's tower	Interval measured on Hollar's etching in mm
DE	0°	0
AHB	12.2°	134.5
TL	8.3°	108.25
TR	10.9°	182.0

Group	Bearing of picture plane calculated in degrees east of true north	
DE – AHB – TL	126.91°	
DE – AHB – TR	126.74°	
DE – TL – TR	126.64°	Average 126.70°
AHB – TL – TR	126.52°	

These results are very precise, showing that Hollar has placed the landmarks in his etching to within a millimetre of their true locations when viewed through a glass set up on a bearing 126.70° from true north. This westerly take is therefore of the utmost significance, for it shows how accurate Hollar could be when he chose. We know that in setting the south bank against the north he did not choose such accuracy, but we can see now that it really was a matter of choice and not of incapacity or lack of interest. Though he must have used a topographical-glass survey of the kind described here he did not feel entirely limited by it when he came to assemble the whole composition of his panorama.

The significance of this point becomes clear when we turn to Hollar's next take, the wide one from Bow Church to St Dunstan's-in-the-East. As usual we can establish the extent of the take by placing a scaled strip across the lines of sight radiating from St. Saviour's: the diagram illustrating the procedure is given in the figure overleaf. These intervals coincide very well with the lines of sight on a picture plane whose bearing is some 103° east of true north, but immediately we see that while they are true for the necessary minimum of four points they are not true – as Visscher's and Norden's were – for St Peter's, Cornhill. Hollar shows that church a little further east than it should be, as if to avoid visual confusion by clearing it away from St

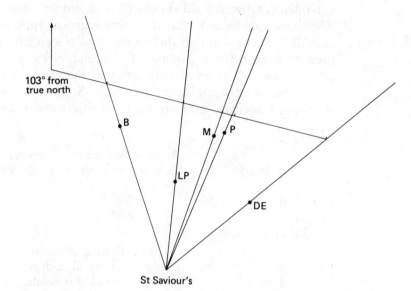

Michael's. Nevertheless the main proportions are correct within very narrow limits, as we may see from the table:

Landmark	Angle subtended at St. Saviour's tower	Interval measured on Hollar's etching in mm
B	0°	0
LP	24.5°	187
M	14.0°	93
DE	31.3°	252.75

Group	Bearing of picture plane calculated in degrees east of true north	
B – LP – M	103.29°	
B – LP – DE	102.99°	Average (none
B – M – DE	102.88°	ill-conditioned):
LP – M – DE	102.66°	102.96°

These results, giving readings for the picture plane consistent to well within one degree, show that Hollar used a glass or frame to establish the main proportions of the segment of his view from Bow Church to St Dunstan's-in-the-East, and that he placed the main landmarks in it to an accuracy of within two millimetres either way. One may test this assertion by imagining that he had drawn St Lawrence Poultney, say, two millimetres to the left of its actual position. It would then have been 185 mm from Bow and 347.75 mm from St Dunstan's. The calculation of the picture plane using these figures yields a bearing of 102.32°, a reading outside the range our measurements have in fact produced.

The next section of the view extends, as we discover from our manipulations on the map of sightlines, from the eastern gable of St Paul's (PE) all the way to the Temple church (T), and gives a picture plane of about 70° east of true north. Most of the major landmarks fall neatly into their correct places: St Paul's east and west gables make precise reference points (PE and PW), as do St Martin's, Ludgate (ML) and St Dunstan's-in-the-West (DW), as well as the Temple church (T).

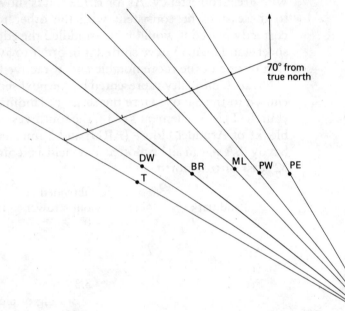

Only St Bride's fails to fit the scale, being displaced a little eastwards of its proper position. The aberration shows up clearly in the trigonometrical calculations, where each of the readings involving St Bride's differs markedly from the rest:

Landmark	Angle subtended at St. Saviour's tower	Interval measured on Hollar's etching in mm
PE	0°	0
PW	8.2°	99
ML	4.9°	64
BR	8.3°	110
DW	5.2°	93
T	3.1°	59

Group	Bearing of picture plane calculated in degrees east of true north	
PE – PW – ML	70.06°	*Ill-conditioned
PE – PW – BR	61.35°**	(includes angle
PE – PW – DW	67.53°	between DW and T,
PE – PW – T	68.30°	less than 4.0°)

PE – ML – BR	58.86°**	
PE – ML – DW	66.73°	**Readings involve
PE – ML – T	67.87°	St Bride's; not
PE – BR – DW	78.43°**	included in average
PE – BR – T	75.89°**	
PE – DW – T	71.75*	Average 68.24°

Even excluding the aberrant St Bride's this take covers five landmarks with great consistency. As for Bride's, it is shown some 8 mm too far to the east to be consistent with the other readings. Had it been correctly placed it would have straddled the edges of two of Hollar's sheets, and he may have shifted it in order to avoid so clumsy a division of one of the more notable and attractive buildings in his view.

No such difficulty is presented by the next sector, from the Temple church to the Savoy. Here the series of landmarks from the Temple church (T) to St Clement's (CL), the southwestern corners of the main blocks of Arundel House (ARU) and Somerset House (SH) and the Savoy (SAV) can all be plotted and yield a picture plane bearing about 32° east of true north.

Landmark	Angle subtended at St. Saviour's tower	Interval measured on Hollar's etching in mm
T	0°	0
CL	3.8°	46
ARU	6.2°	75
SH	3.5°	44.5
SAV	3.3°	43.5

Group	Bearing of picture plane calculated in degrees east of true north
T – CL – ARU	23.67°*
T – CL – SH	26.96°*
T – CL – SAV	28.37°*
T – ARU – SH	32.53°*
T – ARU – SAV	32.49°
T – SH – SAV	32.29°*

Of these groups only T – ARU – SAV does not pose an ill-conditioned problem by involving angles of less than 4.0°; nevertheless the average of all the results is 29.39°, sufficiently close to the only one not ill-conditioned that we may feel justified in accepting them as giving at least a rough indication of how Hollar set up his topographical glass for this take.

Further west than the Savoy our artist seems to have improvised. The Banqueting Hall at Whitehall is compressed a little to the right of its true position on a consistent picture plane of 32°, doubtless because Hollar wanted to centre it in the half-plate that makes up the terminal sheet of the etching.

Each of the three major views of London made in the earlier seventeenth century is based on an accurate survey made according to the principles of the topographical glass. This chapter is not the place to explore the matter as fully as it deserves; the question of the interdependence of the views must sometime be answered (Hollar's panorama often closely approximates Visscher's in the actual measure of the intervals between landmarks, millimetre for millimetre, as may be seen from our composite diagram [p. 171] and of course it is altogether beyond the scope of this book to enquire into such technical matters as how the artists managed to splice their various takes together in order to make a smoothly sweeping view. What we have established beyond doubt is that the panoramas are based on surveys whose accuracy is measurable, and in that fact lies the significance of our discovery. For if the engravings and etchings tend to fill the spaces between the plotted landmarks with passages of invention or formalized representation, the preparatory surveys on which they are based will tell the literal truth within the sort of tolerances we have found to be typical of major intervals in the panoramas. We have none of Norden's preparatory drawings, and only one rough sketch reputedly by Visscher. But from Hollar's hand we have not only the numerous sketches of individual buildings or parts of the scene, not only the newly discovered Evelyn/Pepys panorama, but those two fine pieces which are generally agreed to be the bases of the west and eastern sections of the *Long View*: both pencil and chalk drawings overlaid in ink, the one facing east towards Greenwich, the other the 'West part o[f] Southwarke toward Westminster' [Plate 2]. And there, somewhat to the left of centre, lies the firmly outlined image of the Globe theatre. If this drawing is indeed a study made at the topographical glass we should be able to measure, within the tolerances we have now become accustomed to, the very size and proportions of the theatre built by Shakespeare's company for the acting of his plays.

3 Looking at the Globe

As we look at the two Southwark drawings in the light of the discoveries made in the last chapter one very obvious quality about them strikes us with the force of a revelation: they are not in the least 'composed'. In the Greenwich view particularly [Plate 3] the picture lacks a centre of visual interest; the river cuts off a corner of the sheet and all the rest is filled with a muddle of rooftops. At the bottom edge some of these nudge into view with the inconsequentiality of a snapshot. The roofs of the buildings on the east side of the High Street dominate the foreground, but veer upwards across the sheet in a most unpictorial fashion. To the right a series of parallel roofs make an unseemly gathering of orthogonals which dominates the view and spoils its balance. The westward view is a more satisfactory composition because it has a centre of interest in the two unusual theatre buildings, but here again the angle of the river makes the whole picture restless, and the rooftops of Winchester House in the foreground are allowed far more space than their intrinsic interest can command. Neither drawing looks as if it has been submitted to that process of internal organization by which an artist achieves integrity of design. Instead they look like preliminary surveys, the notes an artist makes before he begins the business of composition.

It is time to leave all the maps and compass bearings behind and climb the tower of St Saviour's to see if we can find where Hollar stood as he set his eyes towards Greenwich and the mouth of the Thames to one side and to the towers of Westminster and Whitehall to the other. So, having duly obtained permission, and accompanied by a very cheerful assistant verger, up we go. Past the gallery overlooking the altar, past the roof of the nave, up beyond the bell-ringing room with its parti-coloured ropes, on beyond the bells themselves all turned rim-upwards, their clappers lolling to one side, up further among the pigeons and out into the blustery sunlight of a busy London afternoon. Here the slope of the leads beneath one's feet tumbles one down to stand in the drainage channel at the foot of the battlemented parapet that surrounds the top of the tower. In each corner a great pinnacle rises, and one is forced to look out over the magnificent scene through the crenellations of the parapet; these, though they were replaced in 1689,[1] are still of the same number and design as in Hollar's time, as may be seen from his numerous drawings and etchings of them.[2] And here is a wonderful thing: if one looks eastward through the southernmost of the crenellations in the eastern face of the tower, the view framed by the stonework is just that encompassed in Hollar's drawing of Southwark toward Greenwich. To the left is the Tower; the river cuts through this side of the scene, leaving a wide area to the right which is now dominated by enormous office blocks. This is the area which Hollar reported as full of crowded rooftops. But if the framing of this eastward view is remarkable, that from the southwest corner opposite is little short of astonishing. Stand immediately in front of the crenellation and you will see, framed in by the quoins to either side, the very view which Hollar records in his 'West part of Southwarke.' There to the right is St Paul's, the river rising upwards across the view to sweep out to the left at Whitehall and Westminster. Almost straight ahead we look down Park Street, Hollar's and Shakespeare's Maid Lane, and from the brewery on its southern side there rises a brick chimney, very grubby and industrial, just about where Hollar marks the Globe. The very extent of his drawing is confined and dictated by the architecture of the church tower, and as one stands there looking out over what Hollar saw, now so much changed and yet so much the same, an angel of history dances among the pinnacles.

Or perhaps it was just a pigeon. We had better retrace our steps and get back to the firmer data provided by maps and straightedges. Our findings in the previous chapter suggest that such preliminary sketches as these of Hollar's will have been made with the help of a topographical glass. Such a device would render accurately both the alignments of buildings as seen from St Saviour's tower and their intervals as seen through a plane set up at a specific and discoverable angle. If we take the view towards Greenwich we find that these criteria are met. To the left we may just make out the main lines of the Tower on the far bank of the river, and we notice that it appears well to the left of St Olave's tower. St Olave's was burned down in 1736,[3] but its site is known and can be located on the modern map just north of Tooley Street in Southwark, close to the site of St Olave's House. The map shows that a line of sight taken from St Saviour's over St Olave's would have run well clear to the right of the Tower, touching instead the curtain-wall bastion to the southeast. Hollar's etching, we may recall, fails to make this alignment true, offering instead the compositional device of the Tower coinciding with the church. On this occasion at least the drawing offers the plain facts which the etching later modifies. To the right of the drawing another church, St Thomas's, may be seen in the middle ground, while beyond and almost directly in line with it lies St Mary Magdalene, among the trees outside the built-up area. Parts of the tower of St Mary's still remain, but the old St Thomas's has gone, to be replaced by an eighteenth-century chapel which is now the chapter house of Southwark Cathedral.[4] The alignment of the two sites with St Saviour's can of course easily be made on the modern maps, and again we find that Hollar's drawing is true. The etching does not reach as far eastward as this, so there is no comparison to be made with it. We can, however, plot the intervals between these two sightlines to St Olave's and St Mary's and also between them and the river at the point where the drawing shows the tangent of its curve as it heads northward opposite Wapping, and arrive by our usual procedure at the conclusion that Hollar set up his glass on a bearing some 28° east of true north. There is insufficient information in the drawing to make a series of supporting calculations, but the one that is possible can refine the manual reading a little:

Landmark	Angle subtended at St Saviour's tower	Interval measured on Hollar's sketch in mm
St Olave	0°	0
River's southern extreme	28°	110
St Mary	34.5°	118

Group	Bearing of picture plane calculated in degrees east of true north
Olave – river – Mary	27.78°

In a moment we shall turn to the exciting westward view towards the Globe, but before that it is necessary to notice that on the verso of this sheet containing the view towards Greenwich is, or rather used to be, a strange diagram apparently of Thames Street in the City. I say that the diagram used to be there because although it was noticed by Sprinzels in his catalogue of Hollar's works,[5] and was photographed and published by Iolo Williams,[6] the drawing's latest cataloguer reports that these intriguing marks have now disappeared and so can no longer be described.[7] That is a pity, but at least we have the photograph which Williams so fortunately published [Plate 27]. The

27.   Wenceslaus Hollar, diagram of Thames Street.

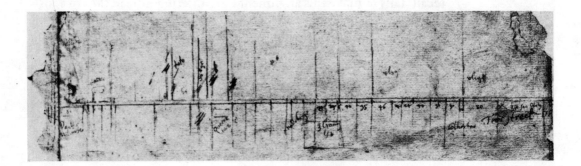

diagram consists of a pair of parallel lines, quite straight, but probably intended to represent the street itself. Reaching upward from these are several perpendiculars, and a greater number depend from it. One knows the difference between up and down because there is a good deal of writing on the sheet, some of it indecipherable but some quite clear: at the centre low down is the name '3 Cranes,' apparently written in a box; to the right is the main title, 'Teme Street'; at the left edge is 'Pauls wharf.' 'Queene hive' and 'Coldharbor' are also marked, as well as other words whose meaning defeats me: 'toto,' 'vlight.' Between the depending perpendiculars in the right half of the diagram only are written figures: '24, 24, 5 . . .' and so on. Plainly these lines and words represent some sort of survey, though not of the topographical-glass kind we have been examining here. Yet neither is this a map of any great accuracy: between the Bridge and Paul's Wharf Thames Street was certainly a fairly straight one, but it was never as straight as Hollar made it here. Moreover the numbers marked beneath Thames Street do not seem to make sense. Assuming that they mark the intervals between lanes running up from the river to the street, they cannot be found to bear any obvious relation to the actual distances between these lanes measured in either yards or feet.

Nevertheless the identifications provided by Hollar at the bottom of the sheet are enough to help us make sense of the whole diagram. Above Coldharbour and somewhat to the right he showed a perpendicular rising to the north (i.e. the upper) side of the street. This, with the help of Ogilby and Morgan's map of 1676, we may tentatively identify as representing Duxford Lane. To the left of this several lines run downwards from the street, and the map shows their names, reading from east to west, as Red Bull Alley, Cold Harbour, Campion Lane, Allhallows Lane, and so on. Fewer roads, at larger intervals, lead northwards from the main street, and these too may be identified: reading leftwards from Duxford Lane we come first to Walbrook, then Elbow Lane, College Hill, Garlick Hill and so forth. On this reading it soon appears that the units of measurement represented by the numbers Hollar attached to the drawing are neither feet nor yards, but paces of $2\frac{1}{2}$ ft each (see OED 'Pace' *sb.* 3), and, allowing for the changes that occurred between it and the time of Ogilby and Morgan's map, Hollar's survey was remarkably accurate, as may be seen from the following table, in which the scaled part of the drawing is summarized:

| From Ebgate Lane to | Distance in Ogilby and Morgan | | Hollar |
	Feet	Paces	Paces
Duxford Lane	200	80	80
Red Bull Alley	36	14.4	10
Cold Harbour	57	22.8	30
Campion Lane	87.5	35	30

Allhallows Lane	87.5	35	40
Steelyard	62	24.8	24
Steelyard	62	24.8	24
Dowgate/Walbrook	113	45.2	46
Brewers Lane	80	32	35
Elbow Lane	123.5	49.4	40
Emperor's Head Lane	13	5.2	5
Brickhill Lane	54	21.6	24
College Hill	54	21.6	24
Total	1029.5	411.8	412

The total distance from Ebgate Lane to College Hill tallies closely, and the proportionate placing of the intervening streets is broadly correct, as may be seen from the similarity of the second and third columns of figures, though of course the realignments and widening of many streets and alleys after the Fire of 1666 will have caused some small changes by Ogilby and Morgan's time. One may go to the City now – I recommend a Sunday morning when the traffic is light – and pace out some of these distances just as Hollar must have done, though perhaps he was equipped with a waywiser. Naturally he did not record New Queen Street, a post-Fire innovation which figures largely in the later map.

To the left of the diagram no pace measurements were given, but they may readily be deduced from the scale of the intervals to the right. Taking only the northward roads we may tabulate the intervals thus:

College Hill to	*Distance in Ogilby and Morgan*		*Hollar*
	Feet	Paces	Paces
Garlick Hill	330	132	134
Trinity Lane	205	82	70
Huggen Lane	102.5	41	45
Bread Street	75	30	30
Paul's Wharf	800	320	322
Total	1512.5	605	601

Here, then, is evidence of Hollar's thoroughness. On the reverse of a preliminary sketch for his *Long View* he took the trouble to work up a detailed scaled diagram – now unhappily lost, so lightly was it all set down – of one of the city's more important thoroughfares, all as background material to be used only indirectly if at all in the finished work. The diagram says nothing about the topographical glass, but it speaks volumes about the painstaking methods the artist used.

The sheet of the view towards Greenwich contains just the sort of information we need as we approach the goal of our investigation, the view to the west which takes in the Hope and the Globe. From that easterly sketch, with its blank literalism, we learn that the earliest stages of Hollar's work were as mechanical as if he had used a pin–hole camera. Through his topographical glass he would have seen just the sort of image that is projected on the plate of a pin–hole camera, each point and each line corresponding directly to the structure of the real scene being viewed, according to the strictest rules of linear perspective. The semiologists speak of the signs used in communication as either symbolic, conventional or indexical. Most pictures are a mixture of the first two sorts, representing reality or the world of the imagination through a code of symbols and conventional signs which we admit as 'standing for' the objects they represent. But in an important sense this drawing of Hollar's is neither symbolic nor conventional, but is rather a direct index of the view he saw from St Saviour's tower, as much an index as a weathercock is an index of the wind. Such signs are actually caused by the objects they represent. The wind among the pinnacles of St Saviour's swings the weathercock there; the shadow on St Paul's is an index of the sun. In just the same way this image of Southwark towards Greenwich is a table of indexical signs, each line caused by a line in reality, each proportion answering to the proportions of the real scene as if it were indeed projected onto a screen by some undistorting lens. In this preparatory drawing, then, we have an image that has – so far as it may be checked – the authority of a photograph. Two last points confirm its accuracy and its superiority to the *Long View* itself simply as a literal record of the facts. The *Long View* errs, like many of the panoramas including Visscher's, in showing Borough High Street as running almost directly in line with the Bridge when in fact it veered quite sharply westward from the South Gate. Although the approaches to the modern London Bridge have obscured this fact, and indeed disrupted the whole area, the angle of the old road can readily be plotted on a modern map, for the more southerly part of it retains its old alignment. We may also plot Hollar's angle of view as he looked out between the battlements of St Saviour's. We have established that he set up his glass on a bearing 28° from true north; Long Southwark ran towards the Bridge on a bearing approximately 39° east of north. It follows that Hollar's picture plane was at an angle of some 11° to the line of the street, and indeed his drawing shows it veering away from the observer to the left, just as it should. Unfortunately the Bridge is not included within this take, so that we cannot judge the angle it made with the High Street.

A second minor point of confirmation lies in the tower of St Olave's, shown in the drawing as having a turret in its northwest corner. When Iolo Williams first published the drawing he pointed out that this configuration fails to agree with the etching, which shows a cupola at the centre of the tower. The drawing shows only one tier of windows in the tower; the etching has two. Williams turned to West and Toms's view of the church, engraved in 1739, three years after the building had been pulled down, to find confirmation of the single-tier structure, and in that respect concluded that the drawing was more accurate than the etching. But West and Toms showed a cupola at the centre of the tower, not to one side. It seemed therefore that the superiority of the drawing was not unmixed, and that sometimes its faults were actually corrected in the *Long View*, presumably from Hollar's memory or because he had other studies to hand which have not survived. We should not, however, trust West and Toms very far. Their picture is a reconstruction, not an eyewitness sketch, and it conflicts not only with Hollar's drawing but with Visscher's engraving, which shows a turret in the northwest corner of the tower [Plate 23]. So too does Claude de Jongh, whose view of London Bridge now at Kenwood includes St Olave's and shows the turret to have been as Visscher's and Hollar's drawing render it. De Jongh's finished painting is confirmed by his preparatory drawing,[8] probably made from a boat anchored in the river, which again shows that Hollar was wrong in the *Long View* to put St Olave's cupola at the centre of the tower. We may now also add the evidence of Hollar's own Evelyn/Pepys panorama, dated 1638, which shows a northwestern turret and a single tier of windows [Plate 5]. Once more his drawing contains accuracies which have been abandoned in the finished etching. Doubtless West and Toms's print was itself influenced by the *Long View*.

Now the moment has come to turn our backs on Greenwich and walk round the battlemented head of St Saviour's tower, past the great pinnacles and widely splayed embrasures, whose bulky forms, replaced in 1689, must have influenced Hollar's choice of position in which to set up his topographical glass. Here before us is the record of what he saw as he stood behind the parapet and looked out through its crenellations over Winchester House to the theatres and beyond them to the great mansions along the Strand. Much of the drawing is meticulously inked in, the clear, precise lines closely following the pencil and chalk sketch beneath them. Among the sharpest passages is that containing the two theatres, the Globe to the left and the Hope to the right. Between and beyond them the trees and rooftops are left in their original lead, so that the distinctive rooflines of the theatres, and especially the Globe, stand out as if crowning the whole composition. The ink lines are like a clarifying interpretation of what lies beneath, as we can see if we look at the rendering of the far bank of the river. Here at first, without the overscoring, all seems practically illegible. The line of the bank can be made out readily enough, but the buildings along it are indicated by pencil marks that have rubbed badly and in any case appear never to have been much more than shorthand indications of landmarks.

When we compare the sketch to the etching we find that, as Iolo Williams put it, 'the angle from which the scene is viewed is slightly different.'[9] It is, as we saw in chapter 1, as if the observer in the etching were standing further to the left than the maker of the sketch. The hall of Winchester House is less sharply foreshortened in the print, and runs somewhat across the view at a more oblique angle. The theatres align differently with the roofs of the courtyard at Winchester House and the sketch seems to keep them pressed further away from the viewpoint than does the etching, which includes rather less of the foreground to the left and rather more of it to the right. We know already that the alignment of the foreground and background in the etching shows a relation of buildings that could not have presented itself to Hollar's eye as he looked out from the top of St Saviour's. Only by hovering in the air somewhere over the nave could he have brought the east gable of Winchester House into line with the crossing of St Paul's, as it is in the etching. And because Hollar was a practical man, not a levitationist, his etching must have been composed like the Evelyn/Pepys panorama in the imagination rather than directly from the facts observed on the spot. It is not surprising that 'the angle from which the scene is viewed' in the sketch is slightly different from that of the etching. If the drawing was made on the spot it could not be the same as the etching; the real, accessible viewpoint gave one picture, while the imaginary viewpoint of the etching gave another. Of course the information contained in the etching is doubtless derived from the sketch, perhaps from additional drawings also, but it is interpreted by the composing faculty of the artist, and we may observe that the beginning of the process of transmutation is already present in the drawing. In general, like the view towards Greenwich, it is a raw piece of perspective, the roofs of the foreground slipping uncomfortably out of view at the bottom edge, the orthogonals formed by the chimneys and ridges at the lower right-hand side disappearing steeply into the angle of the corner. The etching makes all this more horizontal and therefore more stable, and we can see in the bottom-right-hand corner of the sketch how the inked lines begin this process by lifting the rooflines, both ridge and eave, above the levels given by the pencil. Already the ink lines are moving in the direction the whole composition will take in the etching – an indication, by the way, that the lines were in fact inked in by Hollar himself.

I have said that the background of the drawing, its view of the north bank, is almost indecipherable. But if we are to interpret the drawing properly it is of the utmost importance that we should be able to read some of the landmarks there because we need to discover whether they are placed on the sheet in the positions that would be given by the use of a topographical glass. Is this sketch one of the studies actually made at the glass whose use we have had to posit in order to make sense of the spatial intervals revealed in the panoramas? Despite the apparent muddle there is in fact a good deal of information to be found among the pencil strokes along the north bank. The first thing we notice is a dead-straight line running horizontally across the sheet, beneath the line of low hills to the right and above the landline to the left. A moment spent with a couple of straightedges is enough to reveal that this is the horizon line, on which all horizontals in the drawing converge. We shall have to examine the function of the horizon line more fully later on, but for the moment I introduce it as evidence of the methodical way Hollar has gone about making this study. The eaves and ridges of Winchester House do indeed converge on the horizon line, and we note with interest that in the chimneyed block in the right corner it is the pencil, and not the ink, lines that correctly converge. In departing from the pencil sketch here Hollar departs from the method that informed it. A gathering of lines to the right end of the horizon is plainly intended to represent St Paul's, though they are not at all clear in their detail with the one exception of the cathedral's eastern gable. Here, thank goodness, is a piece of certainty: the pitch of the roof, the point of the ridge, even the pinnacles of the angle turrets are all marked with complete precision. Here is a touchstone to guide our exploration westwards along the north bank. As we move from right to left across the sketch we come first to a group of vertical lines apparently intended to indicate the tower and crossing of St Paul's, but their grouping is too ambiguous to leave us in much certainty about what is supposed to be represented by what. Further to the left, at what must be the west end of the cathedral, a great muddle: what looks like a tall tower seems to have a zigzag cancellation through it. Further down towards the river there is no mistaking the outline of Bulmer's water-tower, with its pointed conical roof which at one time supported the sails of a windmill. Above it and a little to the left is a square-headed church tower, identifiable by reference to Hollar's *Exact Prospect* of 1666 as that of St Martin's, Ludgate. There is no sign of the more distant St Andrew's, Holborn, which Hollar gives in the etching in a quite impossible position close to the west end of Paul's, close indeed to the apparently cancelled tower that appears there in the sketch. It seems that in this matter of the placing of St Andrew's he may have been a victim of the unclearness of his own study. Further to the left, under the '-stm-' of 'Westminster' in the title, a random-looking group of lines may indicate Ely Place, but the identification cannot be certain and we must renounce it here. No matter, for to the left of the group, and down on the river bank, there is no mistaking the shape of Baynard's Castle, with its turreted front facing directly across the water. Above this, quite clear, is the precisely stated tower of St Bride's.

Thus far the score is by no means negligible, including as it does the east end of Paul's, St Martin's, the water-tower, Baynard's Castle and St Bride's. But from here westwards locatable points become very

scarce. There are indications of the trees at the Temple just below the
'W–' of 'West' in the title, but these do not give us a very accurate fix.
A few scraps of lines indicate buildings or trees beneath the cancelled
words 'East Part of . . .,' and to the left again is a faint but quite
precisely delineated outline marking one of the great houses along the
Strand. The centre of this dimly rendered façade is directly above the
right side of the round of the Globe theatre, and a careful look at it
under the magnifying glass reveals that it has two turrets to the right
and one to the left of a long horizontal riverside front. Comparison
with the etching reveals that this is the Savoy, and there indeed, too
faint to be visible in any but the clearest of photographs, is its name
inscribed in Hollar's hand exactly above it on the horizon line. It is as
well that this westerly building can be identified, for the sketch of the
north bank offers no further hard information. A group of lines
immediately above the left side of the Globe may indicate another
Strand house, but it is not clear enough to recognize. A slight business
above the shoreline further left suggests another landmark but it is
quite unreadable; beyond that the left-hand corner of the drawing is
cut away and with it any hope of further evidence.

It is fortunate that the Savoy is marked with such precision,
however dim it may be, for it offers us, along with the series St Bride's
– St Martin's – St Paul's east end, the vital datum we need to test
whether the rendering of the north bank shows it to have been
composed at the topographical glass. But first we should consider the
alignments of this sketch. In the etching the east gable of Winchester
House is shown in line with the crossing of St Paul's, an impossible
state of affairs, as we saw in chapter 1. The drawing is much more
satisfactory, showing the gable beneath the area of St Paul's west end.
We do not yet know quite which of the marks in that area indicates the
west end of the church, but a line drawn between the west end of Old St
Paul's and the reconstructed position of the Winchester House gable's
north edge[10] does strike St Saviour's tower if we trace it carefully on a
modern Ordnance Survey map. More of this later; for the moment we
must note that in this matter of the relation between the north and
south sides of the river the sketch offers the literal truth where the
etching gives an expressive interpretation of it. The reputation of the
study as a meticulously accurate document is enhanced. And if
Winchester House is correctly aligned with St Paul's, what of the
building we are now interested in, the Globe? We have already noted
the happy circumstance that places the one recognizable landmark in
the left side of the background immediately above the right side of the
Globe: it enables us to take a sighting along a tangent touching the
Globe's north face and projecting westwards to strike the exact centre
of the river front of the Savoy. This spot lay at the west side of the
modern Lancaster Place, a little to the north of Savoy Place, and if we
draw a line of sight on the modern map joining it to the tower of St

Saviour's we find that it just clears the southern side of Park Street at the point where it is crossed by Southwark Bridge Road. The careful researches of W. W. Braines,[11] together with the subsequent discovery at the London Guildhall of a map of the area,[12] prove that the Globe site lay to the south of Maid Lane (the modern Park Street), projecting a few feet into what is now the roadway. When Hollar's drawing shows the Globe's north face aligned with the centre of the Savoy it shows facts exactly consonant with what Braines discovered. Evidently the theatre was built, as we should expect, toward the northern end of the site, close enough to Maid Lane, along which the audience would come, but not so close as to be cramped for room or to encroach upon the right of way. Again we find that Hollar's study offers the literal facts, rendered as exactly as if they were contained in an actual survey. Once in possession of this insight we are even able to spot the course of Maid Lane through the rooftops in the drawing. At about four o'clock from the centre of the Globe there appears a narrow gap in the buildings. We are looking along a road that cuts, in this foreshortening, diagonally upwards and to the right to turn left past a building whose wall and roof push into view against the background of a tree. This must be Maid Lane, and we can see into it – and hence see the wall against the tree – because for a short stretch it happens to run directly in line with our vantage point in St Saviour's tower, as the Ordnance Survey shows and we can still see to this day from the top of the cathedral. Then, beyond the bend (much accentuated here, of course, in Hollar's regular perspective foreshortening) the Lane runs straight past the northern limit of the Globe, out of sight but presumably parallel to the long roof ridge shown as flanking it to the left. The line of the Lane is thus indicated by the trees flanking the Globe to the right, separating it from the roofs – mostly uninked – of the buildings opposite it on the other side of the road.

In its presentation of the alignments of the south bank with the north the study is correct where the etching is not, and it will be possible to treat the whole view as a coherent unit where the etching has to be considered as a montage of isolated parts. In submitting it to the sort of test I have developed for the panoramas, however, I have restricted evidence about the intervals between landmarks to those on the north bank alone because among those to the south the theatres are the object of this enquiry and to use them as locatable fixes would involve a circular argument, while Winchester House is so close to St Saviour's that the results could be considerably affected according to the exact spot on the tower where Hollar stood when he made his study. This factor has less and less effect the further the observed landmarks are away from St Saviour's, and there is no need to allow for it in measuring bearings to points on the far side of the river. A scaled strip made from the sketch includes the locations of St Paul's east end (PE), the water-tower (WT), St Martin's, Ludgate (ML), St Bride's (BR) and the left or southwest end of the river front of the Savoy (SAV). Baynard's Castle is in line with St Bride's, and so is of little value as an independent fix. We recall that three intersections with lines of sight drawn from St Saviour's will be necessary to show the bearing of a picture plane if a topographical glass was involved in the study, and four will be needed actually to prove that some such device was used. The intervals marked on our strip indicate five possible intersections, and indeed establish the proof we are looking for when placed across the sightlines drawn on the map.

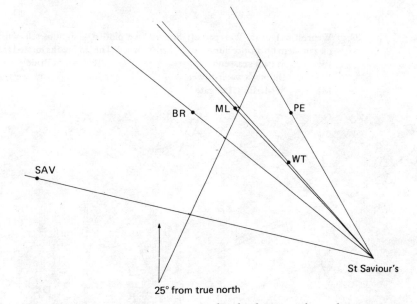

The more exact trigonometrical calculations show how very careful Hollar was in plotting the locations of these five landmarks:

Landmark	Angle subtended at St Saviour's tower	Interval measured on Hollar's sketch in mm
PE	0°	0
WT	12.3°	61.25
ML	0.8°	3.50
BR	8.3°	35.50
SAV	25.1°	100.25

Group	Bearing of picture plane calculated in degrees east of true north	
PE – WT – BR	25.42°	Calculations involving
PE – ML – BR	25.90°	the 0.8° angle
PE – WT – SAV	25.13°	between ML–WT are so
PE – ML – SAV	25.25°	ill-conditioned as not
PE – BR – SAV	25.02°	to be worth reporting

Average 25.34°

These results are as exact and conclusive as any we discovered in the printed panoramas, perhaps because the sketch so directly conveys what Hollar actually saw through the eyepiece of his topographical glass. The average bearing for the picture plane is 25.34° from true north, a figure from which the greatest extreme differs by only 0.58°. The impression of accuracy given by the few checkable alignments of this study is fully confirmed [Plate 28].

Any linear perspective study of this sort will contain a central ray. This is not necessarily located at the centre of the composition, but is that unique line of sight from or to the observer's eye which passes

28.   Wenceslaus Hollar, 'West part o[f] Southwarke' plotted on sightlines drawn to positions marked on a modern Ordnance Survey map, here reduced. The landmarks located are:

PE	St Paul's east end	BR	St Bride's
WT	Bulmer's water-tower	SAV	Savoy, west end of river front.
ML	St Martin's, Ludgate		

through the picture plane at 90°. It happens that in this case the central ray (whose bearing from St Saviour's must be 270° + 25.34° = 295.34°) passes exactly through the centre of the drawing, considered horizontally. The proof is simple: on the scaled strip one merely has to mark the halfway point, and this is found to coincide, when placed on the map, with the bearing of 295.34° from St Saviour's. Here is an indication, as clear as we could wish, that Hollar used a frame of some sort – almost certainly a topographical glass – and that he set it up with the eyepiece exactly opposite the centre of its lateral range. He looked straight through the middle of it, and obliquely through it at everything else. It would perhaps be foolhardy to claim that we know exactly how Hollar made the drawing, whether he used a perspective glass or a drawing frame, whether he inked his locating outlines directly onto the glass or whether he conveyed locating marks by means of compasses to a sheet of paper. That there is no sign of squaring-up on the drawing probably rules out the reticulated frame; indeed it seems more likely that he used a topographical glass as Hopton, Norden, Folkingham and the rest would have enjoined him to do. He must have begun by ruling a line across the glass with a straightedge, so that when he clamped the pane in place he could establish a horizon at the correct elevation when viewed through the eyepiece. When he came to trace the view onto paper he ruled a similar line onto that to start with, as a check against any possible slippage of the sheet against the glass as he worked. The result is a study of the most astonishing accuracy. This drawing signals to the enquirer across more than three centuries with all the precision of an optical instrument. We have long sought a measured survey of Shakespeare's Globe, and here it is, if only we can learn to read it aright.

4 Measuring the Globe

Although the intervals on the picture surface between the major landmarks in Hollar's sketch of west Southwark are exactly consistent with those that would be seen through a topographical glass set at 25.34° from true north it is not quite a necessary conclusion that some such device was used in its preparation. It is just possible that the artist could have arrived at these correct intervals by a mental rather than a mechanical process, but on the whole I think it unlikely. To begin with there is the very narrowness of the limits of precision to account for; then there is the special structure imposed on the whole drawing by the fact that it represents a true and plane intersection of the sightlines; and finally there is the consistency of method with the works of other artists, Visscher and Norden. If we are to suppose Hollar's astonishing exactness to be a product of his steady eye unaided by any instrument, we shall be forced to make similar claims for his predecessors. Thus although in the end it perhaps matters little enough whether Hollar actually used a glass or not – the exactness of the drawing speaking for itself – the evidence shows that he very likely did, and that in doing so he was breaking no new ground.

Much follows from this conclusion. Knowing something of the laws of proportion that govern the study's composition we can identify some of the otherwise unrecognizable marks on the north bank because we now know where certain landmarks *ought* to appear in relation to the ones that can be identified. When the paper strip marked with the known locations is set down across the map of sightlines at the given picture plane of 25.34° the positions of such points as the west end of Paul's or St Clement's can be marked off too, and then carried back to the sketch for comparison. We find that the west end of Paul's includes the tall and apparently cancelled tower which breaks across the horizon line; St Paul's terminates with the left side of that tower, which was evidently intended to mark one of the corner turrets of the cathedral. Further west, under the '-t-' in 'West' in the title, a square-headed tower can now be identified as St Clement's. The group of lines marking a building on the far bank directly above the left side of the Globe turns out to be meant for Durham House, and a similar cluster of marks beneath the cancelled word 'Part' in the title is Arundel House.

One of these identifications is of immediate practical use. Now that the position of the west end of Paul's is known it is possible to deduce just where on St Saviour's tower Hollar stood when he set up his glass.

He must of course have taken up a position on the west side of it, but now that we can see that he chose a spot from which the west end of Paul's lined up exactly with the northeast corner of Winchester House we can tell that he chose the southern or left-hand part of that side of the tower. Only from this position is the alignment correct, as we can tell from the large-scale (1:1250) Ordnance Survey map.[1] Parts of Winchester House remain. From the ruins, which are now built into a warehouse, though they are soon to be exposed in a park opening out towards the river, we can tell that the great hall, with the lovely rose window in its west wall, extended ten feet into what is now the way leading from Winchester Square into Clink Street, and that the north wall of the building stood some four feet forward into the present boundary of Clink Street.[2] The position and size of the gable end shown in Hollar's study are therefore quite precisely known, and by aligning the northern edge of the gable with the west end of Old St Paul's we may discover Hollar's line of sight from St Saviour's and, as I have said, his position in the southwest corner of the tower. The map directs us to the position of the very embrasure through which the artist looked as he made his sketch, and it is the same one we felt impelled towards on our visit to the tower.

Armed with these two pieces of vital information – the bearing of the picture plane and the exact position of the point of view – we are ready to begin the detailed analysis of Hollar's study. The sort of perspective yielded by the systematic use of a topographical glass is known as linear, to distinguish it from other sorts, often more complicated and for our purposes irrelevant. The principles of linear perspective were first described in full by Alberti in his *Della pittura* (1436). They were well known throughout the Renaissance, were developed and disseminated by such masters as Dürer and Holbein, and were without doubt fully understood by an artist of Hollar's technical sophistication. The most convenient modern explanation of them is B. A. R. Carter's exemplary article in the *Oxford Companion to Art*.[3]

Chief among the principles of linear perspective is that the picture represents a plane intersection through the visual pyramid whose base is the object viewed and whose apex is the (single) eye of the observer. The outlines of an object subtend an angle at the point of view and that angle may be larger or smaller according to a combination of the size of the object and its distance from the observer. This object close to me to the left and that object far away to the right both subtend angles at my eye, and these angles are in theory measurable though in practice we hardly ever need to be so deliberate about them. The eye measures for us, estimating size and distance in its own way. A gathering of such angles as these, all subtended at the one motionless eye, constitutes the visual pyramid. A view in linear perspective renders the angles as intervals on a two-dimensional plane by treating the plane as if it were an actual intersection through the pyramid. Of course a topographical glass is exactly that. As I look through my window onto the scene outside I can mark on the glass itself the outline of the Macdonald Hotel and the prettier shape of the Legislature to its left; above them rise the characterless blocks of modern big business and government, each precisely locatable on the glass; below them in the valley of the North Saskatchewan is the inflated plastic dome which covers an indoor tennis court, a necessity here in Edmonton's boreal winter, and that too can be registered on the window. Provided I have kept my eye quite still and know its exact position in relation to the glass I can measure the angle subtended at it by these objects in the landscape. The glass represents the plane intersection of the visual pyramid; the record I have made on it with my felt pen is of exactly the same sort as Hollar's sketch.

It is a characteristic of linear perspective that anything in the scene represented that lies parallel to the plane of the intersection will be represented in true elevation, with no distortion. Not much in Hollar's study runs parallel to the picture plane, though two of the ranges of Winchester House come close to it, and the east gable of the great hall comes fairly close. Everything that is not parallel to the plane of intersection will be foreshortened according to quite specific and immutable principles. All horizontals will converge on a single line which represents the horizon of the view. As we have seen, Hollar established his horizon with a straightedge across the top of his sheet, and because all the buildings on the south bank lie below it their horizontals slope upwards to converge upon it; parallel horizontals such as the ridges and eaves of the straight blocks of the courtyard at Winchester House converge at what later generations than Hollar's would call 'vanishing points' located on the horizon. He does not mark the other vitally important item on the sheet, the central vanishing point. To this point, in another sort of perspective composition, all the orthogonals would converge; the parallel lines, that is, which lay at 90° to the picture plane. Most perspective drawings and paintings make much use of these lines, for they give a ready sense of depth to the composition, like the familiar railway lines rising to a point on a prairie horizon. But Hollar's view is not that sort of ideal, regularized townscape which appears in, say, Piero della Francesca's *Flagellation*, nor does his view give the regular harmony of even such a room as Leonardo's *Last Supper* takes place in. He offers instead the jumble of unmediated reality, and while unmediated reality readily admits to a horizon it offers no such certainty when it comes to a visual centre. This is to be found, then, not by reference to any object that Hollar has drawn, but as we have seen by plotting on a map that line which intersects the picture plane at 90°. This will give us, to put it another way, that part of the horizon line at which Hollar looked as he peered straight through his glass at right angles to it. The bearing thus established from St Saviour's, 295.34°, happens to be close to that of St Clement's church, which is on a bearing of 294.7° from the point of view. Thus Hollar was looking almost straight at St Clement's when he made his study, and for every other point, to the left or the right, up or down, he was looking from his eyepiece through his topographical glass at a more or less oblique angle.

Just as any plane running parallel to the picture plane will appear in true elevation, undistorted by foreshortening, so any horizontal in such a plane will run parallel to the horizon line, failing – unlike all the other horizontals – to converge upon it. It follows that any horizontal line drawn across Hollar's sketch might be plotted on a map as a line bearing 25.34° from true north, parallel, that is, to the picture plane. We may make use of this characteristic to perform a rudimentary test of the drawing's general accuracy. The location of the Globe is known, and a horizontal line drawn through the base of the theatre on the sketch will represent a line on a map bearing 25.34° and passing through the site of the theatre. We project such a horizontal rightwards from the Globe across the sketch until it strikes the north bank of the river and find that it does so beneath a point between the east gable of St Paul's and the edge of the sheet. From the map of sightlines this point can be identified: it lies close to the foot of the modern Bellwharf Lane. Now on the map we project a line from Bellwharf Lane to the south bank on a bearing of 25.34° and find that it strikes the south side of Park Street where it is intersected by Southwark Bridge Road: just where W. W. Braines discovered that the Globe was located. One should not perhaps claim too much for this proof, not only because a certain sketchiness in the drawing of the shoreline beneath St Paul's makes exactness impossible, but also because we do not precisely know the elevation above river level of the site of the Globe in Hollar's time. Our horizontal should be projected from a point *beneath* the Globe at the equivalent of water level in order to register a true bearing to the river's northern waterline. The river's head was a mean 5 ft 4 in. higher before the removal of old London Bridge than afterwards, because of the barrier effect of the starlings;[4] and while the altitude of Park Street where it is crossed by Southwark Bridge Road is known to be a little over 11 ft above mean sea level one look at the area's present state is enough to convince an observer that things have changed in those parts since the day when Hollar made his drawing. Even so, if we cannot draw our horizontal across it with absolute confidence, the general impression of its accuracy remains in its confirmation of Braines's discoveries.

We may perform the same test using the Hope as a point of departure. Here – as we shall see later – there is some difficulty in

determining exactly where to measure the base of the theatre's wall to
the left (the base is altogether obscured to the right); selecting for the
moment the end of the inked line which marks the wall, we run a
horizontal from it across the drawing to the river bank beneath St
Paul's. The reader may repeat this exercise for himself very easily
without going to the trouble of ruling a line if he will take a pair of
dividers, measure the distance of the base of the Hope below Hollar's
horizon line and then, with unchanged dividers, find the point on the
shoreline which is an equal distance below the horizon. He will find it
to be below a spot between the west end and the crossing of St Paul's.
The sightline to this western part of the cathedral from St Saviour's
tower crosses the north bank of the river halfway between Southwark
Bridge and Queenhythe. From that intersection a line plotted on a
map at 25.34° runs southwards across the river to skim along the west
side of Bear Gardens. According to Braines's researches the site of the
Hope straddled the modern lane. Once more Hollar's drawing proves
accurate, and so, we may note in passing, does our finding that its
picture plane is consistent at 25.34°. For the site of the Globe, indeed,
Hollar now provides us with something akin to a grid reference: we
have both the westward bearing towards the Savoy and the southerly
one from Bellwharf Lane. At the intersection of these two lay the site
of the Globe, just where Braines said it was.

Because the locations of St Paul's, the water-tower, St Martin's, St
Bride's and the Savoy are certainly known on the sketch it is possible
to plot on a map the points to which the limits of the view left and right
extend. It is simply a matter of placing the set of intervals from

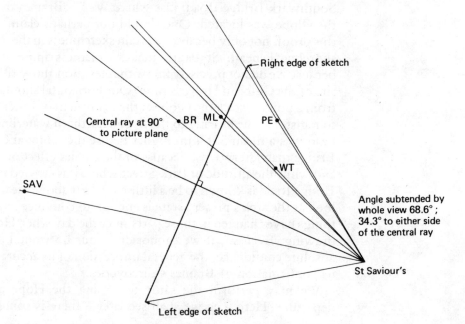

the left edge to the right of the sketch across the map of sightlines. The angle subtended at St Saviour's by the whole view, from its left limit to the right, is 68.6°. The central ray exactly coincides with the centre of the sketch itself, so that the whole arc of the view consists of 34.3° to the left of centre and 34.3° to the right.

We are now in a position to reconstruct the essential facts about Hollar's drawing method. If the sheet before us, measuring 128 mm by 309 mm (the latter measure taken just below the horizon line), is marked with the actual dimensions he took at the glass it follows that the glass itself – or that part of it through which he took this view – was the same size. The central ray, almost exactly coinciding with the bearing of St Clement's and therefore with the position of St Clement's on the sketch, passed through the glass at a point 154.5 mm from its left edge. The angle subtended at the eye is, as we saw above, 34.3°, and the distance of the eye from the glass was 154.4 mm ÷ tan 34.3° = 226.49 mm, or almost 9 in. Hitherto, for the sake of clarity, I have spoken as if the artist's eye was forced, by means of an eyepiece or peephole, to take up a fixed position at the exact point of view. In practice this awkward procedure is neither necessary nor desirable. Some illustrations of the drawing frame show its eyepiece not as a peephole viewfinder, but as a stylus which is simply to be lined up with the objects in the landscape, the viewer looking across its tip from any convenient distance behind it.[5] The effect of this device is the same as that achieved by a peephole, only it is more comfortable and precise. The exact point of view is rigidly fixed by the point of the stylus, but the eye now looks *across* that point, moving a little to the left to note objects to the right of the prospect, right for objects to the left, up for those that are below the horizon and down for those above. An experiment with a homemade glass will quickly convince the enquirer of the value of this arrangement: now that the eye is free to move the whole device is handier to use and less likely to be knocked out of alignment by an importunate nose. Moreover, because the eye can be held well back from it, the stylus can be treated almost like the sight of a gun. Looking across its tip at some distant landmark, the artist registers the point where his line of sight crosses the intervening glass. Let us assume that he is drawing the outline of the view directly onto the glass: as he moves his eye to-and-fro behind the stylus in order to mark the alignments of objects to the left and right of the prospect, so the drawing he makes will appear to depart from the actual view he sees if he simply looks directly at it. Only when he aligns his eye with the stylus tip and this or that particular building will the corresponding point in the picture exactly coincide with the real landscape; the rest of it will not show itself in alignment until he removes the stylus altogether and sets his eye at the very point previously occupied by its tip. Then the pictorial outline on the glass will fit the perceived outline of the view.

The greater precision of the stylus, or gun-sight, method derives from the elementary fact that one can focus more readily on objects which are a fair distance from the eye. The most accurate alignments can be made when the nearer object is at least some feet away from the observer; if it is too close it becomes blurred when he tries to accommodate his eye to it at the same time as he is concentrating on his distant target. In theory a drawing frame of the graticulated sort would allow its user to stand well back so that both the stylus and the network of strings might be held in focus along with the distant subject of the drawing. All the artist has to do is to locate the subject between numbered strings, which he then relocates on a sheet of squared-up paper. There is no need for him to be within reach of the frame itself. But if he is to take measurements from the frame with dividers, or actually to outline the view on a sheet of glass, he must stand close enough to do his manual work. For accuracy of focusing he will want to keep the stylus as far away from his eye as he can, but the length of his own arm will limit his ability to do so. Now I am about middle height, and I can reach a working surface held about 27 in. in front of my eye; I could manage a little more if I were working with a long pencil or brush, but only at the risk of losing some very valuable accuracy. Hollar's working surface, be it graticulated frame or topographical glass, was about 9 in. from his point of view or stylus-tip, and we may conclude that he was able to hold his eye anything up to 18 in. away from that. 18 in. is not a bad distance for this sort of work, though ideally one could do with rather more. It is well beyond the *punctum proximum* where accommodation becomes impossible, and the image of the stylus would blur into uselessness. There is no such difficulty here: precise bearings can readily be taken, as the reader may ascertain for himself if he will set up some sort of stylus 9 in. in front of his window – an unfolded paper clip will do, held between the pages of a book – and with a felt pen trace the outline of the view outside point for point on the glass. In doing so he will, I believe, be reconstructing the essentials of Hollar's method; and he will not fail to be struck by its potential for the most accurate recording of a topographical prospect.

I have said that it is a principle of linear perspective that all vertical planes within the view that lie parallel to the picture plane will be presented in true elevation. Imagine a dead-straight row of billboards ranged parallel to a picture plane on which they are depicted. In linear perspective, as a simple diagram will show, these billboards will appear on the picture in just the same proportions as they possess in reality, even though those to the left and right of the observer are further away from him than those at the centre and ought – so common sense tells us – to look smaller and more closely spaced. They are shown in plan in the following figure:

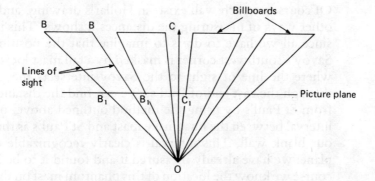

Because the picture plane and the line of the billboards are parallel, triangle O–B–B is similar to triangle O–B_1–B_1, and B_1–B_1 is proportional to B–B as O–B_1 is to O–B or as the distance of the plane of the billboards from the observer (C–O) is to the distance from the picture plane to the observer (C_1–O). OC is of course the central ray of the perspective. If each of the billboards is the same size as the others it follows that each will appear equal in size on the picture plane since each will be proportioned by the ratio O–C to O–C_1. This same thing will apply to vertical dimensions of planes parallel to the vertical picture plane. As we have said, all planes parallel to the picture plane will appear in true elevation. Unfortunately Hollar offers us no such planes of any value, and we must make good the deficiency by imagining them. Imagine, for example, a vertical plane, parallel to the picture plane and intersecting the eastern gable of St Paul's. Clearly such a plane would be marked on a map by a line running through the east end of Paul's on a bearing 25.34° from true north. Extended left and right to take up the whole 68.6° arc of the view that line now marks the actual distance covered by the arc along a plane at a known distance from the observer. Thus the direct distance of St Paul's east end from St Saviour's tower is about 3320 ft, but the distance of the plane which intersects it on a bearing of 25.34° is less than that: 2789 ft according to my best measurement. At this distance from the observer the arc of his view from edge to edge of the drawing covers a measurable quantity of ground: 2789 ft × 2. tan 34.3°. It follows that if we could spot a blank wall, say, somewhere on that plane and by coincidence aligned exactly with it, we could tell its size because its proportion to the whole distance would be known. If it were represented on the sketch by a 20 mm interval its size in reality would be 20/309 times the total distance covered by the plane intersecting Paul's east end, the whole sketch being 309 mm wide, measured below the horizon line. The size of the wall might then be calculated thus:

$$\frac{20}{309} \times 2789 \times 2 . \tan 34.3° = 246.28 \text{ ft}$$

Of course no such wall exists in Hollar's drawing, and we must find other ways of measuring the distances it shows. This is not difficult, since all we have to do is to imagine that the position of (say) the Savoy's southwest corner is masked by a tall mast located at the point where the line of sight to the Savoy intersects the plane that cuts through the east end of Paul's. We can find the distance of that mast from St Paul's by using the method outlined above, only taking the interval between the imaginary mast and St Paul's as the equivalent of our blank wall. This interval is clearly recognizable on the picture plane: we have already measured it and found it to be 200.5 mm. Of course we know the location of this phantom mast on the map, and we can measure in the same place the bearing of the Savoy from St Paul's. With this information we have, as the following diagram will indicate, a useful way of testing the accuracy of Hollar's drawing, for we are able to calculate the distance from St Paul's to the Savoy as he records it and then to compare our findings with the reality.

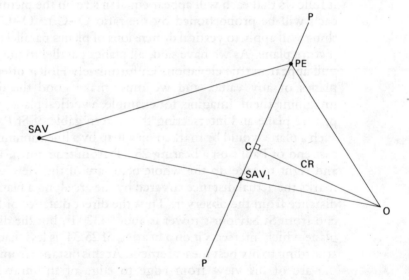

Here P–P is the imaginary plane running through the east end of Paul's (PE) parallel to the picture plane, on a bearing 25.34° from true north. O–SAV is the sightline to the Savoy, O–PE to St Paul's, and SAV$_1$ is our imaginary mast. O–C is the central ray (CR), at right angles to the picture plane. We know from the map that the angle SAV–Ô–C is 13.64° and the bearing of PE from the Savoy is 74.5° from true north. SAV$_1$–PE represents 200.5/309 of the whole distance covered by the plane P–P within its arc of 68.6°. Our first task is to express the distance SAV–PE in terms of the plane P–P, where it is represented by the line SAV$_1$–PE. In the triangle SAV–SAV$_1$–PE,

SAV–SÂV₁–PE is 103.64°; SAV₁–PÊE–SAV is 49.16°, and SAV₁–SÂV–PE is therefore 27.2°. According to the Sine rule, sin 103.64/SAV–PE = sin 27.2/200.5 mm; SAV–PE = sin 103.64 × 200.5 mm/sin 27.2 = 426.27 mm. Thus in terms of the scale of the plane P–P, the distance between the Savoy and St Paul's is 426.27 mm. Now we may treat this distance as if it were indeed on the plane P–P, and find what it represents:

$$\frac{426.27}{309} \times 2789 \times 2 \cdot \tan 34.3° = 5249.08 \, \text{ft}$$

In fact, as measured on the Ordnance Survey map, the southwest corner of the Savoy was 5250 ft from St Paul's east end. Hollar's study gives the distance to an accuracy of 0.92 ft, or 0.02%.

A similar set of calculations for the distance between St Bride's and Paul's east end, the bearing of the latter from the former being 88°, yields a figure of 1930.85 ft, while the measure on the map is 1935 ft: Hollar states the correct distance to within 0.21%. The plane intersecting St Bride's tower runs parallel to the picture plane 4511 ft from the observer in St Saviour's. St Bride's is on a bearing 66.5° from the Savoy, which is 13.64° from the central ray. This is enough information to allow us to calculate the distance between St Bride's and the Savoy as 3366.19 ft. The actual distance was 3345 ft, 21.19 ft less than the figure yielded by Hollar, or within 0.63%.

In a sense these demonstrations of Hollar's accuracy merely confirm the proofs I have presented thus far. If the intervals on his sketch really are precisely where a topographical glass at 25.34° would put them, it is not surprising to find that the results can be used to read distances from as far away as a mile and quarter to within a few feet. We may now, however, move on to another sort of confirmation, one not implied by the figures we have used already. The east gable of Winchester House is finely represented in the drawing, measuring 23.2 mm across on the picture plane. From the large-scale Ordnance Survey map, and allowing for the fact that the wall extended ten feet further east than the present warehouse that has been made of it, we discover that the right-hand side of the gable lay on a bearing of 24.66° from the central ray of Hollar's view, and the plane intersecting it and parallel to Hollar's glass was 335 ft from the observer in the southwest corner of the head of St Saviour's tower, the point we have established as the artist's point of view. The gable itself, which was parallel to the extant west wall of the hall, lay on a bearing 16.0° from true north. This information is enough to make possible the calculation of the width of the gable, using the same method as that we used to check the measurements along the north bank. The accompanying diagram is not, of course, to scale, but it shows the main parts of the procedure.

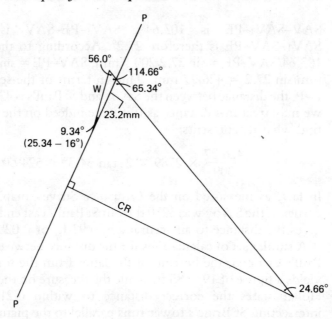

Here the line marked w represents the actual gable of Winchester House, marked on the drawing by an interval of 23.2 mm along the plane P – P. In the triangle of which w constitutes the longest side, sin 56.0/23.2 mm = sin 114.66/w; w = 25.43 mm. The width of the gable may now be calculated:

$$\frac{25.43}{309} \times 335 \times 2 \,.\, \tan 34.3° = 37.61 \text{ ft}$$

Now the actual width of Winchester House great hall is pretty well-known, because the south wall is still extant and so is the stonework of the rose window at the west end. Although the north wall has gone it is reasonable to assume symmetry about the east-west axis marked by the round window, and since the exterior of the south wall is 19 ft from the centre of the window we deduce that the hall itself was 38 ft wide.[6] That is the width, to within 5 in., that Hollar's drawing shows it; his measure is 1.02% off.

We can match it with another dimension derived from Winchester House. To the south, or left side of the buildings a buttressed wall marks the boundary with the park. It is a fair guess, but not as far as I know a proven fact, that this wall marks not only the old boundary of the palace site but also the line of the modern Winchester Walk, somewhat to the south of Winchester Square, itself formed out of the old courtyard of the house. A line of sight from St Saviour's tower to the left side of the Globe, as marked on the map we have developed, runs nearly parallel to the modern wall flanking Winchester Walk to the north, but cutting towards it gradually from left to right. And indeed we do see the left side of the wall in Hollar's drawing, with the left side of the Globe directly above it. Now it is possible to measure the distance along a 25.34° plane from the north side of Winchester Walk to the spot in Clink Street to which the east gable of the hall extended in Hollar's time. That distance is about 254 ft. In the sketch it is represented by a horizontal line running from the base of the gable wall (we have to estimate the position of this because it is obscured by some low buildings) to the face of the wall looking into the park. Because the line is horizontal it runs parallel to the picture plane. It measures 174 mm, not counting the buttresses, and we know already that on the ground it is 335 ft distant from the observer. We calculate the distance thus:

$$\frac{174}{309} \times 335 \times 2 \,. \tan 34.3° = 257.36 \,\text{ft}$$

This is within about 1.32% of the distance we measured on the ground, but it cannot be claimed as any proof of the accuracy of Hollar's sketch, for the identity of the line of the park wall and the north side of Winchester Walk is not established; rather the interest here is the other way round, for we are beginning to make independent deductions from the information Hollar provides. One feels confident enough in the integrity of his study to assert that it gives good reason to believe that Winchester Walk marks the line of the old palace wall.

And there beyond Winchester House lies the goal of our long and I fear rather arduous journey. To the left the Globe, to the right the Hope. Both buildings are neatly inked over, clearly stated considering the smallness of the scale at which they appear. The Globe is about 21 mm wide on the paper, and the Hope about 15 mm. When we come to measure their heights we shall have difficulty, for Hollar has left the groundline of both buildings somewhat obscure, hiding it behind a row of bushes. But these complications may for the moment be postponed as we ask what is perhaps the most important question of all about the Globe: how wide was it? Modern estimates range all the way from 80 ft across to 100 ft, with the consensus tending towards the smaller end of the range. It is hardly satisfactory that the learned should differ in their opinions about the size of so important a building in English theatre history by twenty or twenty-five per cent. Nor does that difference express the full contrast between the two sizes: the 100 ft diameter covers an area 64% greater than the 80 ft, and at a rough estimate allows for over 55% more audience space. The feel of the one house would be altogether different from that of the other. The smaller yard would be a more intimate place than the larger one, but would be heavily overborne by the frame, three-fifths as high as the yard's diameter. The wider yard, with a frame height less than its radius, would feel more spacious yet would not be so large as to lose acoustical effectiveness. It must serve as a sounding-box for Lear's all-shaking thunder, contain the stillness of Brutus's tent at Sardis, even give the strutting player, whose conceit lies in his hamstring, the opportunity

To hear the wooden dialogue and sound
'Twixt his stretch'd footing and the scaffoldage.[7]

We must know how big this theatre was, and now happily we are for the first time equipped with enough information to settle the matter once and for all, though before doing so it is necessary to take note of one more characteristic of linear perspective of special relevance to our enquiry. Broadly speaking it is this: in a correct linear perspective view spheres and horizontal circles will be distorted and overstated at the picture plane unless they happen to be centred on the central ray, and this distortion will increase the further they are away from the central ray. This characteristic was of course well-known to Renaissance practitioners of perspective, who called it anamorphosis. It is most fascinating in the matter of spheres, which ought hardly ever to appear in perspective compositions represented by true circles but nearly always do. If an artist gives the correct distortion to a spherical body, representing it as egg-shaped on his picture plane, nobody believes him. Thus Raphael, in *The School of Athens*, places globes represented by perfect circles well to the right of his rigidly conceived composition. And just as spheres resist the laws of linear perspective because of the quirks of human psychology, so too does the human figure. Raphael makes his portraits in *The School of Athens* as undistorted as his spheres, although they are set in an architectural space which is fully foreshortened. It is, however, neither spheres nor the human figure that concern us here, but rather the horizontal circles of the Hope and the Globe, and their anamorphosis is relatively easy to explain. Earlier, when we touched on the proportionality of a perspective plane intersection, I used the example of a row of billboards set parallel to the picture plane, equal in size and equally spaced. Imagine now, instead of the billboards, a row of circular columns, again parallel to the picture plane and equally spaced. Those to the left and right of the central ray will register on the plane as wider than those at the centre.

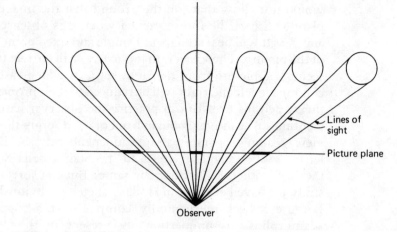

The reason for this anamorphosis is that while we actually see a small fraction less than the whole diameter of any of the columns, we are looking at those to left and right through a plane of intersection which is at an oblique angle to our line of sight. If the plane lies straight across our line of sight to the centre of the column – if, that is, this line of sight is also the central ray of the perspective – there will be no distortion; if on the other hand the lines of sight cut the plane of intersection at an oblique angle the distortion will be great. I confess that when I first thought about this matter I found it difficult to grasp. For some reason I could not shake from my mind the idea of an artist staring fixedly ahead of him along the central ray of his view, and trying somehow to squint left and right without moving his eyes, yet making a record nevertheless of what he saw, distorted at the periphery of his field of vision. Of course that idea was a delusion, nothing whatever to do with linear perspective. In making a view like Hollar's the artist is at perfect liberty to move his angle of vision and so to look straight at whatever he chooses in the scene generally before him, so long as he does not shift his ground in relation to the picture plane. This fixing is achieved in the topographical glass by the stylus across which he must look. But in drawing the picture of the Globe Hollar did not have to squint sideways at it; he looked at it direct, but through a picture plane held at an oblique angle to his line of sight. Consequently, when he marked the positions of the limits of the theatre wall, left and right, on the glass he registered an interval slightly larger than would have been the case had he held the glass straight across his line of sight to the theatre. A small point, perhaps, for so much theory and explanation, but it is of the greatest importance for our enquiry.

Of course, many artists would simply ignore the problem of anamorphosis and show the row of columns in our earlier example the same size as one another. But the strict method of linear perspective would not allow that, on the ground that the image on the picture plane will itself be foreshortened when it is observed at an oblique angle, as it will be if seen from a single and fixed point of view in front of the picture. The viewer, that is to say, will correct the distortion by seeing the picture from the right spot, in which case the over-wide columns to left and right will be reduced to their proper proportions as they reach his eye. But in practice the observer hardly ever reads a painting so; he moves about in front of it, adopting this or that point of view, reading separate passages independently. So Raphael sensibly let his globes stand as circles in the Stanza della Segnatura, and a thousand others have done the same. But the sort of topographical study we have before us in Hollar's sketch is obviously a special case. Because it was mechanically composed at a topographical glass anamorphosis is unquestionably present in the depiction of the theatres, and must be taken into account. Though their walls were probably many-sided polygons, the Hope and the Globe were

29.   Same as Plate 28, but here the bearings of the Globe, the Hope and the eastern gable of Winchester House have been deduced from the drawing.

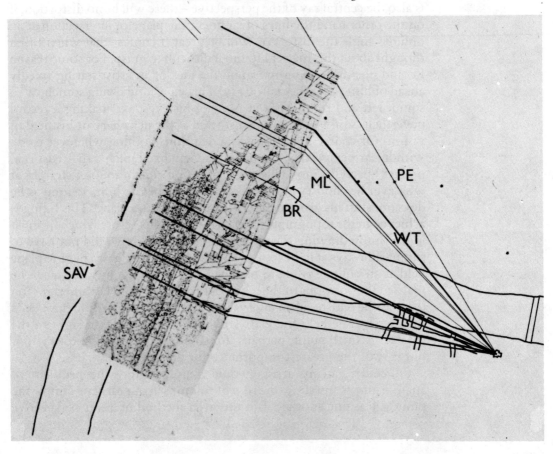

essentially horizontal discs. To determine their degree of anamorphosis we need to know how far they both diverge from the central ray
of the drawing; to discover the angles of the sightlines to both theatres
we must have recourse once more to the scaled strip of paper we used
earlier on to discover the bearing of the picture plane. The positions of
the theatres are marked on the strip, which is then placed in its correct
position on the map, at a bearing of 25.34° from true north and with
the Savoy, St Bride's, St Martin's and St Paul's all meeting their
correct lines of sight. We can now mark the points where the lines of
sight to the theatres, left and right, intersect the picture plane, and
when these points are connected to St Saviour's tower we have the
lines of sight to the north and south sides of both buildings [Plate 29].
In my calculations, because I am interested in the size of the round of
the Globe in the first instance, I have ignored the northerly stair turret
and measured only to the limits of the wall of the main structure. The
Globe lies between 12.5° and 17.5° from the central ray; the Hope
between 1.1° and 5.1°. These figures permit the calculation of the
effect of anamorphosis in each case, expressed as a percentage.
Because later on we shall be measuring the size of each theatre by
reference to an imagined plane running through its centre, it is
necessary to calculate how each would register on such a plane when
viewed under the conditions of Hollar's study. Take the Hope first:

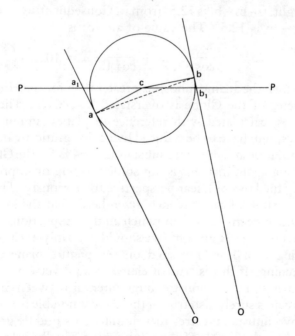

We shall assume that the theatre is 100 units wide. c – b is the radius
(50 units). The imaginary plane P – P lies parallel to the picture plane.

$O - b_1 - b$ is the line of sight from the tower of St Saviour's to the right side of the Hope, passing through the plane at b_1. $O - a - a_1$ is the line of sight to the left side of the building, and while only the segment $a - b$ is actually seen by the observer it registers on the plane $P - P$ as the greater value $a_1 - b_1$. Because the line of sight $O - a - a_1$ is $5.1°$ south (i.e. to the left) of the central ray, the angle $a_1 - ĉ - a$ is also $5.1°$, and $a_1 - c$ may be calculated ($a - c$ being a radius of 50 units):

$$\frac{a - c}{\cos 5.1°} = 50.20$$

Similarly for $c - b_1$:

$$\frac{c - b}{\cos 1.1°} = 50.01$$

The width actually registered on the plane $P - P$ is therefore $50.20 + 50.01 = 100.21$, or 100.21% of the actual width of the theatre. Clearly this distortion is so small as to be negligible, but with the Globe, which is set further from the central ray, the margin is greater. We may use the same unscaled diagram as before [p. 99]. Again the segment actually visible is $a - b$, and again it is registered on the plane $P - P$ as $a_1 - b_1$ whose value may as before be calculated as a percentage of the true diameter of the circle. This time $O - a - a_1$, the line of sight to the left of the Globe, is $17.5°$ from the central ray, while the line to the right, $0 - b_1 - b$, is $12.5°$ from it. Consequently $a_1 - ĉ - a$ is $17.5°$ and $b - ĉ - b_1$ is $12.5°$. The value of $a_1 - b_1$ is

$$\frac{50}{\cos 17.5°} + \frac{50}{\cos 12.5°} = 103.64$$

Here then the anamorphosis is greater than for the Hope, and the true diameter of the Globe is overstated by 3.64%. The widths of the theatres, calculated with reference to planes running through their centres, will have to be reduced by the insignificant amount of 0.21% for the Hope and the more substantial 3.64% for the Globe. It is worth stressing again that this is not some footling or improbable result of taking the laws of linear perspective too seriously. There can be little doubt, after all the evidence given here, that the sketch is indeed a linear perspective study in which all the proportions and locations of the major objects in sight (we should probably exclude the myriad of infilling roofs) are rendered on the picture plane in precise foreshortening. If this is true of elements so diverse as the gable end of Winchester House and the huge interval between St Paul's and the Savoy, it is surely also true of those most notable features of the view, the two unusual theatres that dominate its middle ground. And this being so, the width of the Globe must equally be overstated in the drawing, and by the measurable proportion we have calculated.

In order to discover the widths of the theatres we must measure their widths on Hollar's sketch and establish their distance from his point of view, or rather the distances of the respective planes parallel to his picture plane which intersect the centres of the buildings. First to the measurement of the sketch. Obviously it is most important that this be done as accurately as possible. Even the very thickness of the lines must be taken into account. I assume that we should aim at measuring the distance between the centres of the lines which mark the vertical sides of the theatres, because Hollar would have drawn his lines through, rather than within or without, the outline visible on his topographical glass. Nevertheless, while that may be a preferable measurement, we should determine a range within which the lines may be said to lie. There is some slight evidence to the right of both theatres of uncertainty in the drawing, where a faint, smudged lead line is to be seen within the ink line of the wall. I do not propose to admit these lines as significant evidence. If that in the Globe were taken as more satisfactory than the inked line it would destroy the symmetry of the building and show the wall leaning outwards at an unlikely and dangerous angle. But even the inked lines do present some irregularities: a notch cuts into the left wall of the Globe low down; a bulge of similar size afflicts its right wall high up. The Hope's left wall is very clean, except for its base, of which more later; its right wall is a little foggy, and has a jog in it halfway down. In measuring I have ignored the notch and bulge in the Globe and have attempted to regularize the jog on the Hope. One takes measurements like these with the dividers, and one does it over and over again, transferring the dividers each time to the ruler and making a record of the findings. (Of course, as in all these studies, I have used a full-size photograph of the drawing: the original could not take such punishment. Professor Richard Hosley, however, kindly made available to me the results of his careful measuring of the original drawing at Yale.) The maximum, for the outer sides of the lines marking the wall of the Globe, is 21.2 mm; the open space between them is 20.8 mm and the distance between their centres is 21.0 mm. The Hope is 15.15 mm (maximum), 14.85 mm (minimum) and 15.0 mm between the centres.

Thanks to W. W. Braines we know the positions of the sites on which both the Hope and the Globe were built, and therefore we can measure on a large-scale map the distance from St Saviour's of the planes intersecting these sites and parallel to Hollar's picture plane on a bearing of 25.34° from true north [Plate 30]. The Hope plane is 1513 ft from Hollar's point of view, measured along the central ray; the Globe plane similarly measured is 1144 ft distant. In both cases the distances are to planes passing through the centres of the sites determined by Braines.[8] The width of the Hope registers on the picture plane thus:

$$\frac{15.0}{309} \times 1513 \times 2 \,.\, \tan 34.3° = 100.20 \, \text{ft}$$

This must be reduced by the tiny proportion of 0.21% to allow for anamorphosis:

$$100.20 \times \frac{100}{100.21} = 99.99 \text{ ft}$$

The range of measurements fell between 14.85 mm and 15.15 mm, so we must take the readings for the Hope as lying between limits we can calculate in the same way as a minimum of 98.99 ft and a maximum of 100.99 ft.

The Globe registers on the plane as

$$\frac{21.0}{309} \times 1144 \times 2 . \tan 34.3° = 106.07 \text{ ft}$$

This figure is reduced to counter the effect of anamorphosis:

$$106.07 \times \frac{100}{103.64} = 102.35 \text{ ft}$$

Again we must state the range of possible findings according to the range of our measurements: the minimum is 101.37 ft and the maximum 103.32 ft.

W. W. Braines was able to fix the east-west extent of the Hope's position fairly accurately, but the site of the Globe was an irregularly shaped piece of ground with 156 ft of frontage on the south side of Maid Lane.[9] It is not possible to say whereabouts within this area the playhouse was actually located. Away from the Lane the plot's

30.   An enlargement of the Bankside section of Plate 29, showing the bearings of the theatres and the gable of Winchester House. Drawn on a sixty-inch Ordnance Survey map.

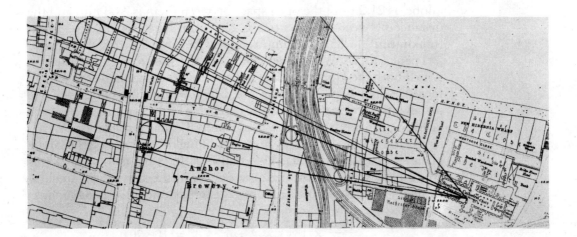

east-west width increased to 220 ft, but the most easterly part of this made a tongue of land too small to take a 100 ft theatre. Thus although the figures I have given above describe the Globe if it were placed mid-way along the whole site's east-west length, it might have been possible to build it a few feet further west or east of the central point I have assumed. If it touched the western boundary of the site it would have been further away from Hollar and so would have been larger to register at 21 mm on his glass; touching the easterly boundary of the northern part of the site it would have been smaller. The furthest possible spot yields a right distance from St Saviour's of 1194 ft and a theatre width of 106.82 ft; the closest possible yields a right distance of 1132 ft and a width of 101.27 ft. Both sets of figures should, I think, be treated with reserve: we have no way of knowing just where on the site the Globe was placed, east and west, but on the whole a central location seems preferable to one pressing against the boundary in any other direction than that perhaps of Maid Lane, along which most of the patrons would come.

In general we have found Hollar's drawing to be accurate to within ± 2.0%. Within that limit lay the readings for Winchester House and the distances indicated between St Paul's and the Savoy, St Bride's and the Savoy, and St Bride's and St Paul's. These plottings range across the greater part of the sweep of Hollar's view, and prove its integrity. It would be churlish to believe that the theatres were for some reason rendered less accurately. We may conclude that the dimensions we have discovered are correct, like the other discoverable measures, to within the same limits of ± 2.0%.

Two things strike one immediately about these dimensions. First, they are rather larger than has hitherto been generally understood; and secondly they are very much the same. At first this conclusion that the Hope was as wide as the Globe seems rather odd, for it looks so much smaller on the drawing, even allowing for its greater distance from the observer. Partly this illusion is caused by the anamorphosis which overstates the width of the Globe, but partly also it is the result of what appears to be the greater height of the Hope in relation to its width. Yet the coincidence of the two diameters at around 100 ft or so is a conclusion that tends to confirm both readings. It happens that we have the building contract for the Hope,[10] and though it fails to give many dimensions it does require that the house be made exactly the same size as the Swan on Bankside. Since these two theatres were built to the same plan at least in their size and shape it is not surprising to find that the Globe was the same size too: it begins to appear that there may have been a standard plan for this kind of auditorium. Thus the Globe shown by Hollar is the second of that name, built on the same foundations as the first after the fire of 1613 and presumably therefore the same size and shape as its predecessor. The first Globe had in its turn been made of the timbers of the first permanent theatre in London, the house which James Burbage built in 1576 in Shoreditch and called simply the Theater. The timbers of the Theater were dismantled in 1598–9 and re-erected in Southwark as the Globe – we shall return to this story later – and it almost certainly follows that the Theater and the first Globe were the same size and shape; the second Globe was the same size and shape as the first; and evidently the second Globe was also substantially the same size and shape as the Hope and the Swan. Hollar's drawing therefore tells us more about the Elizabethan theatre than the particular dimensions of the two houses within sight; it implies that there was a customary plan that had been traditional since Burbage established it in 1576. For our conclusions about the size of the Hope and the Globe – that they were respectively 99.99 ft and 102.35 ft wide within ±2.0% – show beyond doubt that they were *similar* in diameter, and strongly imply that the apparent similarity is probably a matter of actual identity at a few inches over a round 100 ft. The fact that the only public theatre building contract of the period to give a full set of dimensions is that for the Fortune,[11] a square house quite different from any of the others in plan, has led to some unfortunate misunderstandings, the most fundamental of which is that its overall dimension of 80 ft was derived directly from the Globe. Yet the instinct to see the Fortune's design as in some ways based on that of the Globe is perfectly sound; the contract itself makes several explicit references to that playhouse as a model. Since both the extant theatre contracts define the projected structures in terms of their predecessors, the Globe and the Swan, it is again not surprising to find consistency between the second Globe and the Hope. Doubtless the contract for the Swan itself made some such reference to the Theater or the Curtain. Indeed the Hope contract shows that in one case at least the parties to it felt no need to specify dimensions since they were evidently to be found in another theatre; the Fortune contract, being drawn up for a quite new and unusual design, went into details of size simply because it was atypical.

The Hope contract becomes quite particular and specific when it details the scantlings of the timbers to be used in the frame, but only once does it give a dimension relevant to the actual size of the building. This is when it calls for the posts used in the first gallery to be 12 ft tall.[12] We know that at the Fortune the first gallery was 12 ft high, the second 11 ft and the third 9 ft for a total of 32 ft.[13] Since the frame was built on a low foundation wall that rose one foot above the ground the height of the Fortune to the wall-plates was 33 ft, and it has been assumed that because the Hope used first gallery timbers 12 ft long it, too, was 33 ft to the plates. And if the Hope then so also the Globe, since while the plans and widths of theatres might differ their heights, being controlled by such standard requirements as headroom and sightlines, were unlikely to differ very much. On this rather tenuous structure of assumptions have been founded the only attempts hitherto to estimate the widths of the buildings shown by Hollar: if each is 33 ft high to the plates, then by comparing the height to the width in the drawing one may arrive at a rough estimate of the diameter.[14] We could of course now reverse the process and deduce the heights of these theatres from our new knowledge of their widths, but happily we have discovered a more direct way of measuring them. Even so, anyone trying to interpret the heights of the theatres Hollar shows, by whatever method, soon runs up against the difficulty of the ambiguous way in which they are drawn. The right walls of both theatres are obscured in their lower parts by rooftops and trees; only the left walls are visible to the ground, and there the ambiguity intervenes. The base of the Globe wall is lined with shrubs, so that any measurement must become to some extent an estimate. I have measured down to the base of the shrubs but not to the small horizontal line which indicates a shadow beneath the foliage. Read thus, the Globe is 6.33 mm high to the eaves on Hollar's picture plane. With the Hope the matter is complicated by the fact that one line indicates the wall, while another small addition is made slightly within it at its base, thus apparently heightening the wall somewhat. It is not entirely clear that this small line, which seems something of an afterthought and is not very precisely stated, is actually to be included in the height of the wall. Accordingly I give two values for the height of the Hope to the eaves: 4.75 mm without the small line and 5.25 mm with it. Below this again is the lead outline of a bush, and it is perhaps worthwhile considering the measure of this also, on the analogy of the Globe, which is more evidently fringed with shrubs. We may now calculate the heights of the two theatres. Because we are measuring vertical lines on planes of known distances from the observer there is no need to allow for anamorphosis. The calculation for the Hope is as follows:

$$\frac{4.75}{309} \times 1513 \times 2 . \tan 34.3° = 31.73 \text{ ft}$$

For a height on the picture plane of 5.25 mm the figure is 35.07 ft; for 5.75 mm, 38.41 ft. The Globe's height at 6.33 mm works out thus:

$$\frac{6.33}{309} \times 1144 \times 2 . \tan 34.3° = 31.97 \text{ ft}$$

Because of the ambiguities I have noted these figures are less to be trusted than the widths of the two theatres, whose measurement can be more precise, but unless the pencilled bush is included into the height of the Hope it is plain that both playhouses were of similar height to the Fortune, which at 33 ft to the wall-plates would have measured something a little less than that to its overhanging eaves.

In view of the strangeness of our discovery that the Globe and the Hope were substantially of similar width it is perhaps worth asking what Hollar made of this piece of information when he came to etch his panorama far away in Antwerp. His life's work bears witness to the fact that he was an inveterate sightseer, and there can be little doubt that he had at least gone and looked at the theatres close-to. He would have known that they were pretty well the same size, and consequently when he made his etching he would seek to correct the impression given by his preliminary study that one was rather larger than the other. In doing so he would counteract the effect of anamorphosis as it appears in the study, and would instead attempt to give simply a general impression of foreshortening by reducing the size of the Hope in his etching according to his judgment of its greater distance from the observer. Any strict analysis of this part of the etching as linear perspective is impossible because it is simply not regular; nevertheless in general the Hope is shown higher up towards the horizon than the Globe, further away and therefore smaller on the paper. In fact it is 44.0 mm wide, while the Globe is 58.25 mm. If we allow merely for the ratio of the distances of the two theatres from the observer – still taking the plane measures as before from St Saviour's – we can see that Hollar has fully compensated for the anamorphic distortion in his study and made them equal in width:

$$44.0 \times \frac{1513}{1144} = 58.19$$

According to this admittedly rudimentary calculation the Globe is shown 0.1% larger than the Hope. If the ratio is expressed as the relative *direct* distances of the theatres from St Saviour's, instead of the distances of their planes, Hollar's compensation shows up a little less forcefully:

$$44.0 \times \frac{1515}{1184} = 56.30$$

Here the Globe is 3.35% larger than the Hope, still a very small difference. Thus although the etching's status as an imaginative composition precludes the sort of analysis we have been able to bring to the sketch, Hollar does seem to have aimed to convey in it his perception that the Hope was the same width as the Globe. He confirms the general impression to which this chapter has led: that these two theatres and very likely many of the other Elizabethan and Jacobean playhouses were built to a common design whose plan was a circle, or a polygon inscribed within a circle, about 100 ft or so across.

The evidence about the Globe adduced thus far in this book has all come from Hollar, and most of it from his meticulous perspective sketch for the *Long View*. It is time now to turn elsewhere and ask whether the few facts already known about the dimensions of the Elizabethan theatres confirm or deny the conclusions we have come to. By far the most important source of such information is the building contract for the Fortune theatre drawn up in 1600 between the impresario Philip Henslowe and the builder Peter Street, almost certainly the man who had put up the first Globe in Southwark the year before.

5 The plans of the Fortune and the Globe

Of all the documents on which our knowledge of the Elizabethan stage is founded, none is more tantalizing than the Fortune contract. It is unique in giving precise dimensions for a public theatre, but it is in just these specifications that it is most likely to differ from its models, the other theatres of the age and especially the first Globe. Four times it mentions 'the late erected Plaiehowse On the Banck in the saide pishe of Ste Savio^rs Called the Globe,' and on three of these occasions it is to avoid having to go into unnecessary detail when the model is so readily available and its building of such recent memory. It is hard to escape the conclusion that the contract goes into most detail when the proposals for the Fortune differ most from the example of the Globe, and in nothing in this truer than in the very dimensions which give the document its dangerous fascination. Some scholars, anxious to seize on any evidence that will lead towards an understanding of Shakespeare's playhouse, have too hastily assumed that the stage at the Globe was 43 ft across, simply because that is the figure given for the Fortune.[1] Yet on this point the language of the contract is ambiguous, to say the least. It calls for a stage and tiring house to be set up:

... wch Stadge shall conteine in length ffortie and Three foote of lawfull assize and in breadth to extende to the middle of the yarde .... And the saide Stadge to be in all other proporcōns Contryved and fashioned like vnto the Stadge of the saide Plaiehowse Called the Globe ...[2]

'All other proporcōns' may perhaps mean 'in all the other respects *as well as*' the specified width and forward extension, but it more naturally reads 'in all other respects *except*' the specifications just given. That this is the intention of the clause is suggested by the certainty that the remaining dimensions of the Fortune plan were not those of the Globe. The external measurement of the square frame of the house is given as 80 ft, and within this lies a square courtyard 55 ft across. Even without Hollar's evidence it is clear that these dimensions were more appropriate to a square building than a round or polygonal one.[3] Such a plan, inscribed within the 80 ft dimension, would be too small to contain the large audiences described by contemporaries: three thousand, according to the Dutch traveller de Witt, writing mainly of the Swan in 1596.[4] The same number crowded daily into the second Globe to see Middleton's *Game at Chess*, if the dispatches of the Spanish ambassador are to be believed.[5] Again the consistency of these figures goes some way to confirm that the Swan and the second Globe were the same size, and larger than the atypical, square, Fortune.

If the contract gave particular figures for the Fortune's frame because it differed from the model in size as well as in plan, so too for the stage. Any comparative study of the plans of the Fortune and the Globe must begin, then, by laying an old ghost to rest, appropriately enough in the cellarage: the one thing we can be sure of about the Globe's stage is that it was *not* 43 ft across. But where, in that case, does the curious figure in the Fortune contract come from? And where also its companions, 55 ft and 80 ft? I propose in this chapter to offer a rationale for the plan of the Fortune, and then to enquire what relevance our findings have for an understanding of the plan of Shakespeare's Globe.

We must begin with a very practical problem. How is the plan of the Fortune actually to be laid out on the ground? This is a task for a craftsman, not for an owner like Philip Henslowe or the actor Edward Alleyn, the co-signer of the contract. The general idea of the playhouse will doubtless be theirs, but the specific design solution, the particular dimensions and proportions, will be the product of a technical interpretation of their brief. And since their contract is with Peter Street the carpenter it is to him that we must turn for enlightenment. Nobody here is an 'architect' – the term has hardly entered the English language by 1600[6] – but Street is an experienced theatre builder and a man used to working in timber. Poring over the great rolls of the Works Accounts in the Public Record Office we discover Street's name in the accounts for Whitehall for the year 1606–7. There he is recorded as receiving payment for having leased some special equipment to the King's Works for 'boringe the great Collumbes in the Banquettinge house.'[7] The Banqueting House in question was the predecessor of the present one, and it contained Doric and Ionic columns in two orders which must have been of unusual size for London in the first decade of the seventeenth century.[8] Not having their own equipment for this kind of work, the Works turned to 'Peter Streete for the lone of v^e great pumpaugurs . . . ' He was evidently a builder of some importance. Some recent investigators[9] have supposed that his Globe playhouse and indeed the Elizabethan public theatres in general were designed according to the principles laid out in the fifth book of Vitruvius's *De Architectura*, a work not yet translated into English in Street's day, though he might have seen it in a Latin, French or other edition, copies of which were certainly available in England at the time. But however accomplished and experienced, Street was an illiterate man who could only set his mark to his contract with Henslowe and Alleyn.[10] His skill was more likely to be traditional than new-fangled and book-fed. It may be that he had heard of Vitruvius, but it is extremely unlikely that he had read the

De Architectura, or that he would design and build a Vitruvian theatre on the antique model. What he knew about design geometry would be what the generations had known, and if we are to seek for his intellectual methods we shall do better to look for them among the medieval and Tudor craftsmen than to search out the kind of Italian sophistication that would appeal to an Inigo Jones, unless perhaps it might be among the great volumes of practical architectural drawings published, with only a minimal French or Italian text, by Sebastiano Serlio and much used by all sorts of builders during the later sixteenth century.[11]

Elizabethan builders often went by the name of surveyors. Thus Fale's *Horologiographia* (1593), an account of dialling, was intended 'not onely for Students of the Arts Mathematicall, but also for diuers Artificers, Architects, Surueyours of buildings, free-Masons and others.' Leonard Digges's *Tectonicon* (1556) was addressed to 'Surueyers, Landmeaters, Ioyners, Carpenters, and Masons.' In his *English Art 1553–1625*[12] Eric Mercer gives a well-documented account of the relation between the Elizabethan builder and the owner for whom he worked, illustrating by the way how often the term 'surveyor' occurred where now we might be tempted to use the anachronistic 'architect.' These examples show that two senses of the word tended to merge: the overseer (as in Surveyor of Taxes) and the measurer of land (as in Ordnance Survey). The building contractor included something of both skills in his repertoire, but it is the latter that is of interest to us in the present enquiry. The science of surveying was comparatively new in Street's day, but it was developing rapidly while borrowing much of its technical apparatus from the traditions of the builder. Thus although we know comparatively little about the techniques used by craftsmen in the sixteenth century to set out a building, something may be deduced from the nature of their tools and much more from the related skills of the surveyors, which are extensively documented. Here, if anywhere, we shall find Peter Street's intellectual milieu.

The chief measuring instruments of a carpenter were his square and his rod. By the middle of the seventeenth century the carpenter's rod was customarily 10 ft long, a *decempeda* marked off in feet and inches, and used for laying out work.[13] Street may have had a 10 ft rod, but if so it would have hung next to a rather longer one in his toolroom. This rod, like those of the surveyors, was 16 ft 6 in. long, a statute rod or perch. It gave the prime unit of land measurement, used by all Tudor surveyors and interchangeably interpreted as a linear or area quantity, the latter being 16 ft 6 in. square. Simply as a carpenter, Street doubtless thought in feet; but as a measurer of land – a necessary if subordinate part of his craft – he would more naturally have thought in rods. Such a unit was used of the timberwork set up in the tiltyard in 1619–20 at Whitehall, and by custom to measure the amount of brickwork used in foundation walls.[14] But even a 16 ft 6 in measuring stick is not a very handy instrument for accurately laying out such distances as 80 ft, and for that Street would have been equipped with a line marked off, like the surveyors' lines, in rod lengths. Valentine Leigh had put the matter succinctly in his *Science of Surveying* (1578):

> To aunswere by Rodde or by Line, it is at your pleasure, but of them bothe, the line is the spedier, and most commodious, and also of moste antiquite. Your Line beyng fower Perches of length, and at euery Perche ende a knot, would bee well seared with hoate Waxe and Rosen, to auoide stretching thereof in the wete, and shrinkyng in the drought.[15]

A little later, John Norden in his *Surueiors Dialogue* (1610) described the surveyor's chain as three rods long;[16] it was not until 1623, with the publication of Edmund Gunter's *Description and Use of the Crosse-Staffe*, that the chain was first defined as four rods long and divided into 100 links.[17] It is with instruments such as the three-rod chain or waxed line that we must imagine Peter Street setting out the Fortune site early in 1600, not with a Gunter's chain or a measuring tape. They would give him a specialized idea of what he was doing, quite unlike the assumptions we should bring to the task ourselves.

Street will also have had his specialized way of thinking about the frame of the theatre. The contract specifies overall dimensions 'of lawfull assize,' measured from surface to surface to ensure that there should be no ambiguity about the area to be covered by the building or the quantity of materials to be used. But Street built in timber bays, and he was used to thinking also in terms of distances between post centres, since that is the way structural bays must be measured. An eleven-foot bay is defined by the distance, not between timbers, but between the centres of the timbers. Thus for him the frame of the Fortune, while 80 ft across measured overall, was actually some 79 ft 2 in. between the centres, assuming that the posts of the ground storey were 10 in. by 10 in., as they are in the specifications handily provided by the contract for the Hope in 1613.[18] This outer wall of the theatre would be 'beam-filled' with lath and plaster, and the timbers left showing:[19] thus the 80 ft measure refers to the outer surface of the posts. The courtyard within was to be paled 'wth good stronge and sufficyent newe oken bourdes,' and although the scantlings of the boards are not given we may assume that they were 1 in. thick, so that the post centres of the yard were 56 ft 1 in. apart. The construction of the stage was quite different from that of the massive frame, and would have been known to Street simply by its overall dimensions as a piece of ambitious joinery. Thinking in Street's terms, then, rather than the legal specifications of the contract, we see a 43 ft stage surrounded by a timber frame made square, 56 ft 1 in. centre-to-centre for the yard, and 79 ft 2 in. centre-to-centre for the outer walls.

Our next task is to marry these two sorts of traditional thought as they might have been married in Street's mind. The surveyor's line with its rod measurements must somehow be hitched to the very irregular-looking dimensions of the Fortune plan considered centre-to-centre. Of course Peter Street left no record of his theories of design, but we can perhaps come close to them in the sketchy memoranda on architecture drawn up in November 1597 by Robert Stickells, a clerk in the Queen's Works.[20] Stickells appears to have been hardly more literate than Street, but his papers show that he had considered Vitruvius and was acutely conscious of the fundamental difference between Roman and medieval architecture, though he seems not to have been able to make up his mind which he preferred. In one document he condemns Vitruvian modular regularity, with its proportions based on the commensurable repetition of a single unit of measure, as lifeless or 'insencable':

... fore that I see all Buildinges, grownded upon the emperfect sence, the bookes of, Architecktur, victriuces & all thoos Authers have, taken the wronge sence; ther inwardes woorkes ar dead when theay shewe no lif in ther owtward Doweinges.[21]

In a second paper he defends the antique against the modern, using the word 'sence' in a quite different way, to mean the technical rationality of numbers. Vitruvian proportions are usually multiples of a single unit, and so are commensurable; Gothic proportions derive from geometrical figures formed with the dividers (and so called 'cirkler' by Stickells) which involve incommensurable and irrational values such as $\sqrt{2}$, $\sqrt{3}$, and $\sqrt{5}$. This time Stickells is an emphatic Vitruvian:

Thear ar too sortes of byldenges, the on in sence; the other withowt sence; The antikes in sence; the moddarn witheout sence; Because it is from cirkler demonstraction, witheowt sence; for that no cirkell Riseth in evennes of nomber, the antikes allwayes in evennes of nombre be cauese the ar derived from an Ichnographicall ground; it the unevn may be broght into proporctions, as well as the even, &c.

.Ther is no mor but Right & wronge in all things whatsoever, The squear Right the cirkell wronge, &c.[22]

It would be unwise to conclude from this that Street was a Vitruvian too; what matters is that Stickells characterizes the architecture of his own day as un-Vitruvian and irrational in its proportions, and in that tradition we may assume stood the builders of the Elizabethan theatres.

The builder and the surveyor shared a common interest in constructive geometry. In his dialogue on the faults of inexpert surveyors, published in 1582, Edward Worsop regretted that there were no civic geometers appointed in English cities, as there were in Europe:

Masons, Carpenters, Joyners, Paynters, clockmakers, Inginors, and such others vnto whose faculties most needefully appertaine the knowledges of making squares, roundes, triangles, and many other figures, with their transformations according to any proportion assigned resort vnto these professors and Geometers, to learne certaine grounds, & chiefe mechanicall rules.[23]

To judge from the tone of his book Worsop was a crusty and opinionated soul, and there is no need to take his account of the shortcomings of English technicians at face value. But in this passage we have an insight into the methods of Elizabethan craftsmen, including carpenters. They needed to know the sort of geometry the skilled land surveyors could teach them, and indeed we have seen that builders often actually were surveyors as well, capable of 'making squares, roundes, triangles, and many other figures, with their transformations . . .' In describing Street's methods at the Fortune we may therefore begin with an observation that will take some of the mystery from that remarkable figure of the stage width, 43 ft. 43 ft is the altitude (to within about $1\frac{1}{2}$ in.) of an equilateral triangle whose sides are three rods (or 49 ft 6 in.). Such triangles were used in two ways that Street could be expected to know about. They were employed by the land surveyors as a standard technique for measuring area, and they had been used since time immemorial by masons and carpenters in the layout of buildings according to the method called *ad triangulum*.[24] For the surveyor the equilateral triangle was important as one of the simple shapes to which complex tracts of land might be reduced for quantification.[25] Most of the surveyors' textbooks dealt with it, and its proportions were well known to anyone engaged in the measurement of land, since the area of the triangle is calculated from the product of its altitude and half its base. For his part the builder was less concerned with the area covered than with the trueness of the measures he could make by the simple deployment of his waxed lines in triangles. Of course the mathematical geometry was not always very precise, and Street's notion of the altitude of a 49 ft 6 in. equilateral triangle may well have been that it was exactly 43 ft, even though in fact it was not. But since I shall show that he proceeded in the traditional way by staking out his measurements on the ground according to the proportions reached by the use of his line, his interpretation of the exact height of the triangle is irrelevant, except for its translation into the specification given in the contract; what matters is that he used the triangle, and that he appears to have used it well.

We have to imagine Peter Street and perhaps Gilbert East, Henslowe's bailiff, standing on the site near Golden Lane in the early part of 1600. Of the nearby buildings, it may be that one is to abut on the proposed theatre, offering complications to the process I am about to describe.[26] Dealing with them would involve fiddly calculations too confusing to enter into now, but perfectly manageable even so. We can safely ignore them. What Street and East first lay out on the ground is a square whose sides are three rods long. Every Elizabethan surveyor knew how to do that, judging its corners by sighting along the arms of a carpenter's square, and testing its trueness by checking that the diagonals were equal. The line our men use is the traditional surveyor's line, marked with knots for every perch or rod. When the corners of the square have been pegged they use this line with a similar one to erect two equilateral triangles within the three-rod square, thus:

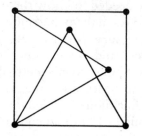

Through the apexes thus formed they run lines parallel to those of the square, so forming a smaller square within the original:

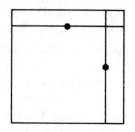

Now with the three-rod lines they drop perpendiculars from the apexes and at their extremes set new pegs, through which they pass new lines parallel to the remaining sides of the square, this time making a larger square within which the others are contained:

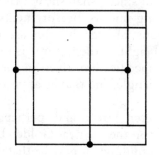

The dimensions of this diagram are as follows: the original square is 49 ft 6 in. each way; the smaller one is 49 ft 6 in. $\times \frac{\sqrt{3}}{2}$ or 42 ft 10$\frac{1}{2}$ in.; and the largest one is the difference between these plus three rods (49 ft 6 in. − 42 ft 10$\frac{1}{2}$ in. = 6 ft 7$\frac{1}{2}$ in. + 49 ft 6 in.), or 56 ft 1$\frac{1}{2}$ in. The smallest defines the width of the stage, while the largest defines the size of the yard, measured between centres. The plan on the ground comes to within $\frac{1}{2}$ in. of what the surface dimensions specified in the contract led us to expect, and yet it has been arrived at entirely by the deployment of the one traditional surveyor's tool, the three-rod line, and by means of only the most traditional of methods.

At one time there was a 'plott' or drawing attached to the Fortune contract, giving details of the layout. It is now lost, but we may be sure that the proportions we have discovered could be checked on it by the manipulation of a pair of compasses set to the equivalent of the three-rod measure. The proportions of the courtyard and the stage could be established and checked on the paper just as they were set out by the line on the ground. Any student of architecture knows how drawings of buildings, especially of centrally planned buildings, will yield information about their proportions to the wielder of a pair of dividers. We have to make something of an imaginative leap to recognize that these patterns are not there merely to please, but to allow the plan to be set out on the ground with a line, and to ensure that once the building is under way its trueness may be readily checkable by the same method. Thus as the Fortune went up the carpenters could run a three-rod line from the sides of the stage foundation to the frame wall opposite and so keep their measurements true. In the same way the dimensions of the stage itself could also be checked.

Having established the central part of their plan, Street and East are now ready to set out the foundations of the outer wall. Like the *ad triangulum* method by which they established the width of the stage, the *ad quadratum* system they are now about to use is of great antiquity. It is described in one of the additions to the Villard de Honnecourt manuscript of the thirteenth century, a work which vividly illustrates the methods and practices of European designers of the Gothic age. The plan of a square cloister is shown, with a radius marked from the centre to one of its inner corners. Against the diagram is the note: 'In this way one lays out a cloister, both with regard to the passages and to the garden.'[27] Paul Frankl describes the technique implied by the diagram, noting its particular value in an age when there were few accurate measuring instruments:

The builder . . . marks off the outer square first, for example, a side length of seventy feet, describes at the end points right angles, and marks off from there the seventy-foot sides. Then he runs two strings along the diagonals, first, to test the right angles and second, to determine at the same time the center.

Next he divides one of the sides into two equal halves, connects the center of this side with the center of the square by means of a string, and marks off this length on the diagonal from the center out. The point so obtained is one of the corner points of the 'garden', that is, the open court. He finds the other three points by the same simple method and can now connect these four points by strings. Thus the mason or stone-mason is enabled to begin setting the stones.[28]

This is not the only way of setting out a courtyard *ad quadratum*, as we shall see, but in its practical geometry it is typical of the work practices of medieval craftsmen. The procedure's main virtue is its simplicity, and in our present study we have no need to follow its history through the proliferating complexities of Gothic church design. It happens that the plan of the Fortune is very like that of a square cloister, and while Peter Street's method differs somewhat from that described by Frankl (in that it works outwards towards the perimeter, not inwards from it) it is in all essentials the same one as that depicted in the Villard manuscript. The Fortune is proportioned *ad quadratum*, just like that thirteenth-century prototype.

The builders at the Fortune site have established their 56 ft square. Now they run diagonals across it to find its centre, and then describe a circle round it, touching its corners. It is simply a matter of one man taking a line in a ring about the site like a pony on a lunge. As he reaches each of the quarters of the circle he drives in a peg, and through these four pegs a new square is set out, tangential to the circle:

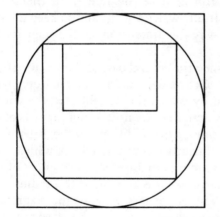

The trueness of this last square is checked by the diagonal test, and also by ensuring that its sides equal the diagonal of the courtyard square, both operations that can easily be performed by the manipulation of a line. This square has been arrived at by the venerable *ad quadratum* method, and its sides are those of the yard times $\sqrt{2}$: 56 ft $1\frac{1}{2}$ in. $\times$ $\sqrt{2}$ = 79 ft $4\frac{1}{2}$ in., or within $2\frac{1}{2}$ in. of what the contract led us to expect. No further specific measure has been used beyond the original three-rod line; the greater dimensions of the outside wall are derived from those contained within the courtyard plan.

The *ad quadratum* method is often met in sixteenth- and early seventeenth-century architectural design, especially in centrally planned buildings. Sebastiano Serlio deals with it briefly in the first book of his *Architettura*[29] where it is also illustrated [Plate 31 I]; for all the gothicism of its roots and its ubiquity in medieval design, Inigo Jones employed it too, for example in his scheme for an anatomy theatre for the Barber–Surgeons' Company in 1636.[30] Its chief merit was its practicality, although it may also have appealed from time to time because it suggested the mystery of the squaring of the circle. We may be sure that Street used it for pragmatic reasons, but John Thorpe in his fanciful design for a triangular house inscribed within a four-rod circle may have thought of it as a symbol: here the house is related to the surrounding terrace *ad quadratum* [Plate 31 II].[31] The method was employed in the design of the cockpit at Whitehall in the 1530s [Plate 31 III]),[32] in Stephan von Hoschenperg's coastal forts for Henry VIII in the next decade,[33] by Robert Stickells in his unexecuted drawing for a lantern at Lyveden New Bield,[34] and in quite another vein by Jones in his project for a Stuart mausoleum, presumably of 1625.[35] How could we ever have missed seeing that it would be the Elizabethan builder's preferred way of laying out a centrally planned theatre? Nothing could be more traditional, more practical, or more secure.

The methods and the measure used to establish the proportions of the Fortune plan have their implications for the Globe, too. The Fortune imitated the first Globe and it is probable that Peter Street built them both. In 1598, as a result of a long argument with their landlord over the lease of the site of the Theater, the Lord Chamberlain's Men took the quite admirable step of taking down their playhouse and shifting its frame, timber by timber, across the river to Bankside. In order to accomplish this sensible but difficult feat they hired the services of Peter Street, whose presence as the site supervisor during the dismantling is attested to in depositions which formed part of the subsequent litigation.[36] Evidently this was no mere rasing or demolition; Street was there to see that the Theater was so carefully taken apart that it could be set up again elsewhere. That this was so is witnessed by the story one of the landlord's agents was fobbed off with. Henry Johnson later told the Court of Requests that he repaired to the Theater when he heard that it was being pulled down:

And when he had soe Charged them not to pull the same Theatre Downe they the said Compl*ainant* [Cuthbert Burbage] and Thomas Smythe and [Peter] Streete the Carpenter tould him this deponent that they tooke yt downe but to sett yt vpp vppon the premisss in an other forme and that they had Couenanted wth the Carpenter to that effecte and Shewed this deponnt the decayes about the same as yt stoode there thereby Colloringe there deceipte.[37]

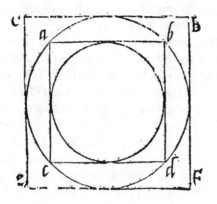

I An *ad quadratum* construction from Sebastiano Serlio, *Il primo libro dell'architettura*, Venice, 1560.

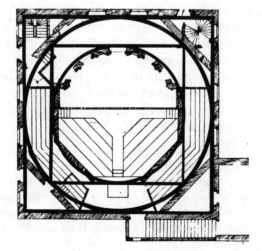

II John Thorpe, plan for a house on a round terrace. I have added the square which relates the two.

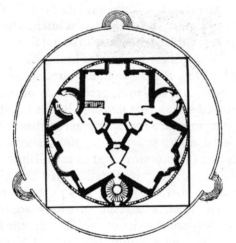

III John Webb, the Cockpit-in-Court at Whitehall. I have added the *ad quadratum* diagram.

There was of course no intention of rebuilding in another form: the real aim was to rebuild in another place,[38] and it is a reasonable assumption that Street was to see to that, too. He supervised the dismantling of the Theater so carefully that bystanders were convinced that he was going to reuse the materials on the spot; all the while he actually had his mind set on the translation to Bankside. And here we must try again to enter into Peter Street's adroit and technically accomplished mind. We must imagine him standing in the old empty Theater in Shoreditch, well before Henry Johnson or his like arrived on the scene, thinking already of how he will put its pieces together again on the new site in Southwark. He has just surveyed the plot of ground there, but the next thing he has to do is to prepare it, sink piles and have foundation walls brought up ready to take the groundsills of the frame of the building. One of his most important tasks, therefore, will be to measure the plan of the Theater with great exactness, so that he can set out the foundation walls at Bankside. The plan will have been developed from a true circle, but it is unlikely to be a circle unadapted. It is true that Hollar shows the second Globe and the Hope as circular buildings, their exterior walls smoothly rounded, but we know that both houses were made of timber, and although a wooden building may be dressed up to look as if it were a true round its structural frame cannot be shaped as one. If the horizontal members of the Globe's frame were curved their own weight, bearing down outside the plane of their supports, would exert enough torque on the joints seriously to weaken them. We shall return to this matter later on, but for the moment we may safely assume that Hollar's rounded auditoria represent a very slightly idealized view of polygonal buildings whose numerous facets expressed the idea of perfect roundness in a material and mode of construction that could not quite achieve it. As Peter Street studies the foundations and frame of the Theater, therefore, he sees a many-sided polygon, and he will measure it most naturally by taking the diameter from one outer post to its opposite, centre-to-centre. Presumably he will do a good deal of detailed checking, but the controlling idea of the plan will be a circle, or rather two circles, in which the inner and outer walls of the frame will be inscribed as polygons. This is the information he will take to the new site, and will use to set out the new polygonal foundation walls there. For we must notice that the reuse of the Theater timbers at the Globe leaves no room for compromise; the Globe plan must have been the same as that of the Theater, otherwise the timbers might just as well have been a job lot of used material, not needing Street's supervision at all. Elizabethan timber structures were not made with entirely standardized pieces. Each joint was individually cut, and although the pieces might fit to perfection they could not be interchanged at will. A many-sided polygonal frame is a fairly complicated structure, and it could not readily be adapted or modified. Once there, there it was. The Globe was the Theater transpontine, but not transformed. What Peter Street saw as he measured the Theater was the plan of what was to become the Globe.

And what did he see? If we are to judge by what he did the following year at the Fortune, we may suppose that he found a building whose layout could be established by the simple deployment of a single measure, possibly the three-rod line. Our evidence suggests that it would be designed *ad quadratum*. It is a characteristic of the *ad quadratum* method that each successive square or circle doubles the area of the one within. Thus the whole area of the Fortune (measured between centres) doubles the area of its yard (similarly stated); or, to put it another way, the area of the ground-floor gallery equals that of the yard. Such considerations were well-known to Elizabethan surveyors and, one surmises, to the owners of theatre galleries. If the Fortune was mostly to be based on the Globe, doubtless it was also in this financially pregnant consideration.

We have reason to believe that the Globe stage was not 43 ft wide. Now, however, our analysis of the Fortune has given us a new figure to conjure with in the three-rod basis of the whole design. Let us suppose that the stage at the Globe was 49 ft 6 in. wide and that the frame was developed from it *ad quadratum*. The result would be a yard precisely 70 ft across and an overall diameter of just 99 ft (that is, six rods), centre-to-centre:

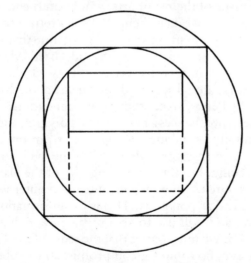

Of course as yet this plan is the merest conjecture, based only on the methods Street went on to apply at the Fortune, and drawing some support from the dimensions now discovered in Hollar's study of the second Globe.

In the previous chapter I remarked that there was reason to believe that the first and second Globes were the same size in plan, because the second was built on the foundations remaining after the fire that destroyed the first. In his 'Execration upon *Vulcan*' Ben Jonson described the fiery god's assault

> Against the *Globe*, the Glory of the *Banke*.
> Which, though it were the Fort of the whole Parish,
>   Flanck'd with a ditch, and forc'd out of a Marish,
> I saw with two poore Chambers taken in,
>   And raz'd, ere thought could urge, This might have bin!
> See the worlds Ruines! nothing but the piles
>   Left! and wit since to cover it with Tiles.[39]

After the depredations of Vulcan had done for Hercules and his load there yet remained the piles and presumably the brick foundation walls of the old house, and on these the new one was erected. Because my argument will depend on this identity of plan between the two Globe playhouses, I must take a moment to establish it. In 1634 at the behest of the Earl Marshal, the Earl of Arundel, a draft was made for a return of new and divided buildings in the parish of St Saviour's, and among them the Globe was mentioned:

The Globe playhouse nere Maid lane built by the company of players, with the dwelling house thereto adjoyninge, built w^t timber, about 20 yeares past, upon an old foundation . . . .[40]

The context of this draft is the series of proclamations issued by James I against new building in and about London. Rendle, who first printed it, remarked that it was drawn up 'at a time when the authorities were insanely jealous of allowing new building'[41] in the London region. The building proclamations form a distinct strand of James's policy throughout his reign, beginning with the year of his coronation. The king took a personal interest in the matter; he intended to restrict the expansion and overcrowding of London, and chose to do so by the doubtless self-defeating means of prohibiting nearly all new building within a certain radius – the distance varies from proclamation to proclamation – of the city.[42] In practice 'new building' came to mean building on a new foundation: merely renewing a building on an old foundation without increasing its size was not disallowed. The frequency of the proclamations shows that there was much law-breaking and consequent need for reinforcement. The Acts of the Privy Council for the period give frequent evidence of the vigour with which offenders were pursued, often to the extent of having their illegal buildings demolished.[43] Theatre owners were by no means exempt: Christopher Beeston was summoned to appear before the magistrates of Middlesex for adding to the foundations of the old cockpit in Drury Lane when he converted it into a playhouse in 1616.[44] Beeston had recently lost a house because he had set it up on a new foundation; now in Drury Lane he stood to lose a theatre. It seems that on this occasion he argued his case successfully, but records in what remains of the Star Chamber papers, in the *Index to Repertories* at the

Guildhall and in the sessions books of the administrative counties[45] attest to the fact that many others were less fortunate, and either lost their houses or else compounded with the authorities at considerable cost. We must note, then, that the Earl of Arundel's survey of 1634 was a serious bureaucratic endeavour, aimed at assessing the amount of new building in and about the city; and that the phrase 'upon an old foundation' applied to the Globe is not some casual remark made to satisfy someone's curiosity, but a technical, official form of words indicating that the building was legally erected on foundations long established.

When the draft reads 'upon an old foundation,' that is precisely what it means. The new building was legal, within the terms of the proclamation, because it did not involve the building of new foundations or even the extension of old ones. Certainly the second Globe was 'far fairer' than the first, but equally certainly it was the same size in plan. It would not, incidentally, have had the jettying galleries specified in the contract for the Fortune; such jettyings were specifically forbidden by a proclamation issued in 1611[46] and in any case cannot have improved the sightlines from the upper galleries. Therefore the upper parts of the walls of the yard directly reflected the proportions of the lowermost parts. The plan of the first Globe is to be found reflected in the second: of that we have Hollar's meticulous survey, and it shows that the theatre was designed *ad quadratum*.

To arrive at this conclusion it is necessary to deduce an actual plan from the information given in Hollar's study. C. Walter Hodges has already done that in *Shakespeare's Second Globe*:[47] there he extrapolates one by conventional and usually reliable means, dropping perpendiculars from various parts of the building shown in the sketch and using their intervals to establish the plan, with the quite reasonable assumption that it is derived from a circle [Plate 32]. Hodges' diagram is perfectly sound within its limitations; as usual in his work the apparent freedom of the treatment belies the rigorous precision that actually informs it. Unfortunately, however, the diagram makes the faulty assumption that the theatre is viewed through a plane of intersection at right angles to the line of sight, when in fact as we have seen the lines of sight intersect the plane at angles ranging from 77.5° (right) to 72.5° (left). Consequently Hodges' plan overstates the width of the theatre in relation to its height (which is undistorted by anamorphosis) by 3.64%. In theory his plan should also make some very small allowance for the relative distortions introduced within the plan itself: a sketch made at the topographical glass ought to stretch the left side of the frame in comparison with the right. But in practice the relative distortion is so minute that we may ignore it. It follows then that Hodges' plan is perfectly good, though 3.64% too big, and its internal proportions soundly stated within the limits we have noted. We may rely on it, and put it to the test to see whether it reveals the *ad quadratum* proportions we have posited.

32.   C. Walter Hodges, 'Diagrammatic projection from the drawing': the plan of the Globe deduced from Hollar's sketch.

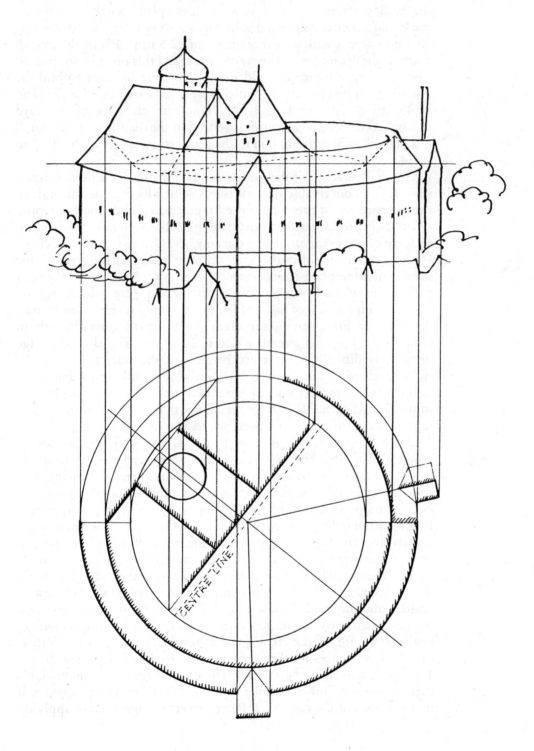

Allowing again, as we did in the analysis of the Fortune, that the conceptual lines of the plan pass through the post centres rather than the wall surfaces, we find that Hodges' plan exactly fits the *ad quadratum* scheme. As printed in his book it shows a circular outer wall 90.5 mm across with a yard diameter of 62.5 mm. 1% of the overall width is the estimated thickness of a post, and this must be subtracted from the larger figure and added to the smaller in order to find the centre-to-centre proportion, which may then be expressed as the ratio 63.405 to 89.595, or 1 to 1.413. Thus the diameter of the yard measured between post centres is related to the diameter of the round in a very close approximation to the proportion of 1: $\sqrt{2}$ (that is, 1 to 1.414).

The exactness of this demonstration is, I confess, a little embarrassing. It is inconceivable that measures which have gone through so many processes of presentation, extrapolation and deduction would retain their precise ratio so unswervingly. The exactness must be an accident of one error cancelling out another. One may however check Hodges on this point quite easily without going to the error-prone trouble of attempting to reconstruct his admirable diagram. We may deduce the width of the yard from the drawing by subtracting the ridge-to-ridge width of the roof from the overall width of the round, doubling the difference and subtracting that from the overall width. In Hollar's drawing the overall width is 21.0 mm. The ridge-to-ridge distance is difficult to measure because of the uncertainty on the right-hand side, compounded by some clumsy inking-in, but a fair estimate is 17.7 mm, from which we deduce that the yard must be 14.4 mm wide. Allowing 1% of the overall width for each measurement to represent the thickness of a post, we have a centre-to-centre ratio of 1.423 to 1. This is not as close to the *ad quadratum* proportion as Hodges' diagram, but quite close enough to carry conviction. As usual the etching is less satisfactory as evidence than the drawing, this time not only because of its status as a composed work of art, but because its presentation of the roofline lacks symmetry, implying a frame substantially wider to the left than to the right. This distortion is greater than any that could have been the result of regular anamorphosis, and in any case Hollar seems deliberately to have countered the anamorphic stretching of the theatre in preparing the etching. Hodges draws his plan from it[48] as a compromise between the two frame widths, and the result is close to the $\sqrt{2}$ proportion, again assuming measurement between the post centres: 1.447 to 1. The ridge-to-ridge test, carried out on the etching itself, produces the ratio 1.395 to 1. Plainly these figures are all approximations to the *ad quadratum* ratio of 1.414 to 1, and all are very close. The conclusion seems unavoidable that the second Globe, and like it the first, was built *ad quadratum*. If that was indeed the case, then Peter Street was not merely applying a familiar principle when he evolved the Fortune design; he was faithfully following his model, as his contract with Henslowe and Alleyn generally enjoined him to do.

There remains the question of the three-rod measure which Street used at the Fortune and may have carried over from his work at the Globe. While we have concluded that the proportions of the Globe derived from the *ad quadratum* method, we still have to discover what the actual measurements were. The evidence presented in the previous chapter led to the conclusion that the width of the Globe lay within ± 2.0% of a range from 101.37 ft to 103.32 ft. Into this range falls neither the 83 ft nor the 84 ft width espoused by John Cranford Adams and Irwin Smith,[49] nor the 92 ft diameter proposed by C. Walter Hodges.[50] But the 100 ft surface-to-surface diameter which results from the deployment of a three-rod line in the layout of the building is entirely consistent with Hollar's evidence. A theatre so proportioned will measure 99 ft centre-to-centre; its yard, according to the *ad quadratum* proportions of Hollar's sketch, will be just 70 ft between post centres, or 69 ft surface-to-surface. And it is a fair deduction that the stage, again proportioned *ad quadratum*, will be 49 ft 6 in. across.

Peter Street, standing in the empty Theater in 1598 and wondering how to go about setting out his new foundations at Bankside, will soon see that the controlling measure of his plan must be a three-rod line, the same line that Burbage used when he set the building out in the first place. At Bankside he will probably begin by pegging out a 49 ft 6 in. square. Around this he will describe the 70 ft circle which will define the placing of the gallery posts. There will be no need to describe a further square around this circle, since he can move directly to the line of the outer wall by using the three-rod measure as a radius centred in the midst of the original square. The circle thus produced will enable him to construct the necessary polygons to take the straight groundsills of the timber-framed wall. We do not know how many sides these polygons had, but the *ad quadratum* method suggests that the figure would be a multiple of four, since then the sides of the stage would meet the principle posts in a direct and satisfactory way, either engaging the posts themselves or coming in neatly at mid-bay.

We notice that the gallery depth at the Globe is some 15 ft 6 in. overall, or 14 ft 6 in. between post centres measured radially. This figure is somewhat larger than the 12 ft 6 in. overall of the Fortune galleries at ground-floor level, and allows a row or two more of spectators, but these are crowded into a similar or perhaps even a smaller headroom, at least at the second Globe (we have been able to discover nothing about the heights of the galleries at the first Globe). The great width of the theatre mitigates the effect somewhat, but doubtless the sightlines leave something to be desired, as they do in most London theatres to this day.

In breaking with the 12 ft 6 in. gallery depth we have abandoned the last of the 'controlling' dimensions of the Fortune contract. Yet in departing from the figures themselves we have looked beyond them to the reasons for their being. Once Street had measured the Theater and set out the foundations for the Globe, all with the single three-rod line, what more natural than that he should have used the same technique for the smaller, square-planned Fortune? There he reduced the width of the stage *ad triangulum*, then by quite logical and economical means established the width of the yard, from which, as at the Globe, he constructed the plan of the outer wall *ad quadratum*. In doing so he produced figures that had to be stated one way to himself as a carpenter and another way to his contractual partners as 'lawful assize,' with the result that we have all been confused. Yet Street himself could hardly have been more direct or economical of means. His design methods had the simple grace of their origins, in the traditions of the masons' lodge, the surveyor and the builder in oak.

6 Seating and capacity

Now that we know the size of the Globe theatre we should be able to estimate its audience capacity. Here, however, direct evidence almost fails us. Hollar's study shows nothing of the seating, and the only hard fact to which we can turn is that the Spanish ambassador reported in 1624 that the second Globe held more than three thousand spectators.[1] Some have thought the figure an exaggeration, others have found confirmation of it in the similar estimate made by de Witt of the Swan in 1596.[2] Those who have sought to test it by applying some sort of body-space formula to the area available to the audience in one or another reconstruction of the auditorium have not been able to agree on the formula or on the resultant capacity. Given our knowledge of the size of the playhouse we are now in a position to apply such a procedure with some confidence, and in this chapter I shall introduce new evidence which will take the formula itself off the shifting sands of theory and place it on a solid historical footing.

There can be little doubt that each of the three levels of galleries was provided with seating space, almost certainly in the form of degrees or bleachers rising stepwise towards the back as shown in the drawing of the Swan. The yard was for standers only. Parts of the frame included gentlemen's rooms which were doubtless less densely occupied than the rest of the house, though not – as we shall see – by very much. Some spectators sat on the stage, but their number would not be great enough seriously to affect the overall capacity. Our main problem, then, lies in the nature and the size of the degrees in the galleries. How many people could sit there?

In the absence of direct information about the seating in the Globe we must turn to the analogical evidence, and our first port of call is the great mass of documentation accounting for the preparation of various royal houses for masques and plays enrolled in the Pipe Office accounts of the Works at the Public Record Office. Year after year in both Elizabeth's and James's reigns carpenters' records were made of the degrees that were set up at Whitehall and elsewhere, but only occasionally do they offer the sort of detailed information we are looking for. Here, for example, is an account for fitting out the Banqueting House at Whitehall in 1621–2, the season of Jonson's *Mask of Augurs*:

Ralphe Brice Carpenter for frameinge and setting upp xj^{en} baies of degrees on both sides of the banquettinge house every bay conteyninge xvj^{en} foote longe, being two panes in every of them; the degrees belowe beinge seven rowes in heighte; and twoe boordes nayled upon every brackett the degrees in the midle gallery beinge fower rowes in heigthe and twoe boordes nailed upon bracketts also with a raile belowe and another raile in the midle gallery beinge crosse laticed under the same; working framinge & settinge upp of upright postes wroughte with eighte cantes to beare the same woorke. . . .[3]

The actual construction of the temporary seating used at Court seems to have consisted of a sloping frame to which wooden brackets were attached; on the brackets deal boards were then nailed. This at least seems to be the method described in the following Works entries:

Whitehall, 1583–4 '. . . sawinge of Brackett*es* and naylinge them uppon the degrees for the greate Chamber . . .'[4]

Richmond, 1588–9 '. . . fframynge postes and Railes for plaies setting up degrees in the greate Chamber Nayllinge one brackett*es* and boordes for the people to sitt one . . .'[5]

Whitehall, 1593–4 '. . . fyttinge of degrees for both sides of the Hall, Cuttinge and Nayleinge of Brackett*es* and Deale boordes on them in the Hall, for the Earle of Sussex and gent' of Grayes Inne to make there shewes . . .'[6]

Hampton Court, 1603–4 'John Bradshawe and John Mardes for sawing of CCth di xx foote of degrees for the hall at ij^s v^d Cth . . .'[7]

In 1635 the hall at Whitehall was fitted up for the performance of a pastoral, *Florimène*, for which a detailed plan survives among the Lansdowne MSS at the British Library.[8] Unfortunately the Works accounts for this occasion do not use their usual formula to describe the seating, subsuming this part of the preparations under the phrase 'sondry other neccīe woorke.'[9] The general arrangements, however, are much like those made in the Banqueting House in 1621–2: ranks of seven or eight degrees arranged in 'panes' of 7 ft 6 in. or 8 ft each flank three walls of the room, and posts are marked capable of supporting a gallery of four or five degrees above them. Most of the degrees are a mere 18 in. deep from front to back: those closest to the floor are only 12 in., while those at the back by the walls are 2 ft 3 in. deep, perhaps to provide some room for circulation. A few years earlier, in 1632, Inigo Jones had set up a temporary theatre in the Paved Court at Somerset House for a performance of Walter Montagu's *Shepherd's Paradise*, and here each degree had a depth of 19 in.[10]

Modern commentators have found some difficulty in believing their eyes when faced with such evidence as this. How could one possibly squeeze oneself into so small a space and sit patiently through the two hours' traffic of the stage, let alone the seven or eight of Montagu's interminable pastoral? Despite the strictures of Leslie Hotson in *Shakespeare's Wooden O*,[11] such eminent scholars as J. Cranford Adams and Richard Hosley could not, at least until recently, bring themselves to accept the evidence at face value: Hosley, for example, allowed 26 in. for each degree in his reconstruction of the Swan in *The Revels History of Drama in English*. Yet the evidence is there for all to see, and in a recent paper Hosley himself has followed it in a reconstruction of the Fortune, whose degrees he places 18 in. apart.[12] If the Caroline courtiers were afforded only that much in 1635 the Elizabethan and Jacobean citizens can hardly have commanded more room at the Fortune in 1600 or the Globe in 1599 and 1614.

Eighteen inches is exactly what they were given at the Cockpit in Drury Lane, converted into a theatre by Christopher Beeston in 1616, the year of Shakespeare's death. Inigo Jones's drawings for this conversion are extant, and show an enclosed U-shaped house much like our idea of the Blackfriars theatre.[13] Degrees are marked in the stage boxes, the galleries and the pit, and they are all 18 in. deep. Like the temporary scaffolds of the palace theatres these seats are constructed on a sloping frame, but they appear to be made box-fashion, and each 18 in. surface is almost evenly divided into a seat at the front with a trough for feet behind it. As in all the extant plans much of the access to the seats is to be had by clambering across them; little specific circulation space is reserved for gangways or steps. The degrees are clearly intended for sitting rather than standing, for the division into seat- and foot-space would otherwise be pointless. Nowhere in the theatre is any room evidently left for standing. We must conclude – what we already knew – that Elizabethans and Jacobeans were smaller than we are, and – what we had perhaps only guessed – that they were prepared to put up with much discomfort in the theatre. In Italy the Teatro Olimpico still stands to remind us that the English were not alone in their astonishing compressibility.

When Leslie Hotson addressed the problem of audience capacity in *Shakespeare's Wooden O* he made a brief reference to an unnoticed drawing of a theatre, catalogued as probably German, among the Additional MSS at the British Library.[14] The drawing shows a plan and section of a royal theatre fitted up in a rectangular hall, and pressing hard about both figures is a mass of writing in a neat italic hand giving instructions for the erection of the auditorium they show [Plate 33]. Among them are many helpful comments on the matter of seat size, distribution, access and capacity. Dr Hotson printed a couple of these, but because their evidence seemed to be foreign and remote he did not make very much of them. As he saw, the handwriting, the style of drawing and the nature of the theatre all combine to indicate a date in the first half of the seventeenth century. Were the drawing English rather than German it would be of breathtaking interest to English theatre historians.

And indeed it is English, not German at all. There is not a word of German on it, nor any allusion to a German place or person. All the writing is in English, and there are allusions to the king – hardly likely

33. The theatre in the hall at Christ Church, Oxford, in August 1605.

in a seventeenth-century German context. The drawing was originally among the Sloane MSS before being transferred to the Additional MSS in the nineteenth century, and it has therefore been in a major collection since at least the early eighteenth century. It is mounted and bound up with a number of miscellaneous German manuscripts, and for that reason alone, it seems, has been thought to refer to a German theatre. But because the English writing on it is prescriptive rather than descriptive it is clearly not the work of a tourist reporting some foreign sight; instead it is an original English design, as may be judged from a sampling of the instructions given on the sheet:

. . . the piazza is 12 foote from the scene to the Center K. it wer better to bee 14 foote, or ^15 [*sic*] that the kinge may sit so much further from the scene. cutting of so much from the ende of the hall

. . . . .

. . . ~~The kings Isl a foote high~~ [*sic*]
. . . the first ~~sta~~ [*sic*] seat behind ~~it~~ [*sic*] ^the Isle 2f½. or rather 3f. high. to looke ouer the Isle.

. . . . .

In anny case remember that a slight Portico bee made eyther at H. or K. of hoopes & firrpoales. wherupon many lights or lamps of seueral coulers may be placed. This portico giues a great grace to all the Theater, & without it, the Architectur is false. . . .[15]

Clearly these are instructions for setting up a theatre, not descriptions of one already built. Since they are in English the presumption must be that they are for an English occasion. The first of the written comments above the section gives the necessary clue to its identity:

1. The hall is a 115 foote longe & 40 broade. . . .

To my knowledge there is only one hall in England that is commonly stated to be 115 ft by 40 ft, and that is at Christ Church, Oxford.[16] In the first half of the seventeenth century English monarchs twice visited it to see plays, once in 1605 and again in 1636. On the latter occasion there was a deep scenic stage which according to Anthony à Wood came almost to the central hearth of the hall.[17] Since one of the comments on our drawing specifies only 33 ft for the stage the design must be for the former occasion, when there was some trouble about the placing of the king's seat, which was found to be too close to the stage and had to be moved back so that the rest of the audience might see more of their monarch than merely his cheek.

An academic visitor from Cambridge, Philip Stringer, made a comprehensive report[18] on the royal visit of 1605 and recorded that at Christ Church the university had the advice of Inigo Jones as a scene designer and of the Comptroller of the King's Works for the layout of the auditorium.[19] This division of responsibilities was quite normal at the time in the royal palaces, and seems on this occasion to have been visited on Christ Church complete. The drawing shows the auditorium in great detail but has little to report on the scene, beyond giving in the section a 4 ft high flat forestage with a raked area behind it. Just such an arrangement is known, from Isaac Wake's Latin account of the event, to have been made at Christ Church in 1605;[20] indeed the raked stage – the first recorded in England, and now also the earliest to be illustrated – made something of an impression on Wake, who noted that the actors gained in dignity by making their entrances down it, as if walking down a hill:

Partem Aulae superiorem occupauit scena, cuius Proscenium molliter decliue (quod actorum egressui, quasi e monte descendentium, multum attulit dignitatis) in planitiem desinebat.[21]

The auditorium established by the carpenters from the Works caused some consternation among the Court officials when they inspected it before the royal visit:

They ... vtterlie disliked the stage att Christchurch, and above all, the place appointed for the chayre of estate because yt was no higher and the kinge so placed that the Auditory could see but his cheeke onlie. this dislike ... much troubled the *Vicechancelor*, and all the workmen, yet they stood in defence of the thinge done, and maynteyned that by the art perspective the kinge should behould all better then if he sat higher. ... in the end the place was removed, and sett in the midst of the hall, but too farr from the stage (vizt) xxviij. feete, soe that there were manye longe speeches delivered, which neyther the kinge nor anye neere him could well heare or vnderstand.[22]

It seems that our drawing shows the auditorium originally planned by the Works and evidently constructed according to the plan, for it places the king's 'Isle' very close to the stage, in front of all the rest of the audience. It appears that the changes insisted on by the Court involved the dismantling of the forward tier of degrees so that the 'Isle' (or rather that part of it marked on the plan by the letter K) might be moved 28 ft from the stage. This would have brought its back edge 36 ft from the stage, exactly in line with the front of the elevated gangway at the foot of the higher tier of degrees. In his description of the auditorium after the alterations, Isaac Wake confirms that there was a gigantic arc of degrees attached to the wall, but reports that the stage was now set in the midst of the hall with boxes for the Lords of the Council to either side [Plate 34]. The front tier of degrees had been rearranged in the area between the throne and the stage:

Ab infimis Aulae tabulatis vsque ad summa laquearium fastigia cunei parietibus ingenti circuitu affinguntur; media cauea thronus Augustalis cancellis cinctus Principibus erigitur, quem vtrinque optimatum stationes communiunt: reliquum inter thronum & theatrum interstitium Heroinarum Gynaeceum est paulo depresstus.[23]

34. The hall, Christ Church, Oxford in 1605. Diagram showing the rearrangements made
in the auditorium after the Court's intervention, with descriptive comments by Stringer
and Wake.

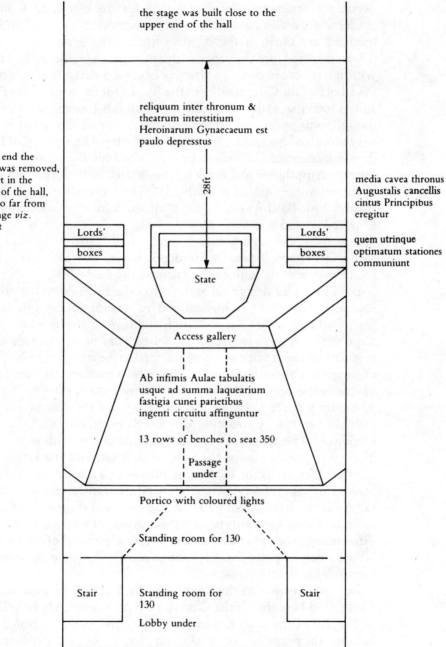

the stage was built close to the upper end of the hall

reliquum inter thronum & theatrum interstitium Heroinarum Gynaecaeum est paulo depresstus

28ft

in the end the place was removed, and set in the midst of the hall, but too far from the stage *viz.* 28 feet

media cavea thronus Augustalis cancellis cintus Principibus eregitur

quem utrinque optimatum stationes communiunt

Lords' boxes

Lords' boxes

State

Access gallery

Ab infimis Aulae tabulatis usque ad summa laquearium fastigia cunei parietibus ingenti circuitu affinguntur

13 rows of benches to seat 350

Passage under

Portico with coloured lights

Standing room for 130

Stair

Standing room for 130

Stair

Lobby under

Here, then, is a drawing of singular interest to the theatre historian. It is not German at all, but an English design made in the period of Shakespeare's greatest flourishing, six years after the building of the first Globe. It is by far the earliest theatre plan we have, showing in detail the arrangements thought fit for an elaborate Court and academical occasion at Oxford, though its origins are in London. Its methods are those of the Works officials: the groundwork for the design is scored into the paper with a pointed instrument, then filled in with ink where necessary. Stringer observed that the university had the advice of the Comptroller of the Works for the scaffolds in the hall, and in 1605 that office was held by Simon Basil, who was shortly – in the following year – to advance to the Surveyorship itself.[24] In this very month of August 1605 he had been ordered by the Earl of Dorset, the Chancellor of Oxford, to prepare plans for the restoration of the lodge at Ampthill,[25] and drawings associated with the project survive in the muniment room at Hatfield.[26] Thus at the time of the Christ Church visit Basil was occupied with work for the Chancellor of the University, and it is not very surprising to discover that, during the debate over the arrangements in the hall, Dorset sided with his architect: 'Their *Chauncelor*,' wrote Stringer, 'also after his cominge, tooke part wth the vniuersitie [against the Earls].'[27]

Basil based his design on Serlio's woodcut of a ducal theatre in the second book of the *Architettura*.[28] The general debt is obvious: like Serlio's theatre, the Christ Church auditorium fronts a raked scenic stage with degrees ranged on a semi-circular plan, and although for practical reasons their curves are reduced to the straight sides of a series of irregular polygons the arcs within which they are described are still visible in the original drawing, scored into the surface of the paper. The empty space between the forestage and the closest seats Basil calls the 'piazza,' borrowing the word directly from Serlio's later editions.[29] The Italian divides his auditorium according to a social hierarchy, with seats for the noblest in front, and the ladies behind them divided from the more agile men seated higher up. At the very back some superfluous space is left for the common people. Much the same scheme is followed by Basil: the king and the lords at the front; ladies and king's servants behind them divided by a gangway from the other men in the upper tier. At the back is a 'portico' of lamps beyond which – cast in outer darkness, presumably – is some standing space for students.

But our business in this chapter is the seating and capacity of the Globe, and here the Christ Church plan is immediately helpful. First to the size of the seats themselves. They are forms or benches, and because they are set on a sloping floor they are provided with 'footesteps.' Here are the relevant comments transcribed from the drawing, the key letters referring to the section of the theatre:

D   the seats for Ladys & the kings servants; the seats D are 8 ynches broade.
     they are two foote distante ech from other. so that 8 ynches therof serues
     for the seate, & the other 16 ynches for the legs & knes.

E   are the footesteps 2 foote vnder the seats D. or G. four ynches broade.
 . . . . .

G.   13 other seats 18 ynches a sunder. wherof the seat conteyns 6 ynches.
 . . . . .

J.   a slopp scaffold for peopl to stande on. which should haue barrs to keepe
     them from ouerpressing one another.
 . . . . .

L.   the roome behinde the skreene wher scaffolds may be made to see
     conveniently.

To these we may add the description of the Lords' boxes, keyed to the
plan:

L.   places for the L^{ds}. of the Counseyle. wherof L.L. is somewhat higher
     then the other L.

At once we notice the tiny ration of space allowed to all but the
Lords of the Privy Council (and of course the royal party itself, whose
'Isle' was 16 ft across). The fore-and-aft space available for the lords
was 30 in. (what Alfred Harbage[30] would lavish on every ostler and
tapster at the Globe); the Court ladies and the king's servants had 24 in.
(two inches less than Richard Hosley would have given the appren-
tices at the Swan); the men in the upper tier had a mere 18 in., the
figure we have found to be standard in Inigo Jones's designs. Beyond
them was undifferentiated standing space. But this wonderful if
delayed gift from His Majesty's Works has not done yet, for it gives us
precise specifications of audience capacity:

> The first seuen seats will conteyne 200 persons to sitt at ease.
> The seconde 13 seats, will conteyne 350.
>   In al 550. to sitt on seats
> The place behinde them. 130 [sic] will hold 130.
> The place behinde the skreene as many.
>   The summe of al 810. without pressing.

A moment with a ruler shows that the front seven rows contain 300
linear feet of seating space and the upper thirteen rows about 530 linear
feet. Obviously the Works formula allowed 18 in. width for each
sitting spectator, whatever the legroom. The standers up above are
grouped into two sets of 130 each, but inaccuracies in the drawing
permit us only to say that each set had about 400 sq. ft or so of space.
This is sufficient indication, however, to make possible an estimate of
the capacity of the Globe using the Works formula and not some set of
dimensions concocted out of modern practices and expectations, such
as that employed by Alfred Harbage in his pioneering study of this
subject, *Shakespeare's Audience*.[31]

Let us pack the yard with standers using the Works formula for the standing-room in the uppermost parts of the Christ Church auditorium. It will not do to be picayune, so we shall take into account only one-half of the area of the yard, leaving aside questions about the size of the stage. In the Globe as described in these pages the yard is 69 ft across; in Appendix A I shall argue in support of Richard Hosley's suggestion that its shape, like that of the Swan, was a polygon of twenty-four sides. Let us anticipate that argument for the moment and calculate half the yard's area as 1848.36 sq. ft. This figure we must divide by 400 and multiply by 130 to arrive at a standing capacity of about 600 people at the density recommended by the King's Works for the students at Christ Church.

When we turn to the galleries we are faced with the intractable problems of how much space to leave for the circulation of the audience, how steeply to rake the degrees, how to manage the ascent and descent from one gallery to another, and so on. Our new Works evidence has some contribution to make to the discussion of these problems, which have been ably addressed by Professor Hosley on the basis of a minimum of evidence and a great deal of alert common sense.[32] It seems likely that a corridor ran round the second Globe, at least, behind the degrees of the middle gallery, for Hollar shows a row of small windows whose function was probably to light it. The lowest gallery had no such windows and was presumably lit from the yard alone. Its space will have been filled with degrees, and the Christ Church drawing shows that the Works, had they been building it, would not have felt the need to provide any special access to the benches, the audience being expected to clamber down to them as best they could. A walkway 2 ft 6 in. wide at the rear of the degrees seems reasonable, since that is the width of the passage marked G. on the Christ Church plan and F. on the section at the back of the lower tier of degrees:

G.   a gallery two foote & a $\frac{1}{2}$ broade to pass betweene the seats. which must bee raysed ouer the passage ∞ 8^y to pass rounde about, leauing 7 foote at least vnder.

If an access passage the same width as that at Christ Church, 2 ft 6 in., ran along the back wall of the bays, there remained 11 ft 6 in. to be filled with seven 18 in. degrees together with legroom for an eighth whose seat consisted of the front part of the passage itself. A similar pattern, though with fewer degrees, appears in Jones's hall plan for *Florimène* and made for both simplicity of construction and flexibility of access and capacity. The audience entered the degrees from the rear, the first-comers stepping down them to the best positions by the rail at the front. The bays then filled up until, if the house was full, the latecomers found themselves perched on the access passage at the rear.

An alternative method, with the audience entering the degrees from a walkway at their front, might occasionally have been used at the Court theatres with their armies of ushers who could make sure that the early arrivals did not sit at the front and so clog the passage to the back seats, but so awkward an arrangement can hardly have been made in the public playhouses.

At the Globe, then, the depth of the galleries was filled with eight degrees, pitched much lower than the 45° shown in the Cockpit drawings and more at the angle of the Christ Church section. Again without prejudging the question of the 'fit' of the stage and tiring house into the frame of the auditorium I propose to apply the Works' formula to only three-quarters of the Globe's circumference, leaving the remaining quarter for the actors and such special seating as the lords' rooms. Three-quarters of twenty-four sides is eighteen, and it is into eighteen bays some 9 ft across at the front and opening out to 12 ft 11 in. at the rear that we must pack our capacity first-gallery audience. Each bay has eight benches averaging some 10 ft 6 in. apiece, for 84 linear feet; the total for eighteen bays is 1512 ft, yielding room for an audience of about 1000 at 18 in. for each person.

In Hollar's sketch the sills of the windows lighting the second-gallery corridor are marked at about three fifths of the height of the frame to the eaves, or about 19 ft 6 in. above ground level. They were high enough, therefore, to light the rearmost degrees if these were set up exactly on the pattern of the lower gallery with a walkway behind, in which case the middle gallery could also have accommodated 1000 people 'to sitt at ease,' as the Works document puts it. The topmost gallery offers many problems. Perhaps it was a standing place like the uppermost tiers at Christ Church; perhaps it mixed standing room with some benches. At any event the sightlines must have been very poor indeed from most parts of this upper level of the house, and one is disposed to reduce its usable capacity accordingly, though in a packed house it probably accommodated something not far short of the other galleries, say 750. When the theatre was filled, then, as it was for Middleton's *Game at Chess*, it was capable of holding

in the yard	600
in the first gallery	1000
in the second gallery	1000
in the top gallery	750
	3350

The Spanish ambassador in his dispatch to Madrid reporting Middleton's furiously anti-Spanish play noted that 'the actors whom they call here "the King's Men" have recently acted, and are still acting, in London a play that so many people come to see, that there were more

than 3000 persons there on the day that the audience was
smallest....'[33] Don Carlos Coloma was an astute and methodical
diplomat. It seems that on this occasion his information was
characteristically sound.

7 *The Globe and the sun*

The technique of the Globe's design was rooted in the practice of medieval craftsmen. Yet there is no obvious medieval tradition of circular or polygonal structures in which the designers of Burbage's Theater can be said to have stood: the most likely candidates are the animal-baiting arenas, but evidence about them is sketchy and what there is of it hardly suggests that the huge three-galleried, 100 ft wide wooden circles or polygons merely imitated their design, which seems if anything to have been rather rudimentary until well after 1576.[1] By one of fate's more appealing little accidents it happens that the great Sarsen circle of Stonehenge arranges its stones so that their dressed inner faces form tangents to a circle just 97 ft 4 in. across. Since the stones average 3 ft to 4 ft in thickness, their centres, again on average, lie on a circle almost exactly 99 ft across, just like the posts at the Globe.[2] When Inigo Jones surveyed the ruin in 1620 he concluded that it was Roman work, designed along the lines of an ancient theatre.[3] It would be pleasant to think that he was led to this obtuse conclusion by some unspoken recognition that the whole thing reminded him of the London theatres, but it would be more than pleasant – it would be hilarious – to claim that Peter Street's tradition had roots in prehistoric Wessex culture. After all, the polygon of the Sarsen stones has thirty sides, almost certainly more than the Globe's;[4] the place is made of very large pieces of stone, not timber; it was some kind of sacred place or memorial, not a theatre; and this solemn disclaimer must cease before it comes to look like a covert suggestion of the opposite. We must look elsewhere for the Globe's architectural tradition.

There has arisen in recent years a school of thought contending that the Globe and other theatres of Shakespeare's age were designed in imitation of the ancient Roman theatre as described by Vitruvius in the *De Architectura*.[5] This textbook of architectural theory and practice – virtually the only one to survive from the ancient world – had great currency after the time of Alberti, and as we have seen was certainly known in England by such practitioners as Robert Stickells, Clerk of Her Majesty's Works at Richmond from 1597 to 1620.[6] The Vitruvian influence on Italian architecture from Alberti to Palladio and Scamozzi is a matter of record, and of course in England there is no doubt that Inigo Jones was in the fullest sense a Vitruvian if also eclectic and pragmatic. His design probably made for the conversion of the

Cockpit in Drury Lane into a theatre in 1616 is proportioned in ways that echo Vitruvian ideas, though rather remotely, and his plans for the adaptation of the Whitehall Cockpit-in-Court as a playhouse in 1629 are full of allusions to the ancient theatre. But if Vitruvianism is plainly evident in Jones's work and his pronouncements – so much so that in *Love's Welcome at Bolsover* Ben Jonson satirized him as 'Coronell Vitruvius'[7] – it is by no means equally clear that men like Peter Street or Henslowe or indeed Alleyn, Burbage or Shakespeare would have thought very much about it. We have found that Peter Street's methods were traditional, akin more to medieval design than Renaissance.

Nevertheless there are many possible points of contact between the design scheme of the Globe and that of the Vitruvian ancient theatre. Discussions of Vitruvius's account of the theatre often overlook the fact that it includes a much more far-reaching exploration of the themes of proportion and harmony, and of their special emanation in the theory of acoustics.[8] For Vitruvius the theatre illustrates how sound works in ways that make palpable the proportionate structure of the cosmos. Just as sound rises in orderly concentric circles from its source, so the theatre ranges its degrees of seats in the *cavea* of the auditorium in a plan developed from the circle. Indeed the whole theatre, *scena*, *proscenium* and *cavea*, is proportioned in imitation of that harmony which the late Hellenistic Platonists posited as the fundamental tendency of the phenomenal world and which so took the hearts and minds of the neo-Platonists in Renaissance Florence. It is while he is making these connexions between Nature and Art, acoustics and architecture, that Vitruvius describes the particular way in which the theatre is laid out according to the pattern of four equilateral triangles inscribed within a circle, a pattern borrowed from the astrologers, who used it to demonstrate the harmony of the heavenly spheres. It was a pattern much illustrated in Renaissance editions of the *Architectura* [Plate 35].[9]

Now in so far as the Globe was an acoustical auditorium, intended to serve the word and the ear more fully than the image and the eye, it is hardly surprising that it bears some resemblance to the ancient theatre as described by Vitruvius. Both served the same cause; what they had in common was not so much a design tradition as the natural laws governing the transmission of sound. Surely what is most interesting about the Globe – what would be most interesting if it were to be reconstructed now – is not the comparatively trivial business of how many stage doors it had, or how high its stage was, or whether there was a 'discovery space' or an inner stage, but what it *sounded* like. Lear's rage and Cleopatra's immortal longings, the old mole in the cellarage, or the music of the god Hercules leaving Antony: can anybody doubt that it was the sound of these things rather than the sight of them that mattered first? The temptation to go beyond noting the mere resemblance of the Elizabethan to the ancient theatre is therefore very great, but I think it should be resisted. Certainly contemporary travellers spoke of the London playhouses in Roman terms, and de Witt went so far as to label parts of the Swan with Latin names: orchestra, arena, proscenium, porticus and so on.[10] He certainly saw the resemblance; but that does not prove that the Swan was a deliberate imitation of the ancient theatre.

The resemblances are indeed many. Like the Vitruvian theatre, the English one was planned within a circle. Vitruvius placed the front of the stage on the diameter; so Peter Street brought his to the middle of the yard at the Fortune,[11] and the crude drawing of the Swan appears to show something similar. At the Cockpit in Drury Lane Inigo Jones made the stage front exactly bisect the body of the theatre, though since Jones was an accredited Vitruvian in any case his example hardly counts.[12] If the Globe's frame was polygonal it might readily have been absorbed into the twelve-point system of Vitruvius. But all this amounts to very little when we reflect that any centrally planned auditorium will make similar contact with the Vitruvian scheme. The diameter will be visually significant because the centre is; the

35.   Andrea Palladio, drawing of a Roman theatre made to illustrate an edition of Vitruvius.

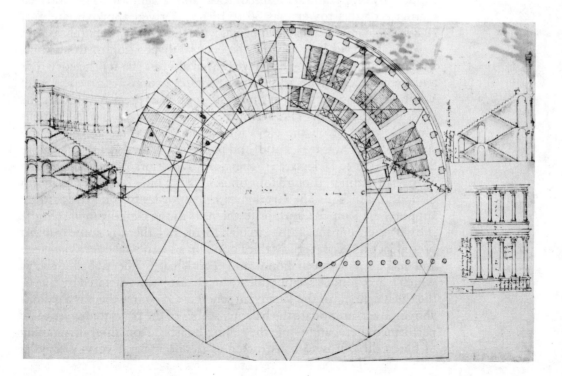

perimeter is bound to have interruptions of some sort such as entrances or windows, and these are most unlikely to be placed there irregularly, with the result that they will probably echo the regular astrological scheme whether they are meant to or not. It is little wonder that the centrally planned. theatres of Elizabethan London reminded contemporary observers of Roman theatres: both were the product of an orderly constructive geometry, bounded by the circle. But there is no specific evidence that the Globe and its like actually alluded to the twelve-point scheme in their plans, nor that their stages came to the diameter in particular imitation of the Romans; nor that the tiring-house façade was placed according to the Vitruvian astrological scheme; nor that the auditorium had seven gangways and the *scena* five entrances, as they do in the *Architectura*.

Inigo Jones was of course an exception to this general rule. At Drury Lane he showed his Vitruvianism by proportioning the width of the stage to that of the whole theatre as 1: $\sqrt{3}$, a ratio which does indeed derive from the ancient plan, though not in any very direct way.[13] At the Cockpit-in-Court at Whitehall he had a fine opportunity to reconcile the Vitruvian scheme with the more traditional or Gothic *ad quadratum* plan of the building he was commissioned to adapt. This simple showplace, built by Henry VIII in the 1530s, consisted of a square main structure probably some 57 ft 2 in. wide within which rose an octagonal tower made of timber and supported on posts, topped by a pyramidal canted roof and a lantern. The internal diameter of this tower was 36 ft 10 in., derived approximately *ad quadratum* from the internal dimensions of the walls of the square, 53 ft 6 in. [Plate 31 III].[14] We know the general disposition of these walls from an elevation of the building drawn about 1606 by the surveyor and architect John Thorpe;[15] their actual proportions are given by John Webb's drawings of Jones's scheme, though their precise scale remains in doubt [Plate 36]. The antiqueness of Jones's intentions here is obvious: marked on the elevation of the *frons scenae* are busts and statues of ancient Greek muses and poets, at the centre is the Horatian tag 'Prodesse & Delectare,'[16] there are five doors of entrance in the Vitruvian manner, though four of them being only five feet high seem of doubtful utility. The Greek Corinthian order of the lower storey supports the Roman Composite above.[17] In the plan the *frons scenae* is shown in an unusual semi-circular form, but there is some ancient precedent for this in Serlio's third book, in a segmental *frons scenae* seen and recorded between Fondi and Terrasina.[18] The five doorways which pierce Jones's scenic wall are located at points dictated by five of the twelve points of the Vitruvian scheme. Of course there is a gallery above, to accommodate the balcony scenes of the plays that were to be performed there, and while the ceiling boasts a Roman-style *velarium* of blue calico, it is so constructed as to allow a not-very-Vitruvian throne of whalebone and wire to descend from above.[19] The theatre was, in short, a marriage of ancient forms with modern stage practice, a deliberate piece of theatrical archaeology in action, as Thomas Heywood confirmed in a speech written for the opening night:

The potent *Caesars* had their *Circi*, and
Large Amphitheaters: in which might stand
And sit, full fourscore thousand, all in view,
And touch of voice: this great Augustus knew.
Nay *Rome*, its wealth, and potency injoy'd,
Till by the barbarous Gothes these were destroy'd.
But may this structure last, and you be seene
Here a spectator with your Princely Queene,
In your old age as in your flourishing prime,
To out-strip *Augustus* both in fame and time.[20]

Yet nowhere in his designs for the Cockpit-in-Court does Jones attempt to reconcile the evident Vitruvianism with the Gothic proportions of the cockpit building itself. His stage front might well have been made to coincide with the centre of the house, but in fact he presses his whole semi-circular proscenium back as far as possible against the posts of the central octagon, ignoring the centrality of the older structure. Webb's drawings [Plate 36 I and II] are, like most architectural drawings of the period, inked over a carefully constructed groundwork of scored lines. In the overall plan of the building [Plate 36 II] a number of these lines converge from the cants of the octagon to a centre just a foot or two in front of the stage rail, while in the larger plan of the stage alone [Plate 36 I] scored radii defining the layout of the segmental *frons scenae* depart from a centre about a foot inside (or upstage from) the rail. The lantern overhead, which might have asserted the original building's centrality willy nilly, Jones obscured by the calico *velarium*; his design of the degrees in the auditorium, though it follows the lines of the old structure, he left unreconciled with that of the stage and *frons scenae*: his plan asserts the separateness of the scheme from the old Tudor structure with its lofty masts springing from battlemented roofs and supporting grotesque images of the King's Beasts. He saw, that is, no reason to assimilate its centrality of design to the Vitruvian centrality he espoused himself. For him, as for Robert Stickells, the ancient and the modern (or Gothic) were irreconcilable. In making this assertion I do not forget such evidence to the contrary as Jones's powerful imaginative work at St Paul's, whose Romanesque nave he recased with serene inventiveness.[21] But that task was a special case, eliciting an unusual and mighty response. At Whitehall the cockpit's festive style called forth no such respect.

Jones's failure, or his refusal, to wed his Vitruvian scheme to the more-or-less regular *ad quadratum* proportions of the cockpit makes it

unlikely that such a marriage had already been arranged at the Globe and the other public theatres of Elizabeth's days. Had the example been there it is at least likely that he would have followed it; since he did not follow it, it is equally likely that it was not there. Indeed in setting the stage front back from the centre of the structure it may be that Jones copied the example of the second Globe precisely in that point where it most obviously differed from any Vitruvian model.[22]

In the Roman theatre only half of the circle from which its plan was developed was actually visible as part of the structure, like the curve in a capital D. The Elizabethan theatre – a wooden O – by contrast expressed its circularity completely; in Roman terms it was an amphitheatre rather than a theatre proper. Yet as we have seen this difference did not prevent contemporary observers from noting a resemblance, though how far this perception was merely a commonplace of the time it is difficult to determine. As early as 1520 the French built an auditorium at Ardres in connexion with the Field of the Cloth of Gold, though in the upshot it was not used. It was described as built

de la façon comme du temps passé les Romains faisoient leur théâtre, tout en rond, à ouvrage de bois, chambres, salles, galleries, trois estages l'un sur l'autre, et tous les fondemens de pierres.[23]

It could have been the Globe! And there is the almost routine observation: 'comme du temps passé les Romains faisoient leur théâtre.' Was this French auditorium Vitruvian? On the whole it seems unlikely that such a structure, antedating by far the Teatro Olimpico of Palladio, should have anticipated that wonderful building's careful Vitruvianism and yet have gone unnoticed by contemporary scholars. Nor do I mean by this that the Globe was built in a French tradition, but rather that the large open centrally planned auditorium naturally suggested the Roman analogy to observers who commented on it in a general way without establishing any serious connexion. In fact the English builders who accompanied Henry VIII to the Field of the Cloth of Gold set up a very similar house at Calais for his meeting with Emperor Charles V soon afterwards, on 10 July 1520, and although like the auditorium at Ardres it was fated never to serve its intended purpose, it too had three timber galleries of standing-places, one above the other and sloping so that those at the back might see over the heads of those who stood in front. It had also a great double roof of canvas, supported at the centre by an enormous pole made up of masts lashed together. The auditorium had sixteen sides, and it was apparently – the evidence is contradictory – some 125 ft across overall, bigger even than the Elizabethan theatres for which both it and the French counterpart at Ardres constituted precedents.[24] But it is a long way and a long time from Calais in 1520 to London in 1576, and it would be hard to prove a more definite connexion. The canvas banqueting houses at Whitehall constructed in the time of Elizabeth in the same festive tradition as the great marquee at Calais differed from it in their rectangular plans, and appear to have had no influence on the design of the public playhouses. The cockpit at Whitehall, though centrally planned and in the same festive style, hardly embodied enough of the features of the Ardres and Calais exemplars to convey them to James Burbage and his like. The trail runs cold.

As yet, we must reluctantly conclude, there is no altogether satisfactory hypothesis to explain the provenance of the Globe, prior at any rate to its first manifestation as the timbered round of Burbage's Theater. The attraction of the baiting-ring theory is that it offers at least the possibility of a continuous design tradition, but because the rings were comparatively primitive and specialized structures they are not very convincing in the role of progenitor of the glorious Elizabethan theatres, of what Thomas White called from the pulpit at St Paul's 'The sumptuouse Theatre houses, a continuall monument of Londons prodigalitie and folly.'[25] The festive court tradition offers a more substantial model, but the particular examples at Ardres and Calais are too far removed from the Theater and the Globe to permit us to assert that they taught Burbage or Street how to build. As to the possibility that the guiding influence was that of Vitruvius, it can certainly be proved that the *Architectura* was available in England in the sixteenth century, that Vitruvius was understood and promulgated by such practical thinkers as John Dee and Robert Fludd, and that he was known to artisans like Stickells as well as to the more Italianate and intellectual patrons. Yet nowhere do we find a specific link between the Globe's design and that of the antique theatre described by Vitruvius in his Fifth Book.

There is no denying the appeal of the Vitruvian idea of the theatre as it was developed by such Renaissance commentators as Daniele Barbaro. It has been forcefully put by Frances Yates:

The entries and exits of the characters take place within a Theatre of the World, cosmic in its ground plan, religious in its meaning . . . . To the cosmic meanings of the ancient theatre, with its plan based on the triangulations within the zodiac, was [sic] added the religious meanings of the theatre as temple, and the related religious and cosmic meanings of the Renaissance church. The Globe Theatre was a magical theatre, a cosmic theatre, a religious theatre, an actors' theatre, designed to give fullest support to the voices and gestures of the players as they enacted the drama of the life of man within the Theatre of the World.[26]

Set against so rich a cluster of suggestive ideas our new interpretation of the Globe's design, based upon patient but I trust diligent enquiry, pales almost into transparency. Can it therefore be true? The Elizabethans, we know, often thought of their theatre as a little world, its stage cover a heavens, its cellarage a purgatory or a hell. In reducing its design to a matter of technical procedures of measurement have I not been guilty of robbing it of its magic?

Yet there is, in the *ad quadratum* idea, as much imaginative force as there ever was in the astrologers' triangles. The most elaborate and weighty discussion of analogical harmony in the *Architectura* is that in Book III where Vitruvius relates the ideal proportions of temples to those of the human body, and especially to the circle and square within which the body may – at least in theory – be described:

. . . in the human body the central point is naturally the navel. For if a man be placed flat on his back, with his hands and feet extended, and a pair of compasses centred at his navel, the fingers and toes of his two hands and feet will touch the circumference of a circle described therefrom. And just as the human body yields a circular outline, so too a square figure may be found from it. For if we measure the distance from the soles of the feet to the top of the head, and then apply that measure to the outstretched arms, the breadth will be found to be the same as the height, as in the case of plane surfaces which are perfectly square.[27]

37. The *homo ad quadratum* in Vincenzo Scamozzi, *L'idea dell'architettura universale*, Venice, 1615, p. 40.

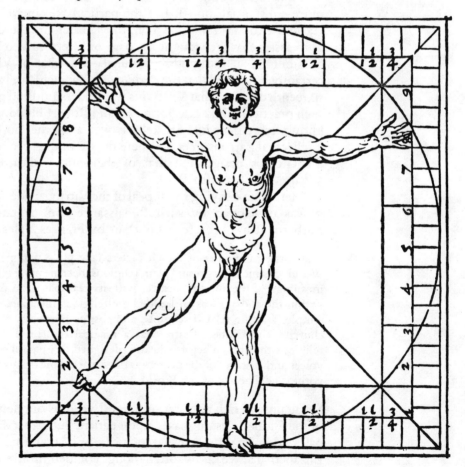

The *homo ad quadratum* and *ad circulum* were so famous that they were repeatedly depicted by artists and by the illustrators of editions of Vitruvius [Plate 37].[28] Some Renaissance painters were fascinated by the $\sqrt{2}$ proportionality of these two figures, Piero della Francesca, for instance, placing Christ at the centre of a floor-circle in his *Flagellation*, and proportioning the major intervals within his perspective in ratios which have been discovered to represent multiples of π.[29] The mystery of the squaring of the circle appears to have interested not a few Renaissance thinkers,[30] and it is of course precisely this mystery which is embodied in Peter Street's very practical *ad quadratum* scheme for the Globe.

Unfortunately we cannot say, on the present evidence, that Street or Burbage or anyone else intended the Elizabethan theatre to echo the Vitruvian idea of the 'homo ad quadratum.' A detailed knowledge of the *Architectura* would hardly be necessary to suggest such an intention; the idea was widely illustrated and vivid enough to appeal in its own right. On the other hand we can be certain that Inigo Jones, in his schematic design for a man-centred anatomy theatre prepared for the Barber–Surgeons' Company in 1636, used *ad quadratum* procedures to develop its oval plan [Plate 38]. At the centre of the little auditorium stands what appears to be an anatomy table just 3 ft wide. The overall width of the building, like the height of its main chamber, is 34 ft; the lateral and end windows are spaced between reveals just 17 ft apart; the attached stair turrets (so reminiscent of the Globe) are 8 ft 6 in. wide, a measure which equals the diagonals of the anatomy table. The main entrance door, shown in the elevation leading into the first-floor chamber, is 8 ft 6 in. by 4 ft 3 in., clear space. These measures are all developed from the width of the anatomy table by an *ad quadratum* process: 3 ft $\times$ $\sqrt{2}$=4 ft 3 in. and so on, for the series 3 ft, 4 ft 3 in., 6 ft, 8 ft 6 in., 12 ft, 17 ft, 24 ft, 34 ft. The copy of the design which we have is in fact by Jones's pupil John Webb, and not by the master himself, though Jones is known to have done the original design work.[31] Someone, Jones or Webb, has pencilled in the outline of a human body on the anatomy table [Plate 39]: it is a kind of Vitruvian *homo ad quadratum* though in this case we must take the proportions of the surrounding building as rendering explicit the idea contained in the famous diagram.

The Barber–Surgeons' theatre is an enlightening *post facto* analogue of the Globe. Its curved walls, designed *ad quadratum*, enclose an audience with man himself surrounded at the centre. The Company had planets and constellations painted on the ceiling, and the signs of the zodiac carved into corbels on the piers between the windows, supporting skeletons and musclemen.[32] This was Inigo Jones's Theatre of the World, just as the Globe was Hamlet's:

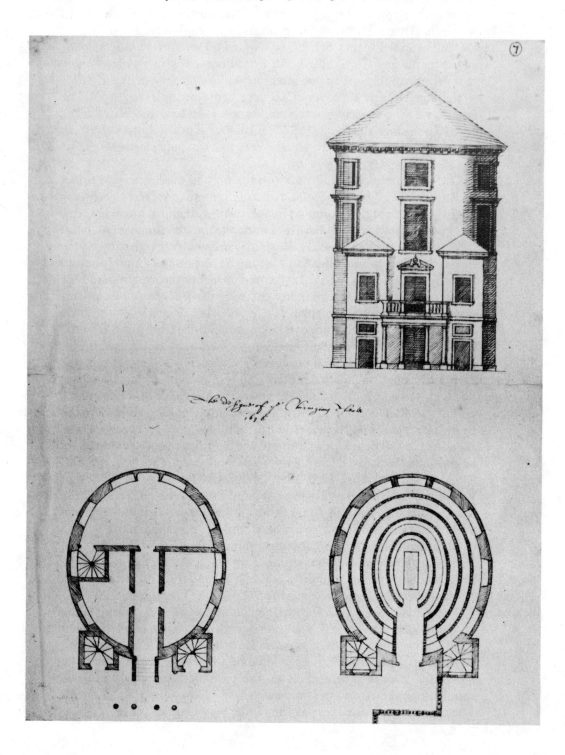

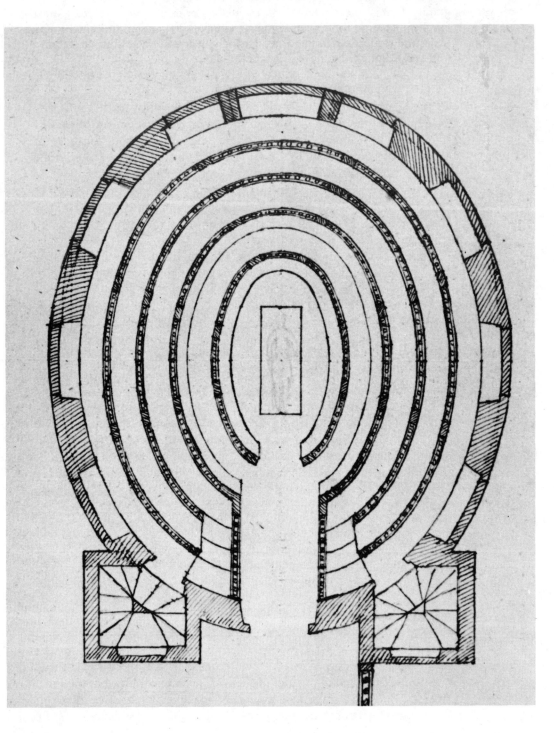

I have of late, but wherefor I know not, lost all my mirth, forgone all custom of exercises; and indeed, it goes so heavily with my disposition that this goodly frame, the earth, seems to me a sterile promontory; this most excellent canopy, the air, look you, this brave o'erhanging firmament, this majestical roof fretted with golden fire: why, it appeareth nothing to me but a foul and pestilential congregation of vapours.

(*Hamlet*, II, ii, 303–11)

At the centre of this little universe, beneath the roof fretted with the golden fire of the heavens, his feet spread on the sterile promontory of the Globe's wooden stage, stands man himself, the paragon of animals, the quintessence of dust. But if Hamlet can turn the Globe through his language into a cosmic theatre for the moment, can it be said to have retained that quality in his absence, or when he characterized it with equal conviction as a specific place like the battlements at Elsinore? Was it *recognized* as the sort of symbolic structure its name suggests?

If we are to rescue the Globe from the pale indeterminacy of a mere scaffold we need some clear indication that its structure had links with that of the cosmos itself. Lacking a plan like that of Jones's anatomy theatre, where the central human body validates the surrounding *ad quadratum* proportions, we turn once more to our substitute survey, Hollar's sketch of Southwark, and find that there is one last piece of hard information to be deduced from it. For it enables us to judge, to within tolerable limits, the actual orientation of the theatre measured in degrees from true north. Here, at any rate, lies a promising path of enquiry, for although the Vitruvian theatre was not oriented in any special way beyond avoiding the unhealthy southern exposure, we know that medieval and Tudor craftsmen were alive to the symbolic implications of direction as judged from the sun: the Great Hall at Whitehall, for example, was aligned due north and south,[33] as was the Banqueting House, where in Jonson's day the monarch sat at the south end and was frequently addressed as a figure of the sun:

'Tis he, that stayes the time from turning old,
And keepes the age vp in a head of gold.
That in his owne true circle, still doth runne;
And holds his course, as certayne as the sunne.   (*Oberon*, 350–3)

If it can be found that the Globe's orientation made some similarly specific contact with the movement of the heavenly bodies a good deal of the 'magic' associated with the potent neo-Vitruvian idea of the theatre may yet be recovered. The particular notion of the cosmic harmony contained in the belt of the zodiac which we find in the Fifth Book is not the only one available to thinkers and builders in Shakespeare's time; the playhouse might have possessed cosmic implications without specifically imitating Vitruvius's idea of the ancient theatre.

We can tell the orientation of the Globe in Hollar's study because the artist presents the plane face of its large superstructure or hut, and emphasizes its precise alignment by drawing across it a line indicating a level beam or fascia board just below the gulley between the twin ridges of the roof. Allowing for the slight lift shown at the left end of the board on the hut, we project a line from its overall direction to the horizon line, which it strikes a little to the left of St Paul's and to the right of the water-tower [Plate 40]. Admittedly this is not a very accurate procedure, so we confirm it by running a similar line from the front peaks of both stair turrets at the Globe and find that it too strikes the horizon line in about the same place. Now it is a characteristic of linear perspective views that all horizontals converge on the horizon, and parallel horizontals converge on one another there. The horizontal from Hollar's perch atop St Saviour's which runs parallel to that of the Globe's face must therefore strike the horizon line at this same point above the water-tower and to the left of St Paul's, at, that is, what the modern map tells us is about 42° west of true north. 42° west of north is therefore also the bearing of the band along the front of the Globe's hut, and it follows that the main axis of the theatre, which ran at right angles to it, lay 48° east of north. This figure may easily be checked by another calculation using quite separate data. C. Walter Hodges' plan of the Globe deduced from Hollar's sketch shows the façade at 52° from the perceived diameter of the building [Plate 32]. The diameter as seen from St Saviour's lay on a line at right angles to the direct line of sight to the centre of the theatre (this being Mr Hodges' assumption as he made his plan): the line of sight is 280.25°, and the diameter

40.   The orientation of the Globe's façade deduced from Hollar's 'West part o[f] Southwarke'.

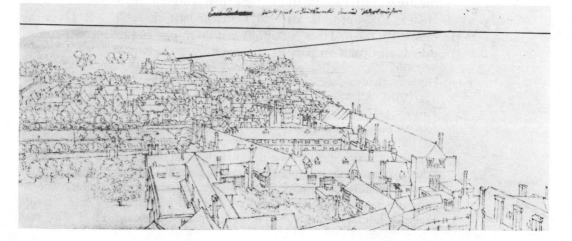

therefore 10.25° east of true north. The façade in the plan is 52° anti-clockwise from that, or 41.75° west of north; the axis of the Globe is therefore 90° from that, or 48.25° east of north. An alternative way of dealing with the information in Hodges' plan is to correct for its mis-statement of the picture plane. The line of sight to the centre of the Globe is 15° south of the central ray of Hollar's perspective as made at the topographical glass. To the 52° divergence from the perceived diameter as reported in the plan we should therefore add 15°, to bring the whole into agreement with the true picture plane (on which the diameter is actually recorded) of 25.34°. The divergence ought to be 67°; from this figure we subtract the bearing of the picture plane (25.34°) to find the bearing of the Globe's façade: 67° —25.34° = 41.66°. Once again the study shows that the main axis of the theatre lay about 48.25° east of true north. Or rather it shows that the axis lay on something like that bearing: our methods of measuring it all stem from the precise angle at which Hollar marked the hut band on his paper, and we should not expect too much of so small yet critically sensitive a gesture of the pen.

Previous discussions of the directionality of the Globe have been restricted to rather broad statements about its stage being in the southwest, and perhaps its main entrance to the northeast.[34] If the figure we now have to deal with may be trusted – and I take some comfort from the close agreement between the conclusions arrived at above – a new element enters the argument. For 48.25° east of north is very close indeed to the azimuth of the midsummer sunrise at the latitude of Southwark.

Here we need expert advice. A word with Professor Douglas Hube of the Physics Department at the University of Alberta is enough to send him into action. We ask him to calculate the point on the horizon where the sun first appeared on St Barnabas' Day, 11 June, the summer solstice, at the time of the building of the Globe. Since the theatre was first put up in 1599 and then rebuilt in 1613–14 we settle on 1610 as a compromise date, and cite the latitude as 51° 31′. Over the phone Professor Hube responds with a figure and then, by request, puts it all down on paper:

I have recalculated the azimuth of the rising Sun for the summer solstice of the year 1610. Allowance has been made for precession (the 'wobble' in the Earth's axis of rotation and the consequent change in the position of the Sun relative to the celestial equator) and for atmospheric refraction.

The procedure is not exact for several reasons: There is no analytical expression which includes the rising angle of an object which is not on the celestial equator; there is uncertainty in the refraction since it is dependent on local environmental conditions; and there is uncertainty in the precessional constants over a period of three and one-half centuries. All these factors together should not produce an error in excess of approximately 0.2 degree.

Local variations in elevation and surface relief would be of greater significance than that in determining first appearance of the Sun.

Azimuth of the rising point of the *upper limb* of the Sun (i.e., first appearance of any part of the solar disc)

=48.7° E of N

Azimuth of the rising point of the *centre* of the Sun

=49.1° E of N

The figure given by Professor Hube for the first appearance of the sun comes to within half a degree of the Globe's orientation as we have deduced it from Hollar's drawing. Is this near-coincidence of any significance? We know of course that the second Globe was considered a summer theatre, and the King's Men played there generally only during the summer months, keeping their winter season at the Blackfriars.[35] Its plan was circular or polygonal. What Jacobean, what Elizabethan indeed, could have resisted incorporating the idea of the seasons and the sun-clock into so dial-like a building? The city he lived in, from Whitehall to the Tower, was decorated with sundials of every sort. The Works accounts report the expenses of fitting up the courts of Whitehall with mathematical and astrological diagrams, our Harleian directory lists the dial pillar surrounded by fishmongers' shops at the centre of the Strand, Edmund Gunter took the trouble to publish a detailed description of one of his Whitehall dials, so that readers might interpret its many and complicated faces.[36] Any student of Elizabethan and Jacobean literature knows how often the poets returned to the theme of the passing year, sometimes constructing their poems in imitation of its phases. Spenser's 'Epithalamion' is just such a piece, a verbal imitation of the midsummer solstice shaped into forms that correspond to the hours of the longest day and the shortest night.[37]

The more-or-less strict tradition of the orientation of churches in much of the Christian world is well known if only scantily documented. It is also well known that the medieval drama inherited some of this directional symbolism from the church. What we have not realized until now is the closeness with which even the Elizabethan and Jacobean theatres appear to have followed this tradition. In a discussion which followed the presentation of his paper on 'Mediaeval Land Surveying' at the Royal Geographical Society, Dr D. J. Price reported some of the conclusions he had reached about the peculiarities of the orientation of English parish churches:

We have the measurements and I think we can show pretty definitely from these that the actual practice was neither to guess nor to make an approximate determination of the meridian by using the sun. On the day when they started building, a date chosen at random, they took as due East the point at which the sun rose; and I think they did this with tolerable accuracy. That is the only hypothesis that will account for the extraordinary results, namely, that churches may be orientated about 45° off the meridian and there is a great preponderance of churches to the north of east rather than south of east. The statistical analysis agrees very nicely with the idea that for the particular longitude [*sic*] and the particular time of year they took the point of sunrise as due east – an ancient method, one theoretically unsound but easy to use.[38]

If there was a tradition of orienting churches on the sunrise interpreted as due east, Peter Street and his kind can hardly have been a part of it. They knew perfectly well where the high east stood; like Casca on the Ides of March they could tell by the time of year where the sun would rise:

Here, as I point my sword, the sun arises,
Which is a great way growing on the south,
Weighing the youthful season of the year.
Some two months hence, up higher toward the north
He first presents his fire; and the high east
Stands as the Capitol, directly here.   (*Julius Caesar*, II, i, 106–11)

Shakespeare wrote those lines at about the time when Peter Street was preoccupied with dismantling the Theater and setting it up again across the river, and it seems likely that the orientation of the first Globe was the source of that of the second. Just as the two playhouses shared the same ground plan and foundations, so they shared the same orientation, the orientation on the azimuth of the midsummer sunrise. This must therefore have been established by Peter Street, possibly as a new contribution to theatre design but more likely – in view of the ubiquity of the northeasterly orientation noted by Hotson among all the known Elizabethan and Jacobean theatres[39] – as a continuation of a tradition established by the Theater in 1576.

When Peter Street set out the foundations of the first Globe in 1599 he could hardly have taken an accurate fix on the sunrise from his position down on the marshy ground at Bankside. The northeastern horizon was obscured by a myriad of buildings across the river, with the tall spire of St Lawrence Poultney and the tower of St Peter's Cornhill just to the left of the crucial line of sight, and the thronging commercial district of Gracechurch Street just to the right. Rather he would have used the old church tradition in a more sophisticated way, looking up the exact azimuth of the midsummer sunrise in an almanack, or consulting a mathematician, or even one of the ubiquitous dials, for the information he wanted. Having found it he would lay out its direction with a line on the ground, aided by a compass, and this axis would become the point of departure for the initial three-rod square which was the basis of his design.

It is difficult to say whether these conclusions about the orientation of the Globe should be dignified with the name of an actual discovery. To be quite sure that the theatre faced the exact point of the sunrise we should have to have exact information about a number of things: did Peter Street or his advisers think of the sunrise as being the moment when the sun's rim first broke the horizon, or when its circle was bisected by the horizon, or when it cleared the horizon altogether? The azimuth of the sunrise differs for each of these. Again, while Hollar's sketch is remarkably accurate, it cannot be expected to offer us information on this subject within limits as narrow as (say) 1.0° either way. The measurement depends on our extending the line of the band on the theatre's superstructure to meet the horizon line, and since the line marking the band is not exactly straight we can only make an estimate. In short, the drawing cannot by any means establish that the Globe was aligned exactly on the azimuth of the midsummer sunrise *and no other*, and in the absence of other confirming evidence only such an exact coincidence could possibly suffice. Nevertheless there is no doubt that Hollar does show that the Globe faced roughly the point of sunrise at the solstice. If by some wonderful quirk of history its shell had survived the depredations of native property developers and foreign bombs and stood today on the southern side of Park Street, we should still be able to observe only that it faced the midsummer sun like Stonehenge, and not tell for sure why it did so or even whether it was positively meant to do so. If history were kinder still and permitted us to enter that goodly frame, to climb onto the promontory of its stage and look upwards at the canopy over it whose majestical roof was fretted with golden fire, then perhaps we could find a clue to the meaning of the building's orientation among the heavenly bodies and the signs of the zodiac painted there. But Clio is a tight-fisted muse, and a tantalizing one. She leaves us, in Hollar's perspective study, just enough information to make possible the assertion that the Globe did more-or-less accurately face the midsummer sunrise; she denies – or she has done so far – the evidence that would make certain the significance of that fact.

But it would be a pity to let her get away with it, and not to snatch at least a hypothesis from the muse's grasp. Here certainly is a theatre designed according to a system which incorporates the unmeasurable quantity of the ratio between the square and its contingent circles, a mystery which fascinated artists and scientists alike in the Renaissance, and which through Vitruvian theory was seen to link the human body to the ideal proportions of the cosmos. This theatre moreover was apparently aligned towards the midsummer sunrise; along the azimuth of the solstice it faced the cosmic centre, just as within its round it contained the proportions which went to make up that other centre of its deepest concern, man himself. Here surely is the true English Theatre of the World.

Appendix A. *Speculations*

Thus far in this book I have tried to offer the reader as little speculation and as much established fact as possible. Because it is a demonstrable fact that Norden, Visscher and Hollar used exact surveys in their panoramic views of London it is possible to discover not only the nature of Hollar's study of Southwark but also the limits of its precision. Accordingly we now know the size of the second Globe to within a very few feet, and have found that it was established by means of a three-rod line. The fact of the *ad quadratum* proportion is established by Hollar's drawing. In a subject where, as Glynne Wickham once remarked,[1] there is 90% speculation to 10% fact we have managed to redress the balance a little. Nevertheless there is no denying the pleasure of speculation, and in this appendix I propose to use the new facts introduced here as the groundwork for some new guesses and fancies about this most alluring of all English theatres.

First to the hut which appears to fill practically one-half of the courtyard's opening to the sky. In Walter Hodges' plan derived from the sketch [Plate 32] the front of this great superstructure almost, but not quite, reaches to the halfway point across the yard. When he comes to interpret this fact in his own reconstruction of the plan, Mr Hodges quite understandably regularizes it, bringing the front of the hut forward to coincide with the diameter of the theatre.[2] Although there is no specific evidence to support this proportioning in this particular case, there is a good deal to show that Elizabethan and Jacobean theatre builders thought of the mid-point of their designs as worthy of some architectural distinction. In the Fortune, according to the contract, the stage was to 'extende to the middle of the yarde'; Inigo Jones, in his conversion of the Cockpit-in-Court at Whitehall into a theatre in 1629 [Plate 36], set the stage front close to the centre of the building (though not quite on it, as we have seen). In the designs probably made for the Cockpit in Drury Lane, erected in 1616, he set it exactly so.[3] It may be that Walter Hodges is right to assume that in the second Globe both the stage and the covering hut extended to the mid-point of the yard, though we can hardly take the matter as proven yet.

There are several things worth noticing about this hut. First there is its great size. Though we cannot perhaps quite see the point where its front engages the frame to our right as we look at the sketch, it certainly looks set to do so. At its widest it must therefore be some 69 ft across, the measure of the diameter of the yard. Then there is its curious double-gabled structure, interpreted by Hodges as a complex roof designed on the hammerbeam principle, open below towards the stage, which is therefore lit by the great lantern nestled in the gulley between the two ridges.[4] This is a fine imaginative theory, and it goes far to explain the presence of that lantern, but it belongs in this appendix of speculations rather than in the previous chapters

158

of fact. It is upheld by persuasive arguments but by no particular evidence. It supposes that there were no posts supporting the superstructure, but in fact we simply do not know whether there were posts or not at the second Globe. Neither do we know for sure whether the superstructure had a floor – and consequently also a ceiling – over the stage. All of that lies in the realm of fancy: what we do know is that Hollar marked a horizontal band across the front of the hut on a level with the ridge of the roof of the frame. The geometry of this arrangement requires that the band must answer to the chord formed by the back of the hut across the ridge behind it, and it therefore offers a clue not merely to the structure of the hut itself but, as we shall see, to the structure of the frame as well.

I shall hardly need to remind the more sceptical of my readers that the sketch we are dealing with shows the Globe as 22.5 mm across overall, hardly bigger than a postage stamp of the modest old-fashioned sort. In the measurement of the width and plan of the theatre the smallness of the image is of no great consequence because Hollar's hand and eye were demonstrably capable of the necessary exactness. But the structural details of the building are another matter. It would, for example, be unwise to pursue the idea of perspective anamorphosis beyond its implications for the extent of the frame and its yard. I have argued that Hollar conveyed the measures of the view to his paper by means of a topographical glass and subsequent tracing. This method would state the intervals between objects and outlines with the correctness we have discovered them to possess. It could hardly be expected to state such matters as the exact conic section of the ridge of the Globe as seen under the conditions of Hollar's linear perspective. It is most unlikely therefore that he would draw the round of the theatre in its 'correct' anamorphic distortion: he would simply do a small-scale foreshortened circle within the limits given by his general outline and leave it at that. Consequently although Walter Hodges' plan derived from the perspective is faulty in not allowing for the scale distortion of anamorphosis, it is right in every other respect, and a sound basis for enquiry about such matters as the structure of the hut.

In the plan [Plate 32] the back of the hut forms a chord across the ridge of the frame roof which subtends an angle of 77.5° at the centre. In a theatre designed *ad quadratum* within a 99 ft circle, post-centre to centre, the diameter of the ridge would be 84 ft 6 in. and the chord at the rear of the hut – and consequently also the band at the front – would be a little under 53 ft ($2.\sin 38.75 \times 42.25 = 52.89$ ft) if it were to subtend the desired angle of 77.5° at the centre of the yard. With the help of the techniques developed in the previous chapters we are now in a position to make at least an approximate measurement of this dimension as Hollar actually shows it in his drawing without the intermediary of Hodges' excellent but deduced plan.

In chapter 7 we calculated that the façade of the Globe's superstructure lay on a bearing some 42° west of north, and we can use this information to determine the length of the horizontal member which runs across it, employing the same method as that which enabled us to calculate the distances along the north bank and the width of Winchester House. On the drawing the band measures 6.5 mm; its bearing as we have seen is 42° west of north; and its right side is on a bearing from St Saviour's some 14.9° south of the central ray of the composition.

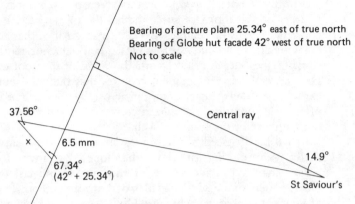

Bearing of picture plane 25.34° east of true north
Bearing of Globe hut facade 42° west of true north
Not to scale

37.56°

Central ray

x

6.5 mm

14.9°

67.34°
(42° + 25.34°)

St Saviour's

x=width of Globe facade decorative band

The calculation of the length of the hut band using this information works out at 52.05 ft, not quite identical with the theoretical figure of 52.89 ft arrived at above, but close enough to encourage further investigation:

$$\frac{\sin 75.1}{x} = \frac{\sin 37.56}{6.5} \qquad x = 10.30 \,\text{mm}$$

Width of band in feet:

$$1144 \times \frac{10.30}{309} \times 2 . \tan 34.3° = 52.05 \,\text{ft}$$

It is generally, though not quite universally, agreed that the Globe was a polygonal rather than a strictly circular building. Hollar shows it as round but in that he is doubtless regularizing a many-sided polygon, the form the building would almost certainly have to have taken were it made of timber. The outer walls of the Globe might perhaps have been circular, especially if they were made of stone or brick: it seems that the Cockpit playhouse in Drury Lane had a semi-circular brick auditorium inherited from the full-circle cockpit building out of which it was converted in 1616.[5] A few years earlier James I had constructed a round brick cockpit at Royston,[6] and in 1621 when the first Fortune had burned down it may have been replaced by a large round brick building.[7] It is not impossible that the second Globe had a round brick outer wall too, but the Hope certainly did not, as we know from its builder's contract, and Hollar uses the same visual convention to present both playhouses. The Earl Marshal's survey of the second Globe made in 1634 said that it was built of timber, with no mention of brick.[8] Furthermore it is most unlikely that a roof ridge would be built circular as Hollar shows it; the circular cockpits had conical roofs or domes with no ridges,[9] and the shape of the roof at the second Fortune is not known. A curved ridge is, as Walter Hodges has observed, a most improbable structure,[10] yet that is how it appears to be in Hollar's sketch. Plainly the artist has reduced a polygon to a circle in this case, and it is likely that he has done the same for the outer wall of the Globe. He would not have done so if the polygon had been of only a few sides – a hexagon, or even an octagon. He clearly indicates, for example, the faces of the Globe's octagonal lantern in the *Long View*. The fact that he fails to distinguish facets in the frame argues that they were many, not few. But how many? It is here that the new information we have about the chord fashioned by the back of the hut may prove critically useful.

It is a reasonable assumption – and I remind the reader that this is an appendix of speculation rather than of fact – that the front of the hut lay on the diameter of the theatre and that it engaged the frame at either end at a point where it was supported by principal posts. It might perhaps have engaged the frame at some other point between posts, but that is unlikely since then it would convey the weight of the hut onto horizontal rather than vertical members. What I have said about the support of the front of the hut goes equally for its back: that too ought surely to engage the frame at the juncture between bays rather than half-way along them. The ridge poles could certainly not take the weight by themselves, and if the hut engaged the ridge at mid-bay it would have to be borne up by extra posts, an unnecessary and rather *ad hoc* addition to the clutter backstage. If both the front and the back of the hut engaged the frame at satisfactory points it follows that there are certain strict restraints on the possible number of sides to the polygon. The chord of the back of the hut in the plan derived from Hollar's drawing subtends an angle in the order of 77.5° at the centre of the theatre. In order to gain direct support from the main elements of the frame the rear of the hut must chord a whole number of bays, and not cover any fraction of a bay. The angle of approximately 77.5° therefore immediately excludes some otherwise attractive polygons: the hexagon, the octagon, and figures of ten or twelve sides. The twelve-sided figure, for example, could subtend only angles that were multiples of 30°, and none comes close to 77.5°. The decagon might provide a chord of two bays at 72°, but that is not really close enough. Three bays of a fourteener would subtend 77.14° at the centre; the angle is very good but the unusualness of the polygon is not. Fifteen sides yield their closest chord at 72°; sixteen yield 67.5° or 90°; seventeen an unsatisfactory 84.71°; eighteen a much more attractive 80°. Nineteen sides provide a possible chord of 75.79°, fairly close; twenty give 72° again, twenty-one far off at 85.71°; twenty-two 81.82°; twenty-three the useful 78.26°, but with a most unlikely configuration; and twenty-four a possible 75° subtended by five bays. Of all these possibilities only one offers a close enough approximation to the 77.5° angle subtended in the plan together with a polygonal configuration that inspires confidence as something likely to be designed by an Elizabethan or Jacobean practitioner, and that of course is the last.

A twenty-four-sided polygon meets many more of our requirements than the one raised in the previous paragraph. It is, unlike some of the others, a regular figure obtained by the subdivision of a circle in ways that were often described in handbooks of constructive geometry, [11] and as we shall see it would have had a special appeal to a builder seeking to lay out its proportions on the ground with the help of a line. It yields, as Richard Hosley has shown, [12] bays of a size that would not demand impossibly large intervals to be spanned by special timbers or doubled up with intermediate posts: at the outer wall the distance between principal posts would be 12.92 ft centre-to-centre; the interval between the centres of the posts around the yard would be 9.14 ft. In addition, twenty-four is apparently the number of bays implied by de Witt in his drawing of the Swan,[13] a theatre which, as we have seen, must have been the same size as both the Globes. And finally it is a sufficient number of facets to justify Hollar's decision to represent the Globe as round.

Unfortunately this conclusion does not end the matter, for if the chord implied by Hollar at the rear of the hut is to be accommodated in the twenty-four-sided figure it must span five bays, thus subtending its angle of 75° at the centre. If it spans five bays one of them must cut directly across the axis of the theatre, since five is an odd number. There must be one central bay and two more to each side, all chorded by the back of the hut. It follows that the diameter of the theatre parallel to this chord cannot, in a twenty-four-sided figure, run through the principal posts, but most cross the frame at mid-bay on either side. In other words, we cannot have our cake and eat it too. If the back of the hut is supported by main elements in the frame, the front, if it is to be a diameter, cannot engage the frame in a similarly satisfactory way. The conclusion must be either that the polygon did not have twenty-four sides or that the front of the hut did not lie on the diameter. Of these the latter is the more likely, since Hollar's study shows the front of the hut to be set back from the diameter by a couple of feet or so. It is true that in the etching which he made in Antwerp he brought the hut well forward of the diameter, but the etching is hardly to be trusted over the drawing. The reconstruction I propose here would set the face of the hut some three feet short of the diameter, or half a bay measured at the perimeter of the yard and allowing for the likelihood that the hut would extend some eighteen inches beyond the centres of the principal posts that took its weight to either side. When Inigo Jones converted the Cockpit-in-Court for the use of the King's Men and others at Whitehall he had no hut to be concerned with, but he set the front of the stage several inches back from the centre of the building [Plate 36 II]. His reason for doing so was probably to make as much space as possible available for the audience, given the other constraints on the design provided by the extant features of the building he was adapting; much the same appears to have been true of the second Globe, if we assume the frame itself to have been a traditional structure.

In the Globe, assuming it to be the 100 ft wide theatre of *ad quadratum* proportions described in these pages, a hut chording five bays of a total of twenty-four would measure 51.44 ft across its back and, so the logic of its design requires, across the ridge-level band that marks its front. This figure is fairly close – I think as close as our methods will allow – to the dimension calculated direct from Hollar's drawing, 52.05 ft. The difference is 1.19%, not by any means an unacceptable figure for so small a feature measured at an oblique angle. The front of the hut of the Globe, then, expressed as part of its structure or decoration a band some 51 ft 6 in. wide. The hut roof itself evidently reached all the way to the eaves of the frame, but here at its centre was a feature of design sufficiently accented for Hollar to recognize it at a range of nearly a quarter of a mile from his vantage point at St Saviour's. We cannot know, on the present evidence, just what it was; but what it marked is obvious enough. It represented that part of the hut which actually covered the stage. In architectural terms, it answered to the extent of the stage as that was set out below. Earlier theatres than the second Globe had evidently provided covers to their stages which related to them as a roof relates to a house, made just a little larger than the area to be protected. De Witt's sketch of the Swan shows the width of the cover thus, though the front part of the stage is left open to the weather.[14] The Fortune contract is specific about the relation between the stage and its roof: the 'coveringe' is to be tiled and adequately guttered to keep rainwater from the area below.[15] At the second Globe, whatever was true of the first, the hut evidently covered almost the whole of one half of the yard, but the horizontal band on its face was like a memory of the extent of earlier covers. It indicated the limits of the earlier kind of cover and in doing so it echoed the dimensions of the stage beneath. At about 51 ft 6 in. its width was sufficient to answer the 49 ft 6 in. of the stage and suggest the extra bit required of a roof. Functionally, of course, the whole cover was much extended; visually its centre part retained something of its old relation to the stage.

If the back of the hut chords five bays of the twenty-four-sided figure, the stage itself must chord six, bearing a simple *ad quadratum* relation to the circle of the yard. But because the stage must be parallel to the hut it cannot engage the frame in such a way that its corners meet principal posts on either side. It must touch the frame at mid-bay, but because there are no loads or stresses to be transferred this is a matter of no structural consequence. It may be that the rhythm of bays behind the stage, $\frac{1}{2}$–1–1–centre–1–1–$\frac{1}{2}$, had some influence on the number and disposition of stage entrances, but that is a matter which awaits further evidence from other sources. For the moment we have only to note that the twenty-four-sided figure designed *ad quadratum* on a three-rod measure could be systematically checked in the course of construction by the repeated deployment of that same three-rod line. Because the yard is of such a size that it will contain a 49 ft 6 in. square, the intervals between its principal posts could be measured by running the line from any one of them in a chord across the arena to the sixth post further round. Any interval of six posts will measure three rods, centre-to-centre. Similarly the posts in the outer wall are disposed at three-rod intervals every four bays, so that the line can be used to check the trueness of every fourth post. This is a particular characteristic of the twenty-four-sided figure, not found in any other polygon with a smaller number of sides, a fact which adds its mite to the accumulation of evidence in favour of this plan. In setting out the Globe Peter Street could use the single measure of the line to establish and check the width of the stage, the radius of the round, the position of every sixth post in the yard and of every fourth post in the outer wall of the frame. Moreover, once the radius of the arena had been established by *ad quadratum* means it could be marked on a line and applied as a measure to check the intervals between every fourth post around the yard and between any yard post and the exterior posts located three bays away in either direction. A twenty-four-sided configuration thus offered a useful chance of simplifying the task of setting out and constructing the main timberwork of the theatre. It cannot have been an easy undertaking to build such large and complex structures as these many-sided frames, but the work would have been made much less daunting by such rational economy of planning.

Yet another indication that the frame was made of twenty-four bays is given by the row of windows which Hollar shows, presumably at middle-gallery level. In the drawing [Plate 2] there are small marks showing their positions all across the visible part of the frame, though they are omitted at the extremities to either side because there they would appear so close together as to cause a jumble. The etching [Plate 1] shows windows regularly spaced across the part of the frame seen to the left of the closer staircase only: the regularity here is clearly a mistake, for it makes no allowance for the increasingly tangential line of sight to the building as the eye moves towards its leftward limit. The Evelyn/Pepys panorama [Plates 4 and 5] gives only the slightest indication of the row of windows all across the theatre, uninterrupted by any staircase. Of these three depictions the Yale study is as always the most reliable, but its placing of the staircase turret has caused some disquiet. Richard Hosley, who was the first to raise this question of the spacing of the windows and the stairs, has attempted to show how their positions as indicated in the Yale study are consistent with a twenty-four-sided plan. Like Walter Hodges he assumes that the staircases must have been attached to the frame at mid-bay, though neither author says why this should be so.[16] Certainly it looks neat in plan and would cause no complications about the introduction of doorways and access passages from the landings onto the various galleries. This consideration leads both scholars to prefer the Antwerp etching over the Southwark drawing in this particular and isolated matter of the placement of the stair turrets. The etching shows them neatly and symmetrically arranged at what appears to be a simple quarter-circle apart, so that the angle they subtend at the centre of the plan is 90°. The regularity of this pattern is most appealing, the more so because it happens to fit a mid-bay spacing for both Hodges' sixteen-sided and Hosley's twenty-four-sided frame. But the stubborn fact remains that the drawing, which on general principles should always be preferred to the etching unless there are compelling reasons to the contrary, presents the stair turrets as more widely spaced, subtending an angle of about 100° at the centre. It is true that the drawing gives a strange and evidently unsatisfactory reading of the further staircase, its perspective thoroughly muddled, but it is not difficult to imagine how such confusion could have entered into Hollar's drawing as he inked over the pencil sketch derived from the topographical glass. The mistaken drawing here does not make reason compelling enough for us to prefer the etching to it.

Let us assume that the drawing and not the etching has the nearer staircase in its correct place. If the Globe's plan was a twenty-four-sided polygon with its main axis running through the centres of bays, as described in the previous pages, the turret will have been located not at the centre of any bay, but spanning two of them, covering just half of one and a smaller part of the other. Starting from the 'front' of the theatre and working clockwise we find bay divisions at 7.5°, 22.5°, 37.5°, 52.5° and so on. The stair turret occurs between 45° and 56°, so that it would bear up against one of the main bay-division structures, with its substantial vertical posts. By this means it would be strengthened, but there would be plenty of room for landings and entrances opening into the part of the frame that lay between 45° and 52.5° (a total of just under 6 ft 6 in., though the space available for the entrances would be rather less; say 4 ft).[17]

Having decided to move the staircase somewhat to the right in order to
bring it to mid-bay, Professor Hosley encounters some difficulty when he
tries to make Hollar's line of windows as shown in the sketch coincide with
the twenty-four-sided plan. He has to relocate these as well as the stairs, with
the result that his final interpretation agrees with neither the Yale study nor
the *Long View*. But if the stairs are left where Hollar shows them in the
drawing the windows distribute themselves neatly into pairs for most of the
visible faces of the polygonal frame. Reading leftwards from the staircase we
have the greater part of the face between 56° and 67.5°: this has two windows.
So do the ensuing bays between 67.5° and 82.5°, 82.5° and 97.5°, and 97.5°
and 112.5°. The next bay, between 112.5° and 127.5°, is viewed obliquely and
only one window is recorded for it; for the last visible bay, viewed almost
tangentially, no window is recorded at all. To the right of the staircase the
story is much the same: the half of the first bay not actually covered by the
stairs has room enough for only one window; then three succeeding bays
have two windows each and the last two bays at the far right have nothing
specific recorded. Of course, in the absence of any actual marks showing the
bay divisions in the drawing these windows are not placed with absolute
correctness, as will be seen from Plate 41, based on Hollar's study but

41.   The Globe with twenty-four sides. Diagram based on Hollar's 'West part o[f] Southwarke'.

showing the bay divisions of a twenty-four-sided polygon aligned as proposed in this appendix.

I have said that the geometry of the hut or superstructure placed within this frame implies a stage beneath it 49 ft 6 in., or three rods, wide, wider than has been proposed before by scholars who have reviewed the available evidence. Most retain something close to the figure of 43 ft given by the Fortune contract, but their argument is *faute de mieux*, and consorts ill with the general agreement that the other dimensions of the plan of the Fortune are far from standard. The notion that Elizabethan and Jacobean playing conditions would have required a more-or-less standardized stage size or shape is a most attractive one, but there is no escaping the fact that the enclosed private theatres at the Blackfriars and the Cockpit in Drury Lane could not offer as much space even as the Fortune. The whole of the Blackfriars was erected in a room only 46 ft across, and the stage at the Cockpit was about 23 ft wide by 15 ft deep.[18] When Inigo Jones converted the Cockpit-in-Court at Whitehall into a theatre for the professional players' royal performances he made the stage 34 ft wide and 16 ft 6 in. deep at its deepest [Plate 36]. Yet plays had often been acted in this building in the decades before its conversion, although the cockfight table itself was only 12 ft wide and was surrounded by seats, a halpace and a gallery, as we know from the Works accounts of its extensive refitting in 1581–2.[19] There could hardly have been room for a large acting area. Square stages were common: those set up in the royal halls for plays and masques ranged from 40ft square for the *Masque of Blackness* (1605) to 14 ft square 'for the plaiers to plaie on' at Richmond in 1588–9.[20] In short, our evidence hardly points to the existence of a standard-sized stage, let alone one 43 ft across and 27 ft 6 in. deep as at the Fortune. A platform or 'Standinge' 43 ft square was set up in the crossing of Westminster Abbey for the Coronation of James I in 1603, but this was made to fit the existing piers of the building, and its dimensions were derived from those of the medieval architecture of the abbey itself.[21]

The evidence about the size of the stage in the famous drawing of the interior of the Swan (c. 1596) is unfortunately ambiguous. Richard Hosley has suggested that we are offered a view of exactly one-half of the frame of the theatre, with four bays visible to the left of the tiring house and three to the right.[22] Counting the bays whose structure is masked by the tiring house front, Hosley concludes that there are twelve in all in the half of the theatre visible to us, for a total of twenty-four for the whole frame. The tiring house is thus judged to mask five bays, and the width of the stage must be defined by the length of a five-bay chord measured between post-centres at the inner or courtyard side of the frame: 42.61 ft in a standard 70 ft yard as described in these pages. This is temptingly close to the Fortune contract's dimension, but de Witt's drawing – or rather Aernout Van Buchell's copy of it, which is all that history has vouchsafed us – is regrettably naive and imprecise. Hosley's method of dealing with it generally has the inestimable advantage of counting the units of various sorts that it shows – pillars, posts, bays, etc. – rather than trying to measure from it direct, but the argument that the tiring house masks five bays, though persuasive enough, is of course just such an argument from measure. It is a pity, therefore, that the naivety of the drawing is such that it shows the front of the stage taking up much more than five-bays'-worth (42.61/69.00) of the diameter of the yard. For all the soundness of Hosley's method there is no escaping the fact that the Swan drawing's depiction of the width of the stage is ambiguous probably beyond recall, and its evidence correspondingly uncertain.

The arguments in support of the larger 49 ft 6 in. width of the Globe's stage therefore deserve to be brought together once more. The first derives from Peter Street's procedures at the Fortune, where he established the width of the stage by reduction *ad triangulum* from an initial square 49 ft 6 in across. His whole design method there began from the basis of this square, moving inwards first to the size of the stage and then outwards to the dimensions of the frame. The frame, that is, was proportioned after the stage, and the stage was a reduction from a three-rod square. Street learned, or at least developed, his notions of theatre design while at work on dismantling the Theater and building the Globe, and it seems likely that these also derived the proportions of the frame from those of the stage, though because they were larger than the Fortune there was no need for the initial *ad triangulum* reduction. The size and the design method of the frame therefore combine to imply a stage within it measuring three rods across.

The second argument for such a width lies in the 51 ft 6 in. length of the architectural feature which Hollar shows on the face of the superstructure covering the general area of the stage; the ordinary felicities of architectural order suggest that this horizontal member answered to the width of the stage beneath. And finally, if it should be thought that 49 ft 6 in. is rather too wide an area for the acting of Elizabethan plays, it might be as well to remember that the theatres, including the Theater, the Swan, the Globe and the Hope, were often used for fencing prizes, an activity that normally required a good deal of room.[23] In 1614, for example, when King Christian of Denmark swept unannounced into the English Court, an outdoor playhouse was hurriedly set up at Whitehall before the king's window at the Banqueting House. There was a halpace for the two kings beneath the window, and there were degrees for other spectators. A standing before the king's window was made for the Master of the Bears at two separate baitings, and for Saturday 30 July a stage was erected in the same place for the fencers. The Works accounted for 'framing and setting vp a great Stage xl^{ti} fo: square vpon trestles iij fo:d[1] from the ground and railed about on the top for the ffencers to play their prizes on.'[24] The area of a platform 40 ft square is of course much greater than that of the stage which appears to have been built at the Globe, whose depth would have been no more than half its three-rod width. If the fencers needed so much room to exhibit their feats of arms it seems likely that the public stages on which they so often performed were normally larger than the Fortune's.

Appendix B. The theatre at Christ Church: British Library Additional MS 15505, fol.21: a transcript of the annotations

[Column above the left of the theatre plan]
The scale is an ynch deuided into 10 parts.

A. the entry into the Hall.

B. easy stayrs to mounte by, in midl wherof which is voyde a lanterne may bee hanged, which will light al the stayrcase.

C. the entrys on eyther side the skreene.

D. a kinde of lanterne or light house, in the hollow places wherof lamps may bee placed to light the vaute E. F.

α. the sides closed that peopl runn not vnder the scaffolde. needles to bee made in the vpper scaffold.

E. is the entry into the passage on the grounde noted with pricks from E to F. through the seats. it must bee vaulted in prospectiue, at the entry E 13 foote high. at F. 7.

[Column above the right of the theatre plan]

F. the ende ~~wher~~[sic] of the vault, ouer which the seconde ranke of seats are heer drawne

G. a gallery two foote & a $\frac{1}{2}$ broade to pass betweene the seats. which must bee raysed ouer the passage ∞ 8^y to pass rounde about, leauing 7 foote at least vnder.

H. from F. to H. you pass in an vncouered gallery because if the seats came ouer it would bee to lowe.

I. the piazza from the scene, to K. the center, 12 foote. or rather 14. or 15.

K. the Isl for the kinge, a foote eleuated aboue the grounde, mounted vnto by 3 degrees 1.2.3. & 4 ynches high a peece. it is vnaequaly deuided to aunswer the angls of the seats.

L. places for the L^{ds} of the Counseyle. wherof L.L. is somewhat higher then the other L.

M. the first stepp two foote & a $\frac{1}{2}$ high. or rather 3^f.

N. stepps wherby to mounte into the seats. which are signified by the hached Lines.

[Right side of sheet, turned through 90°]
[Left column, above section]
The length of the whole Theater.

1. The hall is a 115 foote longe & 40 broade, which I distribut into the parts following.

2. the piazza is 12 foote from the scene to the Center K. it wer better to bee 14 foote, /or 15\ that the kinge may sit so much further from the scene. cutting of so much from the ende of the hall.

3. the Isl is 8 foote semidiameter

4   the passage about it conteineth four $^{f:}$
5   the seuen first seats being two foote broade [*sic*] distant frō the insid to the outside. make 14 foote.
6. the passage F. is 2^f & a $\frac{1}{2}$.
7   the 13 seconde rank of seats, distant only 18 ynches frō inside of the /one\ seat to the ou/t\ side of the next conteyne $19^{f\frac{1}{2}}$.
8. from thoose seats the slope to the skreene is 10f.
9   behinde the skreene 12 foote.
    So the summe of al the length is. 82^f. & ther remaineth for the scene 33^f.
    From C. to H. is 62 foote $\frac{1}{2}$. uidelicet. the Isl $8^{f\frac{1}{2}}$ [*sic*]/8^f.\ the passage 4^f· the /7\ seats 14^f the gallery $2\frac{1}{2}$. the second seats $19\frac{1}{2}$. wherto joyne the piazza 12f, & it amounts to $74^{f\frac{1}{2}}$.

The heigth of the Theater

1. ~~The kings Isl a foote high~~ [*sic*]
2   the first ~~sta~~ [*sic*] seat behind it [*sic*]/the Isle\ $2^f\frac{1}{2}$. or rather 3^f. high. to looke ouer the Isle.
3   the ~~first seuen~~ [*sic*] seats euery one exceeding ech other 8 ynches in heigth. so that the first 7 seats rayse 6 foot & a $\frac{1}{2}$ in heigth. uidelicet the first seat 2^f & $\frac{1}{2}$. the other six. 4^f.
4. the second rank of seats being 13 in number, after the same rate of 8^{yn}, rise 8^f· 8^y· so that the heigth from the grounde to H [*sic*] the seat vnder H is 15^f· 2 ynches. or if half a foote be added to the first seate, then they are 15^f· 8 ^{y}· high.

[Below the section of the theatre]
A. the heigth of next part of the scene; which for the prospectiue of the spectators cannot bee less then 4 foote high. as appears by the prickt line N.
B   the piazza 12 foote broade. rather 14. or 15. 15 as I thinke.
~~C~~ [*sic*] the passage about the Isle & the Isl it self are heer omitted.
C   a rayle to keep peopl from the seats.
D   the seats for Ladys & the kings servants; the seats D are 8 ynches broade. they are two foote distante ech from other. so that 8 ynches therof serues for the seate, & the other 16 ynches for the legs & knes.
E   are the footesteps 2 foote vnder the seats D. or G. four ynches broade.
F. is a gallery to walk betweene the seats. with rayles on eyther side.
G. 13 other seats 18 ynches a sunder. wherof the seat conteyns 6 ynches.
H   a rayle at the back of the seats.
J. a slopp scaffold for peopl to stande on. which should haue barrs to keepe them from ouerpressing one another.
K. a rayle ouer the skreene.
L. the roome behinde the skreene wher scaffolds may be made to see conveniently.
N. the visual line passing from A. to H. shewing that all may see at ease.

[Above, to the right of the section]
The first seuen seats will conteyne 200 persons to sitt at ease.
The seconde 13 seats, will conteyne 350.

In al 550. to sitt on seats
The place behinde them. ~~130~~-[*sic*] will hold 130.
The place behinde the skreene as many.
The summe of al 810. without pressing.

[Note to M on the section of the theatre]
the wall at the end of the Hall behind the skreene.

[Lower down]
In anny case remember that a slight Portico bee made eyther at H. or K. of hoopes & firrpoales. wherupon many lights or lamps of seueral coulers may be placed. This portico giues a great grace to all the Theater, & without it, the Architectur is false If scaffolds bee built upon L. then it must stande on K. if ther bee none, then it must bee reysed on H.

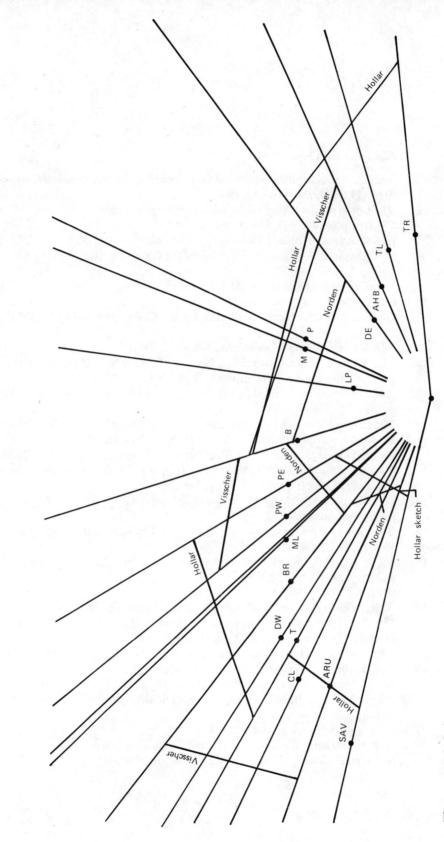

The panoramic 'takes'

A composite diagram showing the 'takes' in the panoramas of Norden, Visscher and Hollar, together with Hollar's sketch of west Southwark. Lines of sight from St Saviour's are drawn through landmarks located on a six-inch Ordnance Survey map (here reduced); the lines of intersection represent the intervals on the panoramas at a common reduced scale.

Notes

Notes to chapter 1 (pp. 1–31)

1. John Taylor's comment is cited in G. E. Bentley, *The Jacobean and Caroline Stage* (Oxford, 1941–68), VI, 183.
2. *The Letters of John Chamberlain*, edited by Norman Egbert McClure (Philadelphia, 1939), I, 544.
3. Iolo Williams, 'Hollar, a Discovery,' *The Connoisseur* 92 (1933), pp. 318–21.
4. I. A. Shapiro, 'An Original Drawing of the Globe Theatre,' *Shakespeare Survey 2* (1949), pp. 21–3.
5. Yale Center for British Art, B1977. 14. 5548.
6. ibid., 4664.
7. Graham Parry, 'A New View of Bankside,' *Shakespeare Survey 31* (1978), pp. 139–40.
8. John Rylands Library English MSS 883, fol. 24^b.
9. Magdalene College, Cambridge, Pepysian Library MSS 2972, fol. 31^b.
10. British Museum Print Room 1882 – 8 – 12 489.
11. *Aubrey's Brief Lives*, edited by Oliver Lawson Dick (Harmondsworth, 1962), p. 317.
12. The first to suggest the identification was C. Walter Hodges, *The Globe Restored*, revised edition (New York, 1968), p. 109. He was followed by Richard Hosley, 'The Second Blackfriars Playhouse (1596),' in *The Revels History of Drama in English*, Volume III: *1576–1613*, edited by Clifford Leech and T. W. Craik (London, 1975), p. 198.
13. Leon Battista Alberti, *On Painting and on Sculpture*, translated by Cecil Grayson (London, 1972), pp. 67–9.
14. *The Literary Works of Leonardo da Vinci*, edited by Jean Paul Richter (London, 1970), I, 317, para. 523.
15. See Joan Gadol, *Leon Battista Alberti: Universal Man of the Early Renaissance* (Chicago, 1969), pp. 189–92.
16. (Rome, 1583), p. 96.
17. A. K. Wheelock, *Perspective, Optics and Delft Artists* (New York, 1977), p. 159. Samuel Marolois's *Perspectiva* was published in 1614; Hendrick Hondius's *Perspectivae* in 1622, the passage cited on p. 17.
18. John Bate, *The Mysteryes of Nature, and Art* (1634), Book III, p. 109.
19. [Jean Dubreuil,] *Perspective Practical* (1672), Sig. Hh ii^b.
20. British Library Additional MS 21111, fol. 15: '. . . he had a defect in one of his eyes, which was the left, so that he always held his hand before it when he wrought; he never had spectacles. . . .'
21. *Aubrey's Brief Lives*, edited by Dick, p. 241.
22. Arthur M. Hind, *Wenceslaus Hollar and his Views of London and Windsor in the Seventeenth Century* (London, 1922), Plate XIV.

Notes to chapter 2 (pp. 32—69)

1. Irene Scouloudi, 'Panoramic Views of London 1600–1666 with Some Later Adaptations: an Annotated List,' reproduced by the authority of the Library Committee of the Corporation of London (London, 1953), typescript.
2. Stephen Harrison, *Arches of Triumph* (1604), reproduced in *Ben Jonson*, edited by C. H. Herford and Percy and Evelyn Simpson (11 vols., Oxford, 1925–52), VII, facing p. 82.
3. Hind, *Wenceslaus Hollar and his Views of London*, Plates XXVI and XXVII.
4. See Ida Darlington and James Howgego, *Printed Maps of London circa 1553–1850* (London, 1964), pp. 8–10, and I. A. Shapiro, 'The Bankside Theatres: Early Engravings,' *Shakespeare Survey 1*(1948), pp. 25–37.
5. British Museum Print Room Crace I, 12 (10).
6. Hind, *Wenceslaus Hollar and his Views of London*, Plates XXVI and XXVII.
7. Darlington and Howgego, *Printed Maps of London*, pp. 10–19 and 54–5.
8. ibid., p. 15 and Plate 2, and Martin Holmes, *Moorfields in 1559* (London, 1968).
9. All this was pointed out by W. W. Braines, *The Site of the Globe Playhouse, Southwark*, revised edition (London, 1924), pp. 51–3. Braines worked before the discovery of the copper-plate maps indicated the source of the so-called 'Agas' woodcut. He saw the parallel – which looked to him like a direct debt – between Visscher and 'Agas', though he evidently did not know that the extant copies of the latter were not published until c. 1633. In any case he posited the existence of the copper-plate map years before its discovery (p. 48).
10. See Darlington and Howgego, *Printed Maps of London*, p. 53 and Shapiro, 'The Bankside Theatres,' pp. 28–9.
11. Shapiro, 'The Bankside Theatres,' p. 28, and Scouloudi, 'Panoramic Views of London.' pp. 19–22.
12. Shapiro, 'The Bankside Theatres,' pp. 25–37.
13. In *The Times*, 26 March 1954, pp. 7 and 14. The whole extent of the panorama is printed in A. M. Hind, *Engraving in England in the Sixteenth and Seventeenth Centuries: Part II, the Reign of James I* (Cambridge, 1955), Plates 52 and 53. Hotson's identification of the playhouse shown at the left of the view as the Curtain has been challenged by Sidney Fisher, who is almost certainly correct in believing it to be the Theater: *The Theatre, the Curtain and the Globe* (Montreal, 1964).
14. *A History of St Paul's Cathedral*, edited by W. R. Matthews and W. M. Atkins (London, 1964), p. 344.
15. P.R.O. MPF 23, transferred from SP 46/36/21.
16. British Library Harleian MS 6850, fols. 31–2.
17. P.R.O. E403/ 2899 B, p. 158.
18. *Vetusta Monumenta* (London, 1789), II, Plate XIV. See the reconstructed plan in H. M. Colvin, general editor, *The History of the King's Works, Volume III: 1485–1660 (Part 1)* (London, 1975), p. 197.
19. See Walter H. Godfrey, 'The Strand in the Seventeenth Century: the River Front,' London and Middlesex Archaeological Society *Transactions*, n.s. 4 (1918–22), p. 217.
20. Hind, *Wenceslaus Hollar and his Views of London*, Plates XLIX and XIV.

21. British Library Harleian MS 3910, fol. 36^b.

22. Henry A. Harben, *A Dictionary of London* (London, 1918), s.v.

23. John Stow, *A Survey of London*, edited by C. L. Kingsford (Oxford, 1908), I, 39–40.

24. See the plan, based on a survey by Wren, in Matthews and Atkins, editors, *A History of St Paul's Cathedral*, p. 344. Wren's scaled original is at All Soul's, Oxford and was published by Margaret Whinney, 'Some Church Designs of John Webb,' *Journal of the Warburg and Courtauld Institutes*, 6 (1943), 143.

25. Stow, *A Survey of London*, II, 11.

26. British Library Additional MS 5095, fols. 209^b and 210^b.

27. Historical Manuscripts Commission, 14th Report, *House of Lords 1692–93*, Appendix Part VI, pp. 323–5.

28. John Stow, *The Survey of London*, enlarged by John Strype (London, 1754), III, 218.

29. ibid., II, 190.

30. Henry Farley, *The Complaint of Paules* (London, 1616), p. 35.

31. Royal Commission on Historical Monuments (England), *An Inventory of the Historical Monuments in London, Volume IV: the City* (London, 1929), pp. 183–4.

32. London County Council, *Survey of London, Volume XII: the Parish of All Hallows Barking (Part 1)* (London, 1929), p. 45.

33. See Haiward and Gascoyne, 'Survey of the Liberties of the Tower,' cited in ibid., p. 55.

34. *The Diary of Samuel Pepys*, edited by Robert Latham and William Matthews, volume VII: *1666* (London, 1972), p. 276.

35. A point missed by John Hayes in his *Catalogue of the Oil Paintings in the London Museum* (London, 1970), writing of the anonymous painting of the *Great Fire of London, 1666*: '. . . the north-east turret of the White Tower is correctly represented as the one circular in shape (where Hollar has the north-west tower as rounded)' (p. 76).

36. Royal Commission on Historical Monuments (England), *An Inventory of the Historical Monuments in London, Volume IV: the City*, facing p. 198.

37. The left edge of the second sheet in the London Topographical Society's facsimile of Visscher's panorama crops 3 mm from the plate; I have corrected the measure between St Bride's and St Dunstan's from the original sheets in the Guildhall Library.

38. In the collection of Fritz Lugt. There is a photograph in the Print Room of the British Museum. The drawing shows London as seen from the west bank of the river at Westminster and does not resemble Visscher's panorama.

39. Shapiro, 'The Bankside Theatres,' pp. 27–8 and 30.

40. Braines, *The Site of the Globe Playhouse, Southwark*, passim

41. The map is printed in Irwin Smith, *Shakespeare's Globe Playhouse* (New York, 1956), Plate 16.

Notes to chapter 3 (pp. 70—83)

1. For the pinnacles and parapet see Nikolaus Pevsner, *London Except the Cities of London and Westminster*, Buildings of England (Harmondsworth, 1952), p. 394.

2. See, for example, Hind, *Wenceslaus Hollar and his Views of London*, Plate XXX.

3. Victoria County History, *Surrey* (London, 1912), IV, 152.

4. The present Chapter House of Southwark Cathedral is built on the site of the old St Thomas's church. See Pevsner, *London Except the Cities of London and Westminster*, pp. 404–5, and Royal Commission on Historical Monuments (England), *An Inventory of the Historical Monuments in London, Volume V: East London* (London, 1930), p.5.

5. Franz Sprinzels, *Hollar Handzeichnungen* (Leipzig, 1938), p. 108.

6. Williams, 'Hollar, a Discovery,' p. 321.

7. Christopher White, *English Landscapes 1630–1850: Drawings, Prints and Books from the Paul Mellon Collection* (New Haven, 1977), p. 4: 'The map of Thames Street and its surroundings, drawn in pencil on the verso, described by Sprinzels, is no longer visible.'

8. Reproduced by Oliver Millar, *The Age of Charles I: Painting in England 1620–1649* (London, 1972), pp. 46–7.

9. Williams, 'Hollar, a Discovery,' pp. 319–20.

10. The location of Winchester House is known precisely from the extant remains. See the Victoria County History, *Surrey*, IV, 147.

11. Braines, *The Site of the Globe Playhouse, Southwark*.

12. Smith, *Shakespeare's Globe Playhouse*, Plate 16.

Notes to chapter 4 (pp. 84–107)

1. Ordnance Survey Plan TQ 3280 SE.

2. See the plan in Victoria County History, *Surrey*, IV, 147.

3. Edited by Harold Osborne (Oxford, 1970), pp. 840–61.

4. See the table in Ll. Rodwell Jones, *The Geography of London River* (London, 1931), p. 71.

5. See for example Dürer's famous print of the artist making a drawing of a nude whom he studies through a drawing frame. Boston Museum of Fine Arts, *Albrecht Dürer: Master Printmaker* (Boston, 1971), Plate 219. Dürer draws the tip of the stylus at just the height of the horizon, which is visible beyond it through an open window.

6. See the discussion and illustrations of Winchester House in London County Council, *Survey of London; Volume XXII: Bankside* (London, 1950), pp. 51–4. The claim, p. 49, that the hall was approximately 36 ft wide appears to be an error. Compare Victoria County History *Surrey*, IV, 147–8.

7. *Troilus and Cressida* I, iii, 155–6.

8. Braines, *The Site of the Globe Playhouse, Southwark*, pp. 44 and 61–2 for the Globe site; for the Hope, p.91.

9. See the map of the site in ibid., p. 40.

10. It is printed in Glynne Wickham, *Early English Stages 1300–1660, Volume II 1576–1660 (Part 2)* (London, 1972), pp. 209–11.

11. The Fortune contract is printed in *Henslowe's Diary*, edited by R. A. Foakes and R. T. Rickert (Cambridge, 1961), pp. 306–15.

12. 'The Jnner principall postes of the first storie to be Twelve footes in height and Tenn ynches square . . . ,' Wickham, *Early English Stages II (Part II)*, p. 210.

13. 'And the saide fframe to conteine Three Stories in heighth The first or lower Storie to Conteine Twelue foote of lawfull assize in heighth The second Storie Eleuen foote of lawfull assize in heighth And the Third or vpper

Storie to conteine Nyne foote of lawfull assize in heigth . . . ,' *Henslowe's Diary*, edited by Foakes and Rickert, p. 307.

14. This procedure is followed by C. Walter Hodges, *Shakespeare's Second Globe: the Missing Monument* (London, 1973), pp. 45–50. Hodges' conclusions are questioned by Richard Hosley, 'The Second Globe,' *Theatre Notebook* 29 (1975), pp. 142–3.

Notes to chapter 5 (pp. 108–26)

1. Some accept the 43 ft width directly: such are Hodges, *Shakespeare's Second Globe*, pp. 78–81 and Hosley, 'The Swan Playhouse,' in *The Revels History of Drama in English*, III, 143. John Cranford Adams, *The Globe Playhouse: its Design and Equipment*, 2nd edn (London, 1961), pp. 90–8 opted for a stage 41 ft across, deriving his measure generally from the Fortune's, a decision in which he was followed by Irwin Smith, *Shakespeare's Globe Playhouse*, p. 66: 'The 41-foot width compares agreeably with the 43 feet specified for the stage of the Fortune. . . .' Richard Southern used a 43 ft width as a controlling measure, though not necessarily a definitive one, in 'On Reconstructing a Practicable Elizabethan Public Playhouse,' *Shakespeare Survey 12* (1959), pp. 23–4.

2. The quotations from the Fortune contract are from *Henslowe's Diary*, edited by Foakes and Rickert, pp. 306–15.

3. Even Adams, *The Globe Playhouse*, p. 23 thought of the Globe as 'an octagonal building 83 feet across,' and with a diameter considerably greater than that figure.

4. 'Theatrorum autem omnium prestantissimum est et amplissimum id cuius intersignium est cygnus (vulgo te theater off te cijn) quippe quod tres mille homines in sedilibus admittat . . . " cited in 'A Note on the Swan Theatre Drawing,' *Shakespeare Survey 1* (1948), p. 24.

5. See Bentley, *Jacobean and Caroline Stage*, VI, 183–4, citing Edward M. Wilson and Olga Turner, 'The Spanish Protest against *A Game at Chesse*,' *Modern Language Review* 44 (1949), pp. 476–82.

6. See the discussion of 'Designers and Craftsmen' in John Summerson, *Architecture in Britain 1530 to 1830* (Harmondsworth, 1960), pp. 56–9.

7. P.R.O. E351/3242.

8. See the account by Orazio Busino cited in Bentley, *Jacobean and Caroline Stage*, VI, 257.

9. For an account of the Globe along Vitruvian lines see Frances Yates, *Theatre of the World* (Chicago, 1969); Richard Kohler has offered an analysis of 'The Fortune Contract and Vitruvian Symmetry' in *Shakespeare Studies 6* (1970), pp. 311–26. See also Ernest L. Rhodes, *Henslowe's Rose* (Lexington, 1976).

10. For Street's mark see *Henslowe Papers*, edited by Walter W. Greg (London, 1907), pp. 4 (the Fortune contract) and 102 (a contract for a building abutting the Bear Garden in 1606). In both contracts the builder sets his mark while the witnesses give their signatures.

11. The various books of Sebastiano Serlio's *Architettura* were published singly and in pairs in Paris and Venice in the 1540s, but were not collected until they appeared as *Tutte l'opere dell'architettura* (Venice, 1566). No English transla-

tion appeared until 1611. See William Bell Dinsmoor, 'The Literary Remains of Sebastiano Serlio,' *Art Bulletin* 24 (1942), pp. 55–91 and 115–54.

12. (Oxford, 1962), pp. 53–9. Compare *2 Henry IV* I, iii, 42 and 53.

13. Joseph Moxon, *Mechanick Exercises* (London, 1677), p. 129 describes the carpenter's ten-foot rod.

14. For the tiltyard at Whitehall see P.R.O. E351/3253: '. . . putting diverse newe postes and pyles and fastening them with spikes to strengthen the grounde-woorke where some of them were rotten being in measure xxij roddes after xj^{en} foote di in length for every rodd at xxvj^{d} the rodd lxvj^{s}.' For brickwork at Royston and Whitehall measured by the rod see P.R.O. E351/3242 and 3244.

15. Valentine Leigh, *The Moste Profitable and Commendable Science, of Surueiying of Landes, Tenementes, and Hereditamentes* (London, 1578), sig. 02^{b}.

16. pp. 121–2.

17. p. 37.

18. 'The Jnner principall postes of the first storie to be Twelve footes in height and Tenn ynches square . . .' Wickham, *Early English Stages, Volume II (Part 2)*, p. 210.

19. The contract calls for the frame to be 'sufficyently enclosed withoute with lathe, lyme & haire,' materials that would be used between the timbers rather than over them. See L. F. Salzman, *Building in England down to 1540: a Documentary History* (Oxford, (1967), pp. 157 and 192.

20. See John Summerson, 'Three Elizabethan Architects,' *Bulletin of the John Rylands Library* 40 (1957), pp. 202–28.

21. British Library Lansdowne MS 84, fol. 25, cited by Summerson, 'Three Elizabethan Architects,' p. 227.

22. British Library Lansdowne MS 84, fol. 26, cited by Summerson, 'Three Elizabethan Architects,' p. 228.

23. Edward Worsop, *A Discoverie of Sundrie Errours and Faults Daily Committed by Landemeaters* (London, 1582), sig. G1^{b}.

24. The *ad triangulum* method is much documented, but see especially Paul Frankl, 'The Secret of the Mediaeval Masons,' *Art Bulletin* 27 (1945), pp. 46–60 and François Bucher, 'Design in Gothic Architecture: a Preliminary Assessment,' *Journal of the Society of Architectural Historians* 27 (1968), pp. 49–71, particularly the comments on the survival of triangulation techniques into the seventeenth century on p. 54.

25. For the equilateral triangle see Richard Benese, . . . *the Maner of Measurynge of all Maner of Landes* . . . (London, 1537), sig. Bii^{b}; for triangulation in general see Leonard Digges, *A Booke Named Tectonicon* (London, 1556), sig. A3^{b}–A4^{b}; Leigh, sig. Oiv^{a-b}; and Worsop, *A Discoverie*, sig. I2^{b}. A critical introduction to these texts is given in A.W. Richeson, *English Land Measuring to 1800: Instruments and Practices* (Cambridge, Mass., 1966), pp. 29–89.

26. *Henslowe Papers*, edited by Greg, I, 15. See also *Henslowe's Diary*, edited by W. W. Greg (London, 1908), II, 57.

27. Cited by Paul Frankl, *The Gothic: Literary Sources and Interpretations during Eight Centuries* (Princeton, 1960), p. 50.

28. ibid., pp. 51–2.

29. Serlio, *The First Booke of Architecture* (London, 1611), fol 2^{b}. The *ad quadratum* diagram is also illustrated on the title page.

30. On the *ad quadratum* method see Frankl, *The Gothic*, pp. 51–2; James S. Ackerman, '"Ars sine scientia nihil est": Gothic Theory of Architecture at the Cathedral of Milan,' *Art Bulletin* 31 (1949), pp. 84–111; and Howard Saalman, 'Early Renaissance Architectural Theory and Practice in Antonio Filarete's *Trattato di Architettura,*' *Art Bulletin* 41 (1959), pp. 89–106. That the courtyard plan of the Fortune could be constructed without adjusting the dividers was in accord with the habits, aesthetic as well as practical, of late medieval builders. See for example Mathes Roriczer's demonstration of how 'to draw a pentagon with unchanged dividers' in *Geometria deutsch* in Lon R. Shelby, *Gothic Design Techniques* (Carbondale and Edwardsville, 1977), p. 116. The scheme for the Barber–Surgeons' anatomy theatre is at Worcester College, Jones/Webb I, 7, and is reproduced in the present volume, Plate 38.

31. Sir John Soane's Museum, T 145–6 (iii-v), reproduced in *The Book of Architecture of John Thorpe in Sir John Soane's Museum*, edited by John Summerson (London, 1966), Plate 67. The plan reproduced here as Plate 31 II is a redrawn version with the four-rod *ad quadratum* square superimposed.

32. Worcester College, Jones/Webb I, 27. John Webb's plan shows the central octagon of the original cockpit surrounded by more recent galleries. The square-planned outer wall was built higher to accommodate the theatre of 1629–30, but appears to have used at least the foundations of an original battlemented wall shown in earlier drawings. The inner surfaces of the octagon posts are located on a circle defined *ad quadratum* (to within a few inches) from the inner surface of the boundary wall.

33. Both Deal and Walmer castles are centrally planned forts constructed in 1539–40. Many of their proportions are developed *ad quadratum*, including the relation between inner and outer surfaces of the massive keep walls, and the relation between the keep and the curtain. See the plans in A. D. Saunders, *Deal and Walmer Castles* (London, 1963), pp. 25 and 33.

34. B.L. Add. MS 39831 fols. 3 and 4, reproduced in Summerson, *Architecture in Britain*, p. 29.

35. Worcester College, Jones/Webb I, 33, reproduced in John Harris and A. A. Tait, *Catalogue of the Drawings by Inigo Jones, John Webb and Isaac de Caus at Worcester College, Oxford* (Oxford, 1979), Plate 88.

36. C. W. Wallace, *The First London Theatre: Materials for a History* (New York, 1969 [1913]), pp. 164–80, 218, 222 and 278–9.

37. ibid., p. 222, citing P.R.O. Req. 2/184/45.

38. The notion that the Globe used the timbers of the Theatre 'in an other forme' (Andrew Gurr, *The Shakespearean Stage 1574–1642* (Cambridge, 1970), p. 92) stems from a misreading of Henry Johnson's deposition in the Court of Requests suit.

39. 'An Execration upon *Vulcan*,' in *Ben Jonson*, edited by Herford and Simpson, VIII, 208–09.

40. William Rendle, 'The Bankside, Southwark, and the Globe Playhouse,' in *Harrison's Description of England* edited by Frederick J. Furnivall, Part II, Book 3 (1877–8), Appendix, p. xvii.

41. ibid., p. xvii.

42. The building proclamations are printed in James F. Larkin and Paul L. Hughes, *Stuart Royal Proclamations* (Oxford, 1973–), I, nos. 25, 51, 78, 87,

120, 121, and 122. For their implementation see Norman Brett-James, *The Growth of Stuart London* (London, 1935), pp. 80–100.

43. See, for example, *Acts of the Privy Council, 1616–17,* 15, 36 and 334.

44. I have rehearsed Beeston's story in 'Inigo Jones at the Cockpit,' *Shakespeare Survey 30* (1977), pp. 161–2.

45. John Hawarde, *Les Reportes del Cases in Camera Stellata 1593 to 1609,* edited by W. P. Baildon (London, 1894), pp. 318–19 and 328–9. See also E. P. Cheyney, 'The Court of Star Chamber,' *American Historical Review* 18 (1912–13), pp. 735–6.

46. Larkin and Hughes, *Stuart Royal Proclamations,* I, nos. 120 and 121, dated 3 August and 10 September 1611. Such jettying was therefore not called for in the Hope contract of 1613.

47. (Oxford, 1973), p. 39.

48. *Shakespeare's Second Globe,* p. 38.

49. Adams, *The Globe Playhouse,* p. 23 suggests that the theatre was 'an octagonal building 83 feet across,' as measured between its opposite sides; its diameter would be considerably larger, though its 'over-all width' is given as 84 ft by Smith, *Shakespeare's Globe Playhouse,* pp. 31–2. The plans published by Adams (pp. 53, 242 and 309) seem to indicate a diameter of about 91 ft 6 in.

50. *Shakespeare's Second Globe,* pp. 45–50. Richard Hosley, *The Revels History of Drama in English,* III, 176–7, estimates the diameter of the Globe as 100 ft.

Notes to chapter 6 (pp. 127–38)

1. Bentley, *Jacobean and Caroline Stage,* VI, 183–4.

2. See 'A Note on the Swan Theatre Drawing,' *Shakespeare Survey 1,* p. 24 and n. 4 to chapter 5 above.

3. P.R.O. E351/3255.

4. P.R.O. E351/3218.

5. P.R.O. E351/3223.

6. P.R.O. E351/3229.

7. P.R.O. E351/3239.

8. British Library Lansdowne MS 1171, fols. 5[b]–6, reproduced in Stephen Orgel and Roy Strong, *Inigo Jones: the Theatre of the Stuart Court* (London and Berkeley, 1973), II, 638–9.

9. P.R.O. E351/3269.

10. See my article, 'The Paved Court Theatre at Somerset House,' *British Library Journal 3* (1977), pp. 13–19. Jones's plan is in British Library Lansdowne MS 1171, fols, 9[b]–10

11. *Shakespeare's Wooden O,* (London, 1959), pp. 291–6.

12. Hosley, *The Revels History of Drama in English,* III, 155–6 and 'A Reconstruction of the Fortune Playhouse: Part II,' in *The Elizabethan Theatre VII,* edited by George Hibbard (Port Credit, 1980), pp. 9–10. Adams, *The Globe Playhouse,* p. 87, places the benches 30 in. apart.

13. For the tentative identification of these drawings see my article, 'Inigo Jones at the Cockpit,' *Shakespeare Survey 30,* pp. 157–68; the identification is confirmed, partly on unpublished evidence supplied by Professor Per Palme, in Harris and Tait, *Catalogue of the Drawings by Inigo Jones, John Webb and Isaac de Caus at Worcester College, Oxford,* pp. 14–15.

14. *Shakespeare's Wooden O,* pp. 295–6.

15. British Library Additional MS 15505, fol. 21. A transcript of the comments written on the drawing is given as Appendix B.

16. E. K. Chambers, *The Elizabethan Stage* (Oxford, 1923), I, 15, unaccountably gives the length of the hall at Hampton Court as 115 ft. In fact it is 97 ft long, and well known for being smaller than its contemporary at Christ Church. See Nikolaus Pevsner, *Middlesex*, The Buildings of England (Harmondsworth, 1951), p. 80.

17. Stroude's *The Floating Island* 'was acted on a goodly stage, reaching from the upper end of the Hall almost to the hearth place . . . .' *History and Antiquities of the University of Oxford*, cited by Bentley, *Jacobean and Caroline Stage*, V, 1191. The hearth was originally at the centre of the hall, beneath the louvre; see Historical Monuments Commission (England), *City of Oxford* (London, 1939), p. 34.

18. Cambridge University Library Additional MS 34. Stringer's account was printed from a transcript by John Nichols, *The Progresses . . . of King James the First . . .* (London, 1828), I, 530–59.

19. 'Ffor the better contrivinge and finishinge of their stages, seates, and scaffoldes in S^t. Maries and Christchurch they interteyned two of his Ma^{ts}. M^r. Carpenters, and they had the advise of the Comptroler of his workes. They alsoe hired on M^r. Jones a great travello^r who vndertooke to further them much and furnish them wth rare devises, but pformed very little to that wch was expected, he had for his paynes as I heard yt constantly reported – 50^{li}' Cambridge University Library, Additional MS 34, fol. 44^b.

20. *Rex Platonicus* (Oxford, 1607).

21. ibid., p. 46.

22. Stringer, Cambridge University Library Additional MS 34, fol. 30.

23. *Rex Platonicus*, pp. 46–7.

24. For Basil see Colvin, general editor, *The History of the King's Works, Volume III 1485–1660 (Part I)*, pp. 106–20.

25. Historical MSS Commission *Salisbury*, XVII 349, letter from Dorset to the Officers of the Works dated 3 August 1605. See M. Girouard, 'Designs for a Lodge at Ampthill,' in *The Country Seat: Studies in the History of the British Country House*, edited by H.M. Colvin and J. Harris (London, 1970), pp. 13–17.

26. See R. A. Skelton and J. Summerson, *A Description of Maps . . . in the Collection made by William Cecil* (London, 1971), p. 84.

27. Cambridge University Library Additional MS 34, fol. 30.

28. (Venice, 1551), fol. 27^b.

29. Sebastiano Serlio, *Tutte l'opere dell' architettura* (Venice, 1566), fol. 43^b. Earlier editions used the word 'proscenio' to describe this space.

30. *Shakespeare's Audience* (New York, 1941), p. 23.

31. pp. 22–3.

32. Hosley, *Revels History of Drama in English*, III, 148–64.

33. See Bentley, *Jacobean and Caroline Stage*, VI, 184.

Notes to chapter 7 (pp. 139–57)

1. On the relation between the baiting-rings and the Theater see Oscar Brownstein, 'Why Didn't Burbage Lease the Beargarden? A Conjecture in

Comparative Architecture,' in *The First Public Playhouse*, edited by Herbert Berry (Montreal, 1979), pp. 81–96.

2. The figures are from R. J. C. Atkinson, *Stonehenge* (Harmondsworth, 1960), pp. 36–8.

3. Inigo Jones [John Webb], *The Most Notable Antiquity of Great Britain Vulgarly Called Stonehenge* (London, 1655). See pp. 1–2 for the occasion of the survey and 'Groundplot' no. 2, facing p. 60, for the Vitruvian interpretation of the stones. A full discussion is given in Yates, *Theatre of the World*, pp. 176–85.

4. See Appendix A.

5. Yates, *Theatre of the World*; Kohler, 'The Fortune Contract and Vitruvian Symmetry,' *Shakespeare Studies 6*, pp. 311–26; and Rhodes, *Henslowe's Rose*.

6. See chapter 5 above, p. 112.

7. In *Ben Jonson*, edited by Herford and Simpson, VII, 809–10.

8. Vitruvius, *The Ten Books on Architecture*, translated by Morris Hicky Morgan (Cambridge, Mass., 1914), pp. 137–57.

9. Plate 35 reproduces Palladio's study of the Vitruvian theatre. Another version was published by the influential Daniele Barbaro in his *M. Vitruvii Polionis de Architectura Libri Decem* (Venice, 1567), p. 188, but similar designs were included in most illustrated editions of Vitruvius.

10. 'A Note on the Swan Theatre Drawing,' *Shakespeare Survey 1*, pp. 23–4 and Plate III.

11. The Fortune contract requires that the '... Stadge shall conteine in length ffortie and Three foote of lawfull assize and in breadth to extende to the middle of the yarde of the saide howse....' *Henslowe's Diary*, edited by Foakes and Rickert, p. 308. Leonie Star has reasonably argued that in the absence of further evidence this aspect of the Fortune's design should not be taken as a standard feature of all Elizabethan playhouses. See 'The Middle of the Yard: a Second Inner Stage?' and 'The Middle of the Yard, Part II,' *Theatre Notebook* 30 (1976), pp. 5–9 and 65–9.

12. The plans are reproduced in my 'Inigo Jones at the Cockpit,' *Shakespeare Survey 30*, Plates II and III.

13. ibid., p. 160 and Plate IIIB.

14. The larger-scale plan of a stage to the left of the sheet shows the forestage to be 34 ft across, as measured against the adjacent scale-bar [Plate 36 I]. There is no clearly inked scale-bar for the overall plan to the right, but because it is approximately half the scale of the stage plan it has often been treated as if it were exactly so (as by Hamilton Bell, 'Contributions to the History of the English Playhouse,' *The Architectural Record* 33 (1913), pp. 262–7). In fact if the 34 ft measure of the forestage is applied as a scale to the overall plan, this latter's scale is found to be almost exactly 1 : 100, for it represents the 34 ft (10.36 m) in 103.5 mm. This is within 0.1% of 1 : 100. My measurements have been made according to this scale, which appears to be confirmed by a pricked-out bar immediately beneath the plan, and show the Cockpit to have been a little smaller than has hitherto been thought.

15. *The Book of Architecture of John Thorpe in Sir John Soane's Museum*, edited by Summerson, pp. 84–5 and Plate 66.

16. See Bentley, *Jacobean and Caroline Stage*, VI, 276. The scheme appears to be thoroughly schematic, countering the binary Latin tag with Greek figures

arranged in pairs: niches for two tragedians (Agathon and Sophocles) and two comedians (Menander? and Aristophanes) flank busts of Thespis and Epicharmos (the reputed founders of tragedy and comedy) at the upper level, while below plinths are set out for the figures of Melpomene and Thalia, the muses of tragedy and comedy. Although the design is certainly by Jones, the drawing is Webb's and dates probably from the Restoration. See Harris and Tait, *Catalogue of Drawings by Inigo Jones . . . at Worcester College, Oxford*, pp. 11–12. In one respect at least it must reflect some changes made to the original conversion of 1629–30, for in the Works accounts of 1633–4 we find the following: 'John de Creetz Serg[t]: Painter Mathew Goodericke Paynter . . . for mending the Statues in the Cockpitt altering the inscriptions and clenzing other woorke there – xx[s],' P.R.O. E351/3267.

17.   Though it is difficult to distinguish between these orders in Webb's drawing they are specified in the Works accounts for the theatre, cited by Bentley, *Jacobean and Caroline Stage*, VI, 271–3.

18.   Serlio, *The Booke of Architecture* (London, 1611), Book III, fol. 25[b]. Serlio's woodcut is similar to a rapid sketch in the *taccuino* of his mentor, Baldassare Peruzzi, now in the Biblioteca Comunale, Siena (S. IV. 17, carta 33 [40][v]).

19.   See the accounts cited by Bentley, *Jacobean and Caroline Stage*, VI, 273.

20.   Thomas Heywood, *Pleasant Dialogues and Dramas* (London, 1637), sig. Q4.

21.   See John Summerson, *Inigo Jones* (Harmondsworth, 1966), pp. 97–106.

22.   See Appendix A for the stage front at the Globe.

23.   Robert de la Mark de Fleurange, *Mémoires*, edited by Michaud and Poujoulat (Paris, 1838), p. 69, cited by Sydney Anglo, *Spectacle, Pageantry and Early Tudor Policy* (Oxford, 1969), p. 140n.

24.   For the Calais banqueting house see Anglo, *Spectacle, Pageantry and Early Tudor Policy*, pp. 159–63 and Richard Hosley. 'The Theatre and the Tradition of Playhouse Design,' in *The First Public Playhouse*, edited by Berry, pp. 60–74.

25.   T[homas] W[hite], *A Sermon Preached at Pawles Crosse on Sunday the Thirde of November 1577 . . .* (London, 1578), cited by Chambers, *Elizabethan Stage*, IV, 197.

26.   Yates, *Theatre of the World*, pp. 188–9.

27.   Vitruvius, *The Ten Books on Architecture*, translated by Morgan, p. 73.

28.   Examples are given by Rudolf Wittkower, *Architectural Principles in the Age of Humanism*, 3rd edn (London, 1962). Plates 2–4.

29.   See R. Wittkower and B. A. R. Carter, 'The Perspective of Piero della Francesca's *Flagellation*,' *Journal of the Warburg and Courtauld Institutes* 16 (1953), pp. 292–302.

30.   See especially Cesariano's *Di Lucio Vitruvio Pollione de Architectura* (Como, 1521), III, fols. xlix and l. In the latter the human figure reaches into the angles of a square inscribed within a circle centred at his navel. See the discussion in Wittkower, *Architectural Principles in the Age of Humanism*, pp. 13–15.

31.   Sidney Young, *Annals of the Barber-Surgeons of London* (London, 1890), p. 133.

32.   On 24 July 1637 the minute book of the Barber–Surgeons records: ' . . . that the Concave seeleing of the Theater shalbe painted with the Constellac̄ons of the Heavens and the 7 planetts over the 12 signes in every peere and sceletons to be wrought and sett up on every one of the 12 signes or Corbells.' Young,

Annals of the Barber–Surgeons, p. 213. In fact it is doubtful whether the scheme was ever completed: see the minutes of the Company for 8 February 1638 and 29 March 1638, pp. 214–15 and 337.

33. See Leslie Hotson, *The First Night of 'Twelfth Night'* (London, 1954), p. 137.
34. Hotson, *Shakespeare's Wooden O*, pp. 258–79.
35. See Bentley, *Jacobean and Caroline Stage*, VI, 194.
36. The dials at Whitehall are often mentioned in the Works accounts; see, for example, P.R.O. E351/3262, in which John Mare, a mathematician, is paid three pounds for directing the painters how to draw 'diverse Lynes wth the planettes and pointes of the Compasse' on a 'Dyall vj foote square to be seene from the privy Lodginges. . . .' For the directory see British Library Harleian MS 6850, fol. 31[b]; for Gunter's elaborate descriptions see Edmund Gunter, *The Description and Vse of His Maiesties Dials in White-Hall Garden* (London, 1624).
37. A. Kent Hieatt, *Short Time's Endless Monument* (New York, 1960).
38. *Geographical Journal* 121 (1955), p. 9.
39. Hotson, *Shakespeare's Wooden O*, pp. 263–6, Alan R. Young, 'The Orientation of the Elizabethan Stage: "That Glory to the Sober West,"' *Theatre Notebook* 33 (1979), pp. 80–5, and R. B. Graves, 'Shakespeare's Outdoor Stage Lighting,' *Shakespeare Studies* 13 (1980), pp. 235–50.

Notes to Appendix A (pp. 158–67)

1. Wickham, *Early English Stages, Volume II 1576–1660 (Part 2)*, p. 119.
2. *Shakespeare's Second Globe*, p. 63.
3. See my 'Inigo Jones at the Cockpit,' *Shakespeare Survey 30*, Plate IIA.
4. *Shakespeare's Second Globe*, pp. 61–6.
5. 'Inigo Jones at the Cockpit,' *Shakespeare Survey 30*, p. 165.
6. The Works accounts for 1609–10 tell of 'makeing and settinge upp a newe Cockpitt' at Royston. William Pettitt, a bricklayer, was paid for 'digginge the foundaċon of the Cockpitt and bringinge upp the same wth twoe brickes di thicke to the water table and twoe brickes thicke the whole heighte . . .' P.R.O. E351/3244. The size and shape of the building were recorded in a survey of the Parliamentary Commissioners in 1649: 'All that Round bricke buildinge called the Cockpitt conteyninge 30[ty]. foote of Assize in widenes, and 17[tn]. foote of Assize in heighte, with a substantiall Tymber roofe couered with Tyles . . .' P.R.O. E317/Cambs. 4.
7. Bentley, *Jacobean and Caroline Stage*, VI, 155, citing Folger Shakespeare Library, Phillipps MS 11613, a document which has, however, recently come under suspicion as a forgery.
8. Bentley, *Jacobean and Caroline Stage*, VI, 186. See also n. 40 to chapter 5 above. It should perhaps be noted that de Witt thought that the outer wall of the Swan was made of flint concrete. 'A Note on the Swan Theatre Drawing,' *Shakespeare Survey 1*, p. 24.
9. See my 'Inigo Jones at the Cockpit,' *Shakespeare Survey 30*, 163–5 and Plate IV.
10. *Shakespeare's Second Globe*, p. 44.
11. See, for example, Benese, *Maner of Measuryng*, sig. Div[b]-Eii.
12. *Revels History of Drama in English*, III, 144–6.
13. ibid., pp. 146–8.

14. For a discussion of the relation between the 'cover' and the stage at the Swan see Glynne Wickham, *Early English Stages, Volume II 1576–1660 (Part 1)* (London, 1963), pp. 299–306.

15. *Henslowe's Diary*, edited by Foakes and Rickert, p. 308.

16. Richard Hosley, 'The Shape and Size of the Second Globe,' in *The Third Globe*, edited by C. Walter Hodges and others (Detroit, 1981), pp. 88–97. See also Hodges, *Shakespeare's Second Globe*, p. 63 for a plan of the theatre showing the staircases attached at mid-bay.

17. In our present reconstruction, Plate 41, a bay division almost exactly coincides with the pencilled ridge of the nearer stair turret in Hollar's sketch. The inked ridge is a little to the right. It is possible that the pencil line here is the more accurate, for stair turrets attached to timber-frame buildings were frequently centred on bay divisions in the early seventeenth century, though not invariably so. Of the ten such turrets shown in the drawings of timber-frame houses in the Thorpe collection at the Soane Museum, seven are centred on bay divisions (T84, upper floor; T121, two turrets; T133, two turrets; T266, two turrets treated as extruded corners, half within and half outside the main frame). Only one (T52) is not centred on a bay division, and this is attached to the corner post of the main frame. A doubtful case is T43, where two turrets are centred on timber extensions of an axial masonry core. None of the drawings shows a stair turret attached to the centre of a structural bay. *The Book of Architecture of John Thorpe in Sir John Soane's Museum*, edited by Summerson, Plates 38, 56, 60, 118 and (the doubtful case) 20.

18. For the Blackfriars see Hosley, *Revels History of Drama in English*, III, 202–3; for a discussion of the Cockpit or Phoenix in Drury Lane see my 'Inigo Jones at the Cockpit,' *Shakespeare Survey 30*, pp. 159–60.

19. P.R.O. E351/3216.

20. For *Blackness* see P.R.O. E351/3240; for the stage at Richmond P.R.O. E351/3223.

21. P.R.O. E407/59, fol. 29.

22. *Revels History of Drama in English*, III, 147–8.

23. See, for example, the allusions to fencing prizes at the Red Bull and Second Fortune in Bentley, *Jacobean and Caroline Stage*, VI, 159, 175, 221 and 238.

24. British Library Harleian MS 1653, fol. 31[b].

Index

(*Page numbers in italic refer to the plates.*)

Adams, John Cranford xii, 125, 128
ad quadratum technique 115–18, 120, 122–6,
    142–6, 148, 149, 152, 163
ad triangulum technique 113, 126, 167
'Agas' map 37–8, 41
Alberti, Leon Battista
    On Painting 21–2, 85
Alleyn, Edward 109
Ampthill 134
animal–baiting arenas 139, 167
Ardres 146–7
Aubrey, John 17, 28

Barbaro, Daniele 147
Basil, Simon 134
Bate, John
    Mysteryes of Nature, and Art 22–3, *24*
Beeston, Christopher 121, 129
Braines, W. W. 63, 80, 87, 88, 101, 102
Browne, William
    Britannia's Pastorals 23
Bulmer, Bevis 45–6
Burbage, Cuthbert 117
Burbage, James 104, 125, 147

Calais 146–7
Carter, B. A. R. 85
chain 111
Chamberlain, John 2, 4
Chambers, Sir William 44
Charles V, Holy Roman Emperor, King of
    Spain 146
Christian IV, King of Denmark 167
Coloma, Don Carlos 108, 127, 137–8

Dee, John 147
degrees (seating) 127–8, 129, 136
de Jongh, Claude 76
Detroit xii
de Witt, Johannes 108, 127, 141, 162, 163,
    166–7
Digges, Leonard
    Pantometria 23
    Tectonicon 110
drawing frame 22, *24*, 83, 90
Dubreuil, Jean
    Perspective Practical 26, *27*
Dürer, Albrecht
    Underweyssung der Messung 21, 26, 85

Earl Marshal, Earl of Arundel 121, 122, 160
East, Gilbert 113–14

Edmonton, Alberta 86
Evelyn, John 6

Fale, Thomas
    Horologiographia 110
Farley, Henry
    The Complaint of Paules 1, 47
fencing 167
Field of the Cloth of Gold 146
Fisher, Sidney xii
Florimène 128, 136
Fludd, Robert 147
    Utriusque Cosmi Historia 22
Folkingham, William
    Art of Survey 23
Fortune contract xii, 104, 108–9, 111, 112,
    115, 126, 158, 163, 166
Frankl, Paul 115–16

Gunter, Edmund 155
    Description and Use of the Crosse-Staffe 111

Hampton Court 128
Harbage, Alfred 135
Harrison, Stephen 36, 59
Hawksmoor, Nicholas 47
Henslowe, Philip 107, 109
Heywood, Thomas 143
Hodges, C. Walter xii, xiii, 26, 122, *123*, 124,
    125, 153, 158, 159, 160, 164
Holbein, Hans 85
Hollar, Wenceslaus xi–xii, 3–19, 26–34, 36,
    37, 44, 48, 58, 62–9, 119, 136
    Evelyn-Pepys panorama 3, 6–10 (*6, 7*),
        12–15, 76, 77, 164
    Exact Prospect 36, 37, 78
    'London and Old St Paul's' 16–19 (*16, 17,
        19*), 26–9
    'London by Milford Staires' 29–30 (*29, 30*)
    Long View of London 1, 3–4, 6, 7, 8 (*8, 9, 10,
        11, 12, 13, 14*), 10–15, 33, 36, 37, 62–9,
        75, 77, 106–7, 164, 165
    Thames Street diagram 72–4, *72*
    View of East Southwark *5*, 5–6, 15–16,
        69–72, 74–6
    View of West Southwark *2, 3*, 4–5, 12–15,
        32–3, 69–71, 76–107 *passim* (*82, 98*),
        122–5, 137, 152–4 (*153*), 157, 158–62,
        164, *165*
Hondius, Jacobus 36, 59
Honnecourt, Villard de 115
Hope contract 103, 104, 111

Hopton, Arthur
  Speculum Topographicum 20–1, 25
Hosley, Richard xii, xiii, 101, 128–9, 135,
    136, 161, 164–5, 166–7
Hotson, Leslie 40, 128, 129, 156
Hube, Douglas xii–xiii, 154–5

Johnson, Henry 117, 119
Jones, Inigo 2, 110, 117, 128, 129, 131, 135,
    136, 139, 141, 142–6, 149, 158, 162,
    166
Jonson, Ben
  'Execration upon Vulcan' 120–1
  Love's Welcome at Bolsover 140
  Masque of Augurs 127
  Masque of Blackness 166
  Oberon 152
Leigh, Valentine
  Science of Surveying 111
Leonardo da Vinci 22, 86
London, Westminster and Southwark:
  Allhallows, Barking 40, 41, 47, 48–65
    passim
  Arundel House 43, 44, 52–68 *passim*, 84
  Baynard's Castle 40–1, 78, 81
  Bear Gardens 40
  Billingsgate 41
  Blackfriars dock 63
  Borough High Street, Southwark 15, 70, 75
  Bridewell 19
  Bulmer's Water Tower 18, 29, 45–6, 60–1,
    78, 81–2, 88, 153
  Clink Street, Southwark 85, 95
  Coldharbour 15, 35, 41, 63, 73
  Drury Lane 121
  Durham House 16–17, 18, 84
  Ely Place 78
  Exchange 41, 63
  Fishermen's Hall 41, 63
  Fleet Street 44
  Gracechurch Street 156
  Guildhall 15, 41, 63
  Lion Quay 41, 63
  London Bridge 15, 18, 29, 38, 41, 62, 63, 75,
    87
  Maid Lane, Southwark 63, 71, 80, 102–3,
    121
  Middle Temple Hall 18, 19, 41, 42
  Milford Stairs 29, 30
  Saint Andrew's, Holborn 78
  Saint Bride's 18, 40, 41, 42, 44, 49–68
    passim, 78, 81–2, 88, 93
  Saint Clement's 41, 43, 44, 84, 87, 89
  Saint Dunstan's-in-the-East 15, 40, 41, 47,
    50–66 *passim*
  Saint Dunstan's-in-the-West 41, 44, 52–68
    passim
  Saint Lawrence, Jewry 7
  Saint Lawrence Poultney 15, 18, 28, 29, 40,
    41, 46, 49–66 *passim*, 156
  Saint Martin's, Ludgate 18, 44–5, 67–8, 78,
    81–2, 88

Saint Mary-le-Bow 7, 18, 26, 29, 40, 41, 46,
    49–66 *passim*
Saint Mary Magdalene, Bermondsey 71–2
Saint Michael's, Cornhill 15, 41, 47, 48–66
    passim
Saint Olave's, Southwark 6, 7, 15, 38, 62,
    71–2, 75
Saint Paul's Cathedral 1–3, 5, 16, 18, 19, 26,
    29, 40, 41, 42, 45, 49–68 *passim*, 77, 78,
    79, 81–2, 84, 87–8, 91–3, 143, 153
Saint Saviour's dock 16
Saint Saviour's, Southwark (Southwark
    Cathedral) 3, 15, 16, 29, 30, 35, 37, 38,
    39, 41, 42, 43–8, 49–68 *passim*, 70–2, 75,
    77, 79–85, 87, 89, 91–4, 99, 103, 106, 153,
    162
Saint Sepulchre 18, 26
Saint Thomas's, Southwark 71
Savoy 16–17, 43, 63, 68, 79, 71, 81–2, 88,
    92–3
Savoy Chapel 42, 43
Shoreditch 40, 104
Steelyard 42, 43
Strand 43, 155
Temple 29, 41, 79
Temple Church 40, 44, 49–68 *passim*
Thames Street 72–4
Tower of London 6, 16, 18, 26, 28, 29, 40,
    42, 47–8, 53, 62, 63, 64–5, 71
Westminster Abbey 166
Whitehall 53, 128, 147, 152, 155
Whitehall Banqueting House 68, 109, 127–
    8, 167
Whitehall cockpit 117, 147;
    see also playhouses: Cockpit-in-Court
Winchester House 5, 11–15, 39, 62, 70, 77,
    78, 79, 80, 85, 93–5, 159
Winchester Walk 94–5
York House 43

Mellon, Mr and Mrs Paul 4
Mercer, Eric 110
Merian, Mathaeus 36, 58–9
Middleton, Thomas
  A Game at Chess 108, 137–8
Montagu, Walter
  The Shepherd's Paradise 128
Moseley, Sir Nicholas 39

Norden, John
  Civitas Londini 32–4, 36, 37, *38*, 39–40 (*39*),
    57, 59–62, 64–5, 84
  Surueiors Dialogue 23–5, 111
  Vicissitudo Rerum 23

Ogilby and Morgan
  map of London 44, 46, 73–4
orientation of churches 155
Oxford (Christ Church) *130*, 131–7 (*133*)

Palladio, Andrea *141*, 146
Parry, Graham 6

Pepys, Samuel 7, 47–8
perspective
 anamorphosis 96–102, 122, 159
 central ray 82–3, 89, 154, 159–60
 horizon line 78, 86, 153
 orthogonals 77, 86
 principles 85–7, 90–1, 96–7
perspective glass: *see* topographical glass
Piero della Francesca 86, 149
Place, Francis 28
playhouses and theatres
 Barber-Surgeons' Anatomy theatre 117,
  149, *150, 151*
 Blackfriars 18–19 (*19*), 129, 155, 166
 Christ Church, Oxford *130*, 131–7 (*133*),
  168–70
 Cockpit, Drury Lane (Phoenix) 121, 129,
  140, 141, 142, 158, 160, 166
 Cockpit-in-Court, Whitehall *118*, 140,
  142–3, *144, 145*, 158, 162, 166
 Fortune 104, 108–9, 111–17, 120, 129, 141,
  160, 167
 Globe xi–xii, 1–8 (*1, 2, 6*), *9*, 32–3 (*33*), *38*,
  40, 62–3, 69, 76, 79–80, *82*, 87, 88, 95, 98
  (*98*), 99–106 (*102*), 117–26 (*123*), 127,
  135, 139–42, 146, 147–8, 152, *153*, 156,
  165
   capacity 108, 127, 134, 135–8
   diameter xii, 96, 99–104, 106–7, 120
   frame 3, 96, 141, 161–2, 163, *165*
   galleries 4, 125–6, 127, 136–7
   height 104–6
   jetties 122
   lantern 4, 5, 158
   orientation 152–7 (*153*)
   stage 4, 108, 120, 166–7
   stair turrets 4, 5, 99, 149, 164
   superstructure 3–4, 5, 153, 158–61,
    166
   timbers 104, 117, 119, 161–2
   windows 4, 5, 164
   yard 3, 96, 120, 158
 Hope 5, 8, 62, 76, 87–8, 95, 98, 99–106,
  160, 166
 Paved Court theatre, Somerset House 128
 Rose 40
 Swan 40, 103, 104, 108, 127, 135, 141, 162,
  163, 166–7
 Theater, Shoreditch xi, 104, 117, 119–20,
  125, 126, 139, 147, 156, 167
Price, D. J. 155–6
proclamations on building 121–2

Raleigh, Sir Walter 17
Raphael 96, 98
Rendle, William 121
Richmond 128, 139, 166
rod as unit of measurement 110–15, 125,
 166
Royston 160

Sackville, Thomas, Earl of Dorset 134
Scamozzi, Vincenzo
 L'idea dell'architettura universale 148
Scouloudi, Irene 35–6
Serlio, Sebastiano
 Architettura 110, 117, *118*, 134, 142
Shakespeare, William
 Hamlet 149–52
 Julius Caesar 156
 Troilus and Cressida 96
Shapiro, I. A. 4, 60
Smith, Irwin 125
Southern, Richard xii
Spenser, Edmund
 'Epithalamion' 155
Sprinzels, Franz 72
Stickells, Robert 112, 117, 139, 143, 147
Stonehenge 139, 157
Stow, John
 Survey of London 45–6
Street, Peter 107, 109–20, 124–6, 139, 140,
 141, 156–7, 163, 167
Stringer, Philip 131–2, *133*
Strype, John 46
surveyor's line 111–12

Taylor, John 2, 4
Thorpe, John 117, *118*, 142
topographical glass 20–30 (*27*), 48–9, 60, 66,
 69, 75, 77, 83, 84, 86, 87, 89–90, 97, 122,
 154, 159

Van Buchell, Aernout 166
velarium 142, 143
Vertue, George 43
Vignola, Giacomo Barozzi da
 Le due regole della Prospettiva Pratica 22
Villiers, George, Duke of Buckingham 43
Visscher, Claes Jan
 London 32–7 (*32, 33, 34, 35*), 40–2, 49–58,
  59–60, 64–5, 69, 76, 84
Vitruvius Pollio
 De Architectura 109–10, 112, 139–49 (*141*),
  157
Von Hoschenperg, Stephan 117

Wake, Isaac
 Rex Platonicus 132, *133*
Webb, John *118, 144, 145*, 149, *150, 151*
West and Toms 76
Wheelock, A. K. 22
White, Christopher 72
White, Thomas 147
Wickham, Glynne 158
Williams, Iolo 4, 72, 75–6, 77
Wood, Anthony à 131
Worsop, Edward
 A Discoverie of Sundrie Errours 112–13
Wren, Sir Christopher 44, 45, 47
Yates, Frances 147